ADVENTURE SPORTS C

Coaching adventure sports is part of the core work of many adventure educators but has been largely neglected in the adventure studies literature. This is the first book to link contemporary sports coaching science with adventure sports practice. It examines the unique set of challenges faced by adventure sports coaches, such as the dynamic natural environment and the requirement to train athletes to levels of high performance outside of traditional structures of competition, and explores both key theory and best practice.

The book covers major topics such as:

- Skill acquisition and skill development
- Models of learning and teaching
- Performance analysis
- Tactics and decision-making
- Training principles
- Mental skills techniques
- Goal setting and progression
- Risk management

Each chapter contains applied examples from a range of adventure sports, including mountaineering, rock climbing, canoeing, kayaking, surfing and winter sport, as well as practical coaching techniques and a guide to further reading. Written by a team of authors with wide experience of coaching, teaching, researching and high-performance participation in adventure sports, this book is invaluable reading for any student or practitioner with an interest in adventure, outdoor education, sports coaching or lifestyle sport.

Matt Berry is a lecturer at the University of Chichester, West Sussex, teaching on adventure education and physical education programmes. Matt is an active adventure sports coach in a variety of sports but with a specialist interest in white water kayaking.

Jane Lomax is a lecturer at the University of Chichester, West Sussex, teaching on adventure education and physical education programmes. Jane is an active ski and netball coach and is also a British Association of Sport and Exercise Sciences (BASES) accredited sports scientist dealing with mental skills training.

Chris Hodgson is a lecturer at the University of Chichester, West Sussex, teaching on adventure education and physical education programmes. Chris is qualified as coach in skiing, paddle sport, mountaineering and windsurfing. His particular area of research interest is in human performance and environmental stress.

ADVENTURE SPORTS COACHING

Edited by
Matt Berry, Jane Lomax and Chris Hodgson

LONDON AND NEW YORK

First published 2015
by Routledge
2 Park Square, Milton Park, Abingdon, Oxon OX14 4RN

and by Routledge
711 Third Avenue, New York, NY 10017

Routledge is an imprint of the Taylor & Francis Group, an informa business

British Library Cataloguing-in-Publication Data
A catalogue record for this book is available from the British Library

Library of Congress Cataloging in Publication Data
A catalog record for this book has been requested

ISBN: 978-0-415-74600-7 (hbk)
ISBN: 978-0-415-74602-1 (pbk)
ISBN: 978-1-315-79757-1 (ebk)

Typeset in Bembo
by FiSH Books Ltd, Enfield

CONTENTS

FIGURES AND TABLES

Figures

Tables

CONTRIBUTORS

Matt Berry is a Lecturer at the University of Chichester teaching on adventure education and physical education programmes. Matt is an active adventure sports coach in a variety of sports but with a specialist interest in white water kayaking.

Dr Pete Bunyan is Head of Department of Adventure Education at the University of Chichester. Pete's specialisms are sailing and paddlesport. He is also heavily involved in coach education for the Swim Teachers Association.

Ed Christian is a Lecturer at the University of Chichester teaching on the Adventure Education and Physical Education programmes. Ed has a broad range of experience in adventure sports and specialist interest in paddlesport coaching and coach education.

Prof Dave Collins heads the Institute of Coaching and Performance (ICaP) at the University of Central Lancashire. His interests are in high-level sport, encompassing training and preparation, expertise in coaching and support science disciplines, skill development and refinement and talent development.

Dr Loel Collins is a Lecturer at the University of Central Lancashire with specialist interests in white water kayaking, surf kayaking, sea kayaking, canoeing and safety and rescue. His research interests are in adventure sports coach education and development.

Paul Gray is a Lecturer at the University of Central Lancashire and programme leader for Adventure Sports Coaching. Paul has a broad range of experience in adventure sports and specialising in paddlesport coaching and is an active competitor in white water rafting.

Dr Chris Hodgson is a Lecturer at the University of Chichester teaching on adventure education and physical education programmes. Chris is qualified as coach in skiing, paddlesport, mountaineering and windsurfing. His particular area of research interest is in human performance and environmental stress.

Dr Phil Kearney is a Lecturer at the University of Chichester in Sports and Exercise Science. Phil is an active coach and his research interests are in motor learning and motor control.

John Kelly is a Lecturer at the University of Chichester teaching on adventure education and physical education programmes. As well as an active mountain bike competitor and endurance athlete, John's specialism is physiology and physical training.

Jane Lomax is a Lecturer at the University of Chichester teaching on adventure education and physical education programmes. Jane is an active ski and netball coach and is also a (British Association of Sport and Exercise Sciences) BASES accredited sports scientist dealing with mental skills training.

Dr Islay McEwen is a Lecturer at Manchester Metropolitan University. With an interest in developing professionalism, she specialises in physiotherapy and the science of injury.

Dr John Metcalfe is course leader for BA (Hons) Sports (Studies) and BA (Hons) Exercise and Fitness Management at the University of Central Lancashire. His sporting and research interests are in surfing, ultra-endurance exercise and strength and conditioning. He is also a qualified mountain bike coach, personal trainer and strength and conditioning coach.

David Pears is course leader for BSc Sport Science and Coaching at the University of Bedfordshire. Dave is an active football coach but had a misspent youth teaching paddlesport and skiing! His research interest is in naturalistic decision-making in coaching.

Craig Pulling is a Lecturer at the University of Chichester teaching on Adventure Education and Physical Education programmes. Craig is an active coach and his specialist area is performance analysis.

Sid Sinfield is a Senior Instructor at Plas y Brenin the National Centre for Mountain Sports for England and Wales. He is an active coach of all non-competitive paddlesports. He is also a coach educator and mountaineering instructor.

Dr Bill Taylor is Programme Leader for the MA and MSc Exercise and Sport programmes at Manchester Metropolitan University. Bill is well known for his contributions to coach education in paddlesports in particular and has a major interest in developing professionalism in coaching.

INTRODUCTION

Matt Berry, Jane Lomax and Chris Hodgson

Aims of the book

This book aims to present theoretical and practical approaches to adventure sports coaching and practice. Present texts in adventure tend to focus on adventure and outdoor sports for educational purposes rather than adventure sports in their own right and therefore tend to provide a philosophical overview of topics rather than a practical guide the coaching process. With the exception of our first book in this series, *Adventure Education: An Introduction* by Berry and Hodgson (2011), there has been little attention given to contemporary sports science skill acquisition and coaching. Current texts underplay the skill-based, sport nature of many adventure education programmes, preferring to address matters in general terms. Actual approaches to coaching adventure sports are often omitted completely despite this being the core work of many adventure educators.

The aim of this book is to provide a clear link between established coaching science theory and recent developments in coaching, and adventure sports practice. All current texts work on the premise that high-level performance is typically linked to competition, which is not the case in adventure sports for the most part. More typically in adventure sports participation and coaching, high-level performance is dictated by the challenges posed by the environment without constructed rules or an opposing athlete. Skiing steep off-piste runs or kayaking grade 5 white water are examples of high-performance demands without overt competition. While there are some excellent technical manuals for specific sports there are no texts that explore this paradigm or make best use of the advances made in coaching science research from more established fields.

Who is the book for?

The challenge for any author is to consider the reader, for it would be a fruitless challenge to attempt to write such a specific text with universal appeal. Therefore, we have made some assumptions about the reader to create the best fit in terms of content, tone and style. First, we have written for students studying coaching courses linked to adventure sports, outdoor education and adventure education. We also hope the way that we have linked theory to more specific contexts may also prove useful to students of coaching science, sports science and physical education programmes. Finally, as adventure sports coaches ourselves we have kept the practising adventure sports coach firmly in mind. We expect that this text will help those engaged in coaching adventure sports to reflect on their current practice and provide a tool for critical evaluation. In adventure sports there is often sound support from the relevant professional governing bodies and their respective technical manuals about 'correct' practice or techniques. These approaches are concerned with an accepted standard of coaching that can be replicated and therefore tend to follow a prescribed formula that supports the respective coaching schemes. In this book we aim to go a stage further and provide the means for coaches to understand and evaluate their current practice within a wider context. We hope we have achieved this by providing:

- Strong links between theory and practice throughout
- Examples in a range of adventure sports. We apologize if we have not accounted for your sport or under-represented it. We have picked examples that we think help best explain the theory
- A critical search of existing coaching literature to highlight differences and similarities for adventure sports coaching

While any claims that adventure sports are unique or special is easily contestable, there are undoubtedly very specific challenges that an adventure sports coach needs to meet. Our motivation to write this book stems from our own experiences as performers, learners, coaches and academics of adventure sport. We have all been involved in applying coaching science theory within an adventure setting and found many benefits and problems along the way. A major characteristic of adventure sports is the level of complexity and dynamic nature of the environment and classic theories often need to be adapted or might not even fit at all. This book represents our best efforts to date to share the benefits of our knowledge and experience. We hope that you the reader will continue this process of applying coaching knowledge in a critical way.

Do we need this book?

The last 20 years or so has seen an unprecedented growth in the development of sports programmes at every level of study. The initial growth centred on degrees related to sports science followed by the development of coaching science, community sports coaching and sport development programmes. Indeed, sport has a major function in society and is clearly here to stay. In fact, organized participation and highly developed coaching structures in sport are significant social indicators of more developed countries. Adventure sport is now a key part of this larger picture with a growth in facilities and opportunities to participate in activities that can provide a lifelong interest. Public awareness of adventure sport has never been higher and adventure sports have become integrated into the everyday lives of individuals and families who enjoy the physical and mental challenge of activities such as skiing, sailing, kayaking, surfing, mountain biking and rock climbing.

Sports science, sports physiology and sports psychology have seen growth in terms of research and publications to support the growth in opportunities to study sport worldwide. Sports such as skiing, rock climbing, sailing and mountain biking in particular have contributed to this scientific knowledge base. In fact, Doug Ammons, editor of the journal *Perceptual and Motor Skills* has remarked that adventure sports can even provide an insight into processes behind human behaviours and performance that have been difficult to examine in other ways. Furthermore, adventure sports have enjoyed impressive rates of growth gaining media coverage through events such as the X Games and Olympics. The recent inclusion of board and ski cross and slope-style events in the Winter Olympics arguably reflects the growing interest in activities more deeply rooted in adventure.

What do we mean by an adventure sport?

Sport and adventure are both contested terms with a variety of definitions. In Chapter 1 we go into some detail in terms of conceptualisation of adventure sports coaching but there is a value in outlining what we have construed as adventure sport. In this book we have used adventure sport to embrace activities that are typically characterized by:

- Interaction with the environment. (Meteorological conditions such as tide, sea state, snow, white water)
- Challenge by choice/self determination. Not selected by coach to compete
- An awareness of risk as a critical element demanding attention
- Independence and autonomy
- Journeys
- Often not overtly competitive and relatively free from arbitrary rules (although may be self-governed by a set of ethics)

Consequently, we would see adventure sport as a continuum e.g. sail racing with safety boat support is less adventurous than an unsupported sail journey, but is still characterized by independence, autonomy, risk and a continuous interaction with the environment. Along these lines, the coach will regularly be operating in less adventurous contexts in order to develop the skills of learners in order to facilitate progress into more adventurous environments and higher levels of challenge.

The popularity of adventure sports is set to grow as more people are attracted to the spirit of adventure supported by the growth in clubs and independent businesses dedicated to adventure sports coaching. We hope that this book serves to aid this development by supporting existing coaches and the next generation of adventure sports professionals who are studying this exciting and dynamic field.

1

CONCEPTUALIZING THE ADVENTURE SPORTS COACH

Loel Collins and Dave Collins

This chapter explores the challenges that adventure sports present for the coach. The adventure sports environment, participants' varied motivations and different perceptions of adventure are explored, as is the idea of adventure-centred performance without competition. We present the view that adventure sports make specific and additional demands on the coach that differ from those in 'traditional' sports coaching practice. Our contention is that the adventure sports coach role necessitates the possession and application of a crucial blend of sophisticated beliefs about good learning and coaching, a domain-specific knowledge and pedagogic skill. These elements are synergized via a specific professional judgement and decision-making mechanism, and epistemological position. Typically, adventure sports coaches are well informed and practiced with respect to the technical aspects of their disciplines but are comparatively naïve about coaching adventure sports as a discipline.

Many factors have influenced adventure sports over the last ten years where increased participation (Royal Yachting Association [RYA], 2009), 'sportification' (Crum, 1991) and 'commodification' (Loynes, 2001) have generated a demand for high-quality coaching. Accordingly, adventure sports coaching has emerged as a subgroup of sports coaching and outdoor education. Unfortunately, this emergent position has led to the lack of a defined role. This chapter considers the factors that characterize adventure sports coaching in an attempt to clarify the question, 'what is an adventure sports coach?'

For the purpose of this chapter, adventure sports are considered to be physical activities with a degree of risk that are non-competitive in origin and guided by their own ethics (without specific rules). Adventure sports require specific technical skills, possess an element of physical challenge and take place within a continually changing dynamic environment.

The demand for adventure sports coaching

Adventure sports are a growing worldwide business. In the UK, over 7 per cent of sports coaches are involved with adventure sports coaching (Sports Coach UK, 2011), meeting the needs of an estimated 150,000 climbers (British Mountaineering Council, 2003) and over 1,200,000 canoeists and kayakers (RYA, 2009). The demand for adventure sports coaching is also growing, with a reported 48 per cent of the UK population taking part in adventure sports at least once a year. There are a number of agencies involved in meeting the consequent need for more and, of course, better trained coaches. In Britain, for example, the United Kingdom Coaching Certificate (UKCC) scheme and long-standing National Governing Body schemes such as the Mountain Leader Training Board. The increase in undergraduate and post-graduate degrees in outdoor and adventure education also contribute to the labour pool.

A desire to take part in adventure balanced with the demands of an increasingly busy lifestyle, access to venues and social acceptance of coaching may all encourage the participant to seek out coaching in order to maximize experience, development of skill and meet their own personal motivations for participation. Unfortunately, however, politically driven shifts in the profile of sports coaching in the UK and an alteration in how adventure is perceived has resulted in movement from the traditional, informal and somewhat *ad hoc* development of adventure sports skills in the past towards a more 'sportified' (Crum, 1991) and 'commodified' (Loynes 2001; Brown, 2000) perception of adventure. Historically, the outdoor instructor had served the adventure industry in a variety of guises and these specialisations have further diversified as we see the impact of the factors stated above. It seems likely, however, that a semantic debate will continue at a range of levels going forward.

Other pressures notwithstanding, the 'sportification' (Crum, 1991) and 'commodification' of adventure sports (Loynes 2001; Brown, 2000) has evolved amidst an increasingly litigious culture (Young, 2010). Notably, however, the philosophical position espoused by these social agendas appears at odds with the epistemological position identified by Collins, Collins and Grecic (2014) in which the stated aim of the adventure sports coach is to generate participants who are capable of independent participation in their own adventure experiences rather than that of a guide.

Delineation by goal – considering the target outcome

It is clear that multiple definitions of coaching in general have lead to ineffectual conceptual frameworks of coaching activity in adventure sports (Collins and Collins, 2012). Some commonality in definitions of coaching activity does occur in terms of coaching being a long-term participant-centred process. The nature of the relationship is driven by the interaction of the participant, adventure sport and environment and is individualized. In common with many sports, however, the length, pace and content of the relationship is governed by an individual's motivation for participation. Therefore, to fully understand the role of the adventure sports coach, the client's motivations for participation must be considered.

Typically, when faced with a group wanting coaching, a range of motivations emerges early in the coaching relationship: those wanting to develop their skills, those wanting to be taken into adventurous environments and those seeking interaction with fellow performers.

Miller and Kerr (2002) acknowledge the motivations for participation beyond the pursuit of medals, while Vallerand (2004) states that "motivation represents one of the most important variables in sport" (p. 427). Extending these broad differences, Bailey *et al.* (2010) proposed that participation reflected a range of motivations: *elite referenced excellence* (i.e., I am the best in XXX), *personally referenced excellence* (i.e., I am getting better than I was) or *participation for personal wellbeing* (i.e., I do this because I enjoy it and it makes me feel good). Balancing coaching practice to meet the provision of these three motivations, are crucial (see Figure 1.1). How do these targets fit within the current picture of adventure sports?

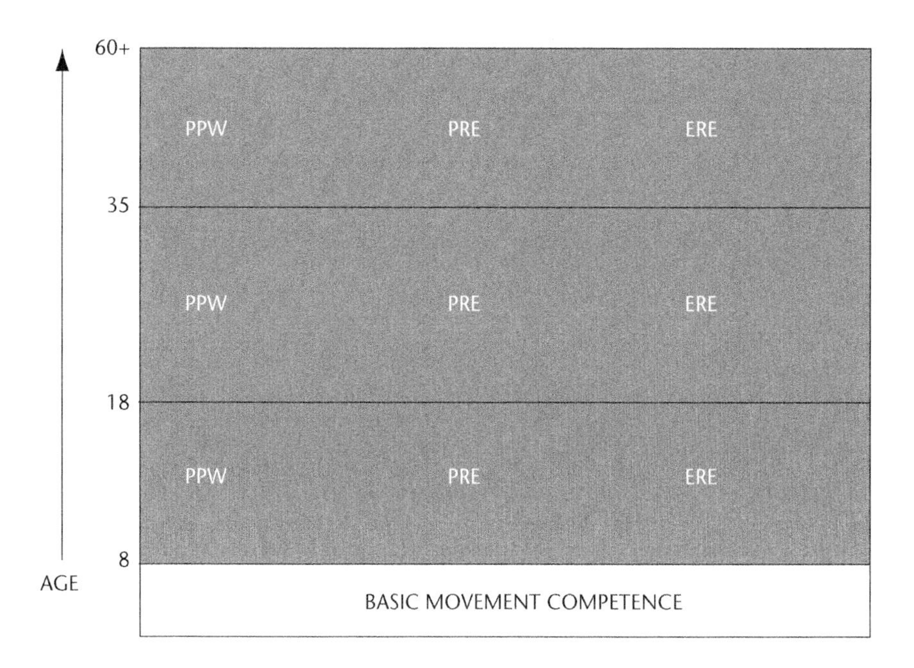

FIGURE 1.1 The 'three worlds continuum'

Source: Based on an original idea in Adventure Sports by Jess and Collins, 2003; cited in Bailey *et al.*, 2010. ERE = elite referenced excellence; PPW = participation for personal well-being; PRE = personally referenced excellence.

Competition has certainly resulted in an increase in participation for the 'more conventional' sport motivations such as elite referenced excellence; however, the debate surrounding the adventurous nature of these sports will surely remain. This category also clearly includes those individuals motivated to be the first among their peers to ascend, descend or cross a mountain, rock face, river, cave, gorge, sea, ice cap or continent.

Personally referenced excellence also emerges as a strong driver for participation in adventure sports. In similar fashion, performers who are attempting to 'push their grade' have replaced the stopwatch with the guidebook or by the attention created by media glamorization of performance in adventure sports; indeed, the latter may be just another type of elite referenced excellence, with the awards made 'virtually' through the various media.

Personal wellbeing and the motivation to 'stay in shape' factor, is shared with many sports and represents a final category. Undoubtedly, and with regard to the third, the motive for participation in adventure sports is clearly not limited to the pursuit of excellence.

Delineation by participant motivation in adventure sport

Bailey *et al.*'s (2010) grouping seems to resonate with many reasons for participation in a range of sports; however, other motives should also be considered that may be more specific to adventure sports. For example, many organisations use the skills developed to participate in adventurous activities to translate directly into a professional context. In the UK, a long history within the military, business and outdoor education have all traditionally used the adventure domain to generate transferable skills.

Sensation seeking (Zuckerman, 1994) has received a lot of attention and is perhaps a consequence of the desire for and seeking out of risk as an element lacking in today's society. However, the pursuit of sensation should not be viewed as just the 'buzz'. For many, the activity, solitude, peace and quiet, isolation or social contact with friends drives a person to seek out coaching, which then enables them to participate at higher levels. In adventure sports, the intensely personal nature of motivation will ensure this aspect remains complex and multi-dimensional (Vallerand, 2004). As an example, skiing a red run before and after coaching may not change the outcome but the performer may have enjoyed the same run more through higher levels of knowledge and skill leading to the sensation and 'flow'.

Brymer and Gray (2010) recognize that these motivations will alter over time, resembling Bailey *et al.*'s (2010) recognition in traditional sports that participation throughout a sport career has to allow for varied motivations. Extending this idea, Hopkins and Putnam (1993) highlight a well-documented and historical use of the outdoors for 'character building' and spiritual development, within the UK. This 'character building' function has long established and strong tradition in organizations such as Outward Bound. Identification of this wide range of motives, only *some* of which find strong resonance in mainstream sport, supports the notion that a coach in the traditional definition may not address the full range of possible motivations an adventure sports coach is required to address. As such, a clear delineation from other coaches exists.

Delineation by context – how does the adventure sports coach fit in to existing roles within adventure and outdoor education?

Defining the role of an adventure sports coach is not without its own challenges. The dynamic environment, risk and varied motivation for participation ensure that the adventure sports coach is not a stand-alone role. In reality, the adventure sports coach's role (i.e., performance development) operates in conjunction with the roles of guide (i.e., experience development) and teacher (i.e., personal development). The adventure sports coach needs to draw on skills for performance development, in addition to some that are shared with the guide or teacher. This enables the adventure sports coach to take on a role that may, outwardly and at different times, appear adventure sports guiding, teaching or coaching. Notably, however, it has an overarching, performance development focus that is supported by a more specific set of pedagogic skills. Equally, the respective positions of guide or teacher have both unique and shared skills but operate from different philosophical stances. Thus, for example, while *guiding* a three-week canoe expedition my role is to provide the experience for my clients (experience development), ensure they are safe and to take them from the start to end. As an adventure sports coach, the three-week expedition becomes the vehicle that I use to teach the students how to plan, prepare and undertake a canoe expedition (performance development). I am successful if they undertake their own expeditions after this one. As a teacher the challenges encountered on the expedition act as metaphors and analogies for the *real* world, I am successful if the tools developed to deal with these challenges *'on trip'* can be transferred into the student world on return.

Considering the position of the adventure sports coach alongside those of teacher and guide may enable us to conceptualize the position of adventure sports coaching activity in the broader context of adventure, and may also help to clarify a definition. Guiding, teaching and coaching are closely related and share common skills (i.e., technical, tactical and pedagogical; see Figure 1.2). The adventure sports coach shares competencies while also having some skills that are shared with other coaching domains.

Figure 1.2 contextualizes the adventure sports coach as a development of the model proposed in Collins and Collins (2012). This revised model utilizes professional judgement and decision-making (PJDM) as the 'glue' that synergizes the three possible roles and domain-specific skills. The three circles represent three major professional areas of adventure activity, superficially these areas of practice are associated with specific roles; however, these may be better considered in terms of the desired outcome:

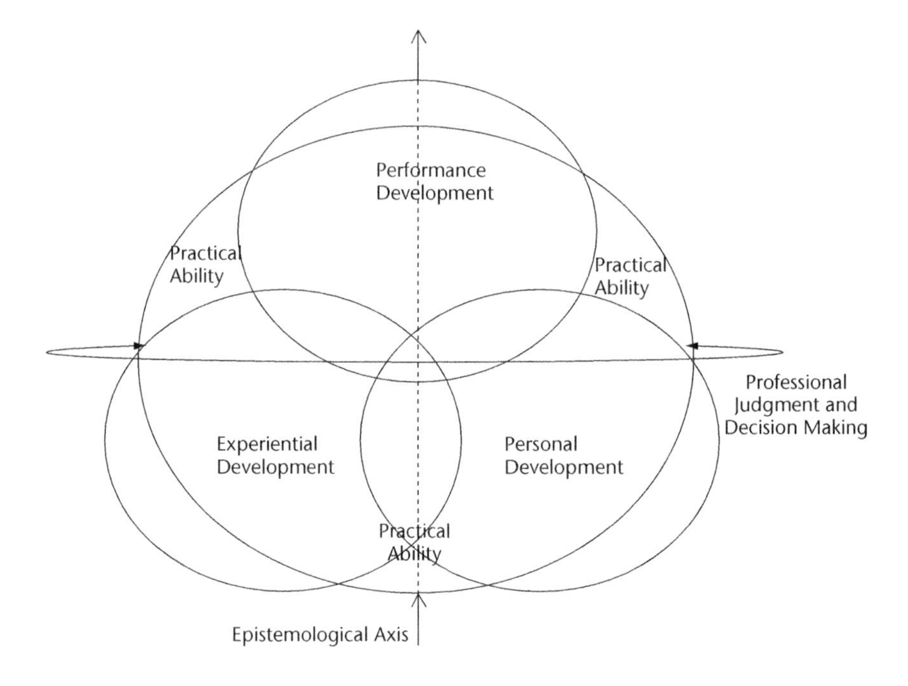

FIGURE 1.2 Conceptualizing the adventure sports coach model

- Guiding is focused on taking others into adventurous settings, offering those desirable experiences and, potentially, *experience development* for their own, sometimes unstated, purposes.
- Coaching aims to offer *performance development* in the adventure sport.
- Teaching uses the outdoors as a vector for *personal development*, sometimes at school, as part of a youth group, in management development, or in therapeutic domains.

The outdoor professional will clearly have a tendency towards a particular function that is dependent on the context of their work domain, philosophy and the students' motivation. It seems likely that this may even become a default setting for the individual, reflecting their epistemological stance. Individuals within an overtly educational setting being in the lower right, expedition leaders and guides in the lower left and coaches upper central. Of course, these roles are clearly not mutually exclusive and the individual coach will be required to select the aspect of development that the learner requires. In this respect, the function (performance, experience or personal development) may differ depending on different student motivations, impact of environment and/or longer term goals. In teaching transceiver search techniques to a group of skiers the adventure sports coach is meeting a clear safety requirement before venturing off-piste (impact of environment). The client who simply wants to be taken to the best powder that day and put in some 'fresh tracks' is learning the use of a transceiver for that day as a means to an end. The client whose motivation is to be able to ski off-piste independently is learning the skills with a much longer-term goal in mind. The nuances of the teaching, actual techniques taught and even the equipment used may differ but outwardly may look similar. The first client will perhaps focus on the use of the transceiver, probe and shovel while the second client may also be taught to recognize the conditions and locations that are prone to avalanche. The adventure sports coach makes the decisions regarding the first client, (slope, gradient, line, pitch length, etc.) while the second student is engaged with the decision-making process, perhaps via a cognitive apprenticeship type of approach.

To operate within the context of the activity (i.e. to be alongside the participants in the adventure), practical skills are essential. As guide or teacher, roles all involve the requirement to be skilfully independent in the environment in which they practice. While adventure sports coaches do not routinely coach on the hardest routes or rivers, as this appears to be the domain of the guides and meeting the 'experience development' needs, a desired aim to create independently skilful performers logically sees performers with the independence and ability to operate in harder environments, so that they may develop away from the adventure sports coach.

This independent skilfulness has a clear relation to managing safety, leadership (Priest and Gass, 2005) and, increasingly, as an aspect of pedagogic skill (Collins, Collins and Grecic, 2014). This requirement results in personal skill becoming an essential attribute rather than the 'nice to have' status that, prejudices/expectations notwithstanding ("of course he's a good coach, he's played in the premiership"), exists in traditional sports. We are not advocating that adventure sports coaches need to be high-level performers, our point is that the adventure sports coach has to be independent, safe and have a capacity to deal with unforeseen issues (e.g. an injured client, long detours, hideous portages, etc.)

The adventure sports coach may move between different positions on Figure 1.2 in response to the learning demands of their students, the task at hand and/or demands of the environment. The ability to be mobile in this respect is enabled by a set of PJDM skills and a clear coaching philosophy (epistemological axis). It seems likely that the clearer and stronger this belief, the easier the adventure sports coach will be able to move around the different roles but still be able to retain a clear focus on the outcome. This epistemological framework provides the philosophical scaffolding to the adventure sports coach's actions and is manifest in links between philosophy and practice (Collins, Collins and Grecic, 2014).

As an example, an adventure sports coach may use an individual rapid for an explicit coaching session and electing to utilize, by guiding, the following section of river, as part of an overall approach that has a focus on slow holistic skill development and potential long retention retains a clear focus on developing an independent, skilful performance. This would differ from teaching in the first rapid so the skill can be used immediately in order to get safely through the following section. The approach therefore requiring a fast albeit temporary acquisition of skill and is perhaps an approach that could be associated with a guide or leader instead.

In reality, most 'outdoor professionals' will inhabit a centralized position that is illustrated by the overlapping areas in Figure 1.2, moving towards a particular position based on student, task and environmental demands. It is only as the outdoor professional specializes and develops a more defined and stronger epistemological position that their role and work pattern gravitates more permanently towards the extremities of the model. Crucially, the demands of the environment, task and student necessitate the coach to move around the model. For example, will the adventure sports coach recognize the need to guide rather than coach in risky situations, while simultaneously focusing on performance development?

Delineation by relationship not just content

Adventure sports coaching shares skills and knowledge with fellow outdoor professionals and a wide variety of coaching contexts. Traditionally, these skills are introduced during a formalized training process. However, Saury and Durand (1998) identified that many coaches are left to contextualize and make sense of the pan-sport theories that are presented in formal training. The uniqueness of the adventure sports coach lies in the complexity of the interactional relationship between both the shared and the discrete components. In short, it is not so much the different skills required but how those skills and other factors interact.

The notion of this interaction may provide an explanation in which the components of adventure sports coaching can be conceived and related. The interaction is clearly a cognitive structure that utilize both the knowledge schema (generalized collections of knowledge) required for the face-to-face, interpersonal coaching encounters and an understanding of the context in which that knowledge schema is applied. The constantly changing action of adventure sports coaching links the interaction to the aforementioned concepts of interactive expertise (Collins and Evans, 2002) and adaptive expertise (Hatano and Inagaki, 1986).

Knowledge schemas are organized into related knowledge groups pertinent to an environment (e.g. when organizing safety for a three-part rapid, I may apply the C.L.A.P. principles that are advocated by Ferrero, 2006). Clearly the practicalities of *Communication* (C) between the group and the coach has a direct relationship with *Line of site* (L); namely if you cannot see the group you cannot communicate with them. However, if you use paddle signals to communicate you can communicate with the top of the rapid but not have line of sight. This raises questions of gradient and, therefore, effects anticipated (A); problems such as boats becoming pinned in a drop, which will effect position of maximum usefulness (P).

As stated, the interaction of the knowledge schema (in this case the C.L.A.P. principles) and the context (the gradient of the rapid) provides a scaffold of broader principles (e.g. the basic principles of protecting a danger point are ...). In the traditional, *ad hoc* development of adventure sports professionals this interaction may be unique to an individual adventure sports coach, created from personal experiences, adventure sports associated to reflective practice and, quite possibly, be tacit in nature.

In more formalized learning environments, however, the notion of interaction is rarely explicitly addressed, where instead the emphasis is placed on knowledge schema in preference to developing more overarching judgement and decision-making skills. We would advocate that if the interaction can be made explicit, both the knowledge schema and context can be reflected throughout development where in practical terms the interaction and knowledge schema are developed alongside each other. Due to the complexity of this interaction a coach's development in this regard will therefore rely more heavily on developing skills in reflection and also highlights the need for experienced coaches with effective mentoring skills.

How might interaction be developed?

When observing and listening to an experienced coach, the aspirant coach can begin to develop a conceptual model of the interaction of the processes involved through a process of cognitive modelling which is, in effect, an interactional schema (e.g. articulation of the application of C.L.A.P. earlier). The developing coach can then apply these principles at the next rapid and be coached on the behaviours in context. Clearly, in activities that are repeated identically (e.g. buckling up a specific type of climbing harness) the interactional schema can be comparatively simple. However, in more varied tasks (e.g. skiing off-piste), the interactional schema will need to be complex and flexible simply because of increased number of variables (snow condition, gradient, mood of the group, etc.) Within this complex and flexible interaction an additional factor, the coach's beliefs about learning, knowledge and adventure add to this mix. For instance, the belief that challenge and adventure is positive will logically influence the level at which the adventure sports coach pitches a particular task or selects the nature of the practice environment. It seems logical to consider that the environment may have greater significance in the coaching process or that the level at which a task is set compared with the performer's skill level may be more complex, therefore knowledge around goal setting will be given greater value.

What is the impact of the adventure sports coach's epistemological position?

The epistemological framework is important because it is fundamental to how we think, perceive, value and learn about knowledge. In turn, the ability to understand how knowledge is created, constructed, acquired and developed forms the foundation of our thinking and decision-making processes as a coach. On this basis, the interaction of epistemological framework and our professional judgement and decision-making appears important as it synergizes the differing functions of a practicing adventure sports coach and differentiates the adventure sports coach from the philosophies of the guide or teacher. The effect impacts on the aims, methods and evolution of the coaching process in both practical and philosophical terms. In essence, these are the values and priorities placed on the interactions.

The influence of these constructs on behaviour is well documented. For example, both Perry (1981) and Schommer (1994) highlighted epistemological development as a continuum, with beliefs being naïve or sophisticated at the poles as illustrated in Table 1.1.

What is the epistemological chain?

In a study of high-level adventure sports coaches, Collins, Collins and Grecic (2014) found that the epistemological chain was demonstrated as a consistent, logical relationship between philosophy, modus operandi, aims and session content. Further to the epistemological chain, Collins, Collins and Grecic (2014) identified a definable epistemological position in a group of high-level adventure sports coaches. This position rests on a belief in positive adventure that stems from influential adventurous experiences, a sophisticated epistemological position and value placed on an individualized coaching process. Implicit within this is recognition that adventure is a personal construct and can differ from individual to individual that, in consequence, contributes to a differentiated coaching process.

This differentiated process is apparent in highly individualized teaching to meet the learner's needs and wants in context. The clearly defined ultimate goals are set to generate an independent performer, capable of undertaking their own adventures. The epistemological position, plus exposure to hyper-dynamic contexts, creates a highly cognitive professional judgement and decision-making ability in the adventure sports coach who, in response, actively creates 'space' in the coaching process to audit actual student development against anticipated development (Collins, Collins and Grecic, 2014). This acts as a measure of the effectiveness of the coaching and drives the professional judgement and decision-making process.

Professional judgement and decision-making

The decision-making processes in adventure sports coaching are complex and varied (Collins and Collins, 2013). Decisions that are not time pressured and that have access to comprehensive information on which to base the decision are best made utilizing analytical/classic decision-making processes, these are frequently pre-activity planning decisions, such as venue choice (a decision outside the realm of most other coaching situations). By contrast, during activities the decision-making process is more naturalistic and demonstrates elements of heuristic simplification and pattern recognition (Klein, 2008); for example, recognizing the differences in water direction based on the colour of the water surface in complex tidal conditions. This could be considered as a distinctly dual process (which is either/or if conceptualized as a graded continuum. Notably, however, we can more easily

TABLE 1.1 Epistemological perspective

Epistemology	*Views of knowledge*	*Views of learning*	*Consequences for teaching*
Naïve	Clear Specific Held in authority Fixed Prescribed Reinforced by authority	Coach centred Coach adventure sports 'expert' Knowledge resides with the coach Learning is procedural and routine based Transactional relationship	Explicit learning defined practices that facilitate rapid knowledge uptake The coach owns the knowledge, manages and censors its dissemination and constant reinforcement Success of failure determined by tangible markers or results set by the coach Constant coach's revision of targets, technique, results Coach-led modifications to be practiced, re-learned and embedded Coach prescribed, subjective to coach's beliefs Coach dependent Autocratic, disciplined, power relationship, dominant coach, compliant athlete
Sophisticated	Complex Changing Dynamic Learned gradually Constructed by the learners	Constant journey of discovery Learning environment created to allow experimentation with safety (physical, pedagogic and cognitive) Two-way flow of ideas sports Experimentation and reflection to create new knowledge(both coach and learner) Future path determined by student	Constructivist teaching strategies, randomized practice Problem-based sports self-analysis Reflective practice Challenges set for and agreed with learner Creating learning episodes Learner-led discussion Trusting and autonomy-supportive behaviours Supported through the use of coaching tools, such as delayed/bandwidth feedback, the development of intrinsic feedback mechanisms and questioning that encourages autonomous and independent performance Dependent on how the player develops as a person Decisions based on 'Is the student autonomous and confident?' Question the status quo, engage in performer- and learning-centred coaching Encourage deep learning and understanding of performance in students

recognize that a single 'big' decision has nested – interactive decisions within it that can be combination of both processes. Thus, for example, selection of a particular section of a white water river for a coaching session the night before may be based on a simple alignment of grade of river with ability of group in algorithmic terms (grade 3 paddlers = a grade 3 river section). During the river trip, however, the selection of teaching locations (specific rapids) would be based partially on the characteristic of the rapid (suitability for the task at hand), on the benefits of a given activity against the risk to the participant (Collins and Collins, 2013) and on the time constraints. Equally, a decision to move quickly through a section without explicitly teaching may be based on a 'gut feeling' to make up time.

Within professional judgement and decision-making, and at the heart of flexibility and adaptability, is a constant auditing cycle in which the anticipated results of a course of action are compared with the reality presented to the coach. This actually follows a simple process: What is happening? What does that mean? What do I do now? It seems logical to consider that the adventure sports coach will utilize differing processes (reflection on action, extrapolation and projection) within that *what, now what, so what* structure to facilitate the auditing function, and that these are required skills for the adventure sports coach. Hence its conceptualisation as a multi-looped and nested process by Abraham and Collins (2011) who recognize the interactional nature of professional judgement and decision-making (see Figure 1.3).

FIGURE 1.3 The complexity of the environment and context for learners is a significant factor in the professional judgement and decision-making process for coaches

The complexity of the environment and context therefore becomes a significant factor in the professional judgement and decision-making process. Chow *et al.* (2006) and Renshaw *et al.* (2010) define complex natural systems as having two or more interrelated parts. Clearly the interaction of learner, environment and task could be defined as complex and, presumably, the management of the learning in that context reflects that complexity. This raises practical problems for the adventure sports coach, not to mention the potential of cognitive overload!

The timing and physical location in which the decision is made has a clear influence on the process. Decisions made in the field appearing more naturalistic/intuitive while decisions made as part of the planning or review processes appear more classical in nature. McCammon (2001) highlights that apparently classic decisions can frequently become naturalistic in nature if a conclusion is not reached. Equally as the decision-maker's experience grows, we also see a propensity to make decisions in naturalistic ways, presumably as the professional judgement and decision-making skills evolve and refine.

Clearly, the quality of the professional judgement and decision-making process is linked to the quality and authenticity of the decision-maker's experience and the learning from those experiences. Deficiencies in the learning from those experiences are manifest in decision-making traps. In this regard, McCammon (2001) recognizes traps of familiarity, authority, social proof, commitment/consistency, liking/conforming and scarcity and expertise and analytical traps – all of which affect the decision-making processes. McCammon (2001) describes the predominance of naturalistic decision-making approaches as a default trap in itself, which stems from the need for authentic experience by the decision-maker. Thus, professional judgement and decision-making is a double-edged sword, both synergizing the complex interactions of the adventure sports coach, student task and environment, while equally being at the mercy of decision-making traps that can only be considered once recognized by the decision-maker.

Within professional judgement and decision-making, sub-process are largely 'in action'; that is, carried out while the activity is being planned or in progress. The first, an overarching meta-decision that relates to how best to make a given decision and a second, subordinate, that balances the risk and benefit of a given course of action (reflecting the positive nature of adventure). For example, in selecting a route for a back country ski trip in an unknown area, the adventure sports coach will not want to rely on the heuristic rules developed for their own local area regarding snow conditions and may rely on more classic approaches. Decisions on route will then consider the risks of a proposed route against the potential learning benefits.

Once en route, the professional judgement and decision-making process focuses on a further two parts. First, recognizing the individual needs of the student (reflecting the individualized nature of the coaching process) that is facilitated by utilizing a combination of observation and questioning of the student to build a learner profile for the individual (Collins, Collins and Grecic, 2014). Second, opportunistically utilizing and specifically creating time in the coaching process to undertake professional judgement and decision-making (facilitating the differentiation of the coaching process). Thus, while following a broken trail, skinning up a peak, the adventure sports coach may move around the group, watching students' skills, fluency of movement, co-ordination and balance, fitness, etc., and talking with the students to get an idea of motivations, understanding and personality. At safe points in the adventure ascent, the group may need to fit ski crampons at which point the coach audits the suitability of the next part of the route or, as the group waits behind a student who is struggling with a kick turn to the right, the coach may take the opportunity to audit the suitability of the route choice.

Having reached the high point the professional judgement and decision-making process focuses on the differentiated coaching process of the downhill sections and specifically the utilisation of environment, individual and task constraints to facilitate variation in practice and to identify affordances and integrate them into the coaching process (Vickers, 2007). The adventure sports coach may first identify a short, safe, 'off-piste' pitch that has a consistent snow covering. In skiing the pitch first and organizing the group to descend one at a time, the coach can then observe each skier in turn over a number of turns. From this, emerge the needs of each individual in that the route up has allowed the adventure sports coach to work out a pedagogic approach. The adventure sports coach can then decide how to approach each pitch that follows: length, location, safe spots and the teaching content. This, in turn, links back to the macro risk benefit assessment of the given course of action.

How is professional judgement and decision-making developed?

McCammon (2004) highlights that decision-making is rarely taught, either formally or informally, during training and results in the aforementioned *ad hoc* development of the interactional elements of skilful coaching. Exposure to the informal learning process via approaches such as the cognitive apprenticeship provides possible approaches for development. McCammon (2001) proposes that part of this process must involve recognizing and addressing (make explicit) the decision-making traps identified earlier.

Decision-making abilities rely on a synergy and interaction of knowledge, experience and self-reflection. The sub-conscious 'construction' of tacit knowledge acts to interpret and simplify complex information, supporting a heuristic element to the decision-making process, while creating explicit knowledge groups and relating variables together supports recognition-primed elements of the process. We are left with a question as to how best might this development be achieved in the formal development setting, especially given the aforementioned preference for non-formal training. Many pedagogic strategies espouse to develop skills and understanding such as 'learnacy' (Claxton, 2002), meta-cognition (Boström and Lassen, 2006), epistemology and criticality. Collins, Brown and Newman (1987) identified six teaching strategies that, when used in combination, can effectively address this need. Three adventure sports are listed, (modelling, coaching, scaffolding), that are core to cognitive apprenticeship and develop the cognitive and meta-cognitive skills required; two (articulation and reflection) that develop awareness of problem-solving strategies and refine the cognitive and meta-cognitive process; and a final step (exploration), which guides the novice towards independence and the ability to problem solve in context.

Clearly a broad, structured and considered experience has the potential to generate the desired interactional, tacit and explicit knowledge, practical and pedagogic skills for the adventure sports coach.

Reflection in professional judgement and decision-making

Martin *et al.* (2006) stress the significance of reflection in the development of good judgement. The simplistic notion that good judgement comes from experience and that experience comes from bad judgement fails to recognize the value of reflection and a requirement for authenticity in that experience. It appears sensible to conclude that effective reflective practice on previous 'bad judgements' would, if appropriate in style, structure and impact, support both professional judgement and decision-making and future meta-decision-making for the coach. For example, a coach may reflect on a sea kayaking session in which an individual student was unable to respond to coaching as anticipated and identify that the physical environment intimidated the student to a point that their capacity to learn was reduced. This may impact on several factors, either solely or in combination, such as venue selection in the future with that student, duration of activity to limit physical fatigue, content of related sessions to manage potential overload of the student and/or the timing of the session within the tidal cycle to gradually allow the environment to develop. These all impact on the selection of a pedagogic approach. Thus, decision-making in this context is complex and a synergy of processes facilitated by reflective practice is essential if lessons are to be genuinely and effectively internalized.

Reflection in this context needs to take place both on action–in action (Schön, 1983) and on action–in context, especially given the time and environments associated with adventure activities and the nested nature of the process. The challenges of the environment (e.g. time pressure, danger, lack of control if things go awry) prevents the 'stop and think' approaches espoused in more 'conventional' sports (Schön). Accordingly, the reflective process must be positioned within, and possibly away from the changing environment, linking the environment and drawing decisions based on prior experience in that environment and situation, while anticipating the future decisions, events and student performance that may develop, therefore utilizing 'out of context off line activity' in support of contextual activity (see Figure 1.4).

Reflection-in-action (Schön, 1983) allows the adventure sports coach to reshape the coaching process during the session. It is the ongoing experimentation that helps to refine, adapt and make delivery sufficiently flexible to meet the student's needs. For example, if a demonstration of a skill is not working correctly

FIGURE 1.4 Off-line activity with an adventure sports aspirant sea kayaking coach may still be contextual

(does not seem right, does not seem to move the student closer to the goal) then the adventure sports coach reflects on the success of that task in the action-present (Schön, 1987). This assumes that the knowing in action is not the action itself, but what that action indicates that we know through application. In this respect, knowing-in-action is similar to tacit knowledge and is revealed in a more skilful performance.

By contrast, reflection-on-action was originally described as, "We reflect *on* action, thinking back on what we have done in order to discover how our knowing-in-action may have contributed to an unexpected outcome" (Schön, 1983, p. 26). It is clearly separate from the physical activity. It has been suggested that Schön's (1983) original definitions of in- and on-action reflection lack a desired clarity (Moon 1999, Court 1988). Clearly 'thinking on our feet' (Schön, 1983) appears part of the coaching practice in adventure sports in terms of simply 'reflecting on the phenomenon before him' and 'in context' (Schön, 1983 p. 68). Other authors recognize the need for an opportunity to reflect in practice (Killion and Todenem, 1991; York-barr *et al*, 2001) while Moon (1999) comments that a congested curriculum may prevent this reflective pause. Both the need for a pause or space and the congestion it counters are conditions that are clearly recognisable in adventure sports coaching and reflect the extended nature of the coaching interaction and the highly dynamic environment that creates a cognitive and practically 'congested' coaching environment.

Summary

Adventure sports coaching is a broad-ranging, complex field, which utilizes concepts and skills associated with leadership, teaching in the outdoors and traditional coaching skills. The adventure sports coach also has a unique need to combine pedagogic skills and personal performance, aspects that also pertain to the teaching and guiding domains. This interaction of requirements creates the complexity that, in turn, reflects and caters for a diverse range of client aspirations and motivations. Contextualizing the position of coaching in adventure sports highlights the cross-domain nature of the skills required. Adventure sports coaches need to be leaders, teachers and coaches to fulfil their role. Adventure sports coaches coach people to undertake adventure activities as the mechanism for their own adventure. The highly personalized nature of adventure and the related perceptions of, and response to, risk are factors that are specific to the role. We suggest that, to operate in and utilize the challenging environments that characterize adventure sports, coaches are required to have a skilful technical performance, to have skilled coaching, leadership and developmental skills, a sophisticated epistemology and enhanced professional judgement and decision-making skills if they are to exploit benefits these environments.

Building from these demonstrable differences, this chapter introduced the notion of an interactional schema for the adventure sports coaching process, in which the main notion of interaction applies to the inner processes of coaching, and not solely to the confluence of a number of components. In the coaching process, the interactional schema emerges within a nested, multi-looped, auditing cycle made possible by the professional judgement and decision-making process. It should be noted that the notion of an interactive schema is speculative and needs empirical verification, but it appears to describe the interaction within the coaching and decision-making process in a pragmatic way.

In attempting to conceptualize the adventure sports we also acknowledge a number of challenges for the future through continuing shifts in perceptions of adventure, the political shifts in coach education, continued increase in demand and an increasingly litigious culture affect practice before we even 'step off the path'. Despite this challenge, interest in adventure sports and coaching them continues to grow. Perhaps, the task of synthesizing all the factors we have described in view of these challenges is precisely why people continue to be attracted to coaching adventure sports!

References

Aron, A. and Collins, D. (2011). Taking the next step: ways forwards for coaching science. *Quest*, 63(4), 366–384.

Boström, L. and Lassen, L, M. (2006). Unraveling learning, learning styles, learning strategies and meta-cognition. *Education + Training*, 48(2/3), 178–189.

Bailey, R., Collins, D., Ford, P., McNamara, A., Toms, M. and Pearce, G. (2010, March). Participant development in sport: An academic review. Retrieved from Sport Northern

Ireland website: www.sportscoachuk.org/sites/default/files/Participant-Development-Lit-Review.pdf (accessed 6 November 2014).
British Mountaineering Council (BMC) (2003). Participation statistics. Manchester. Retrieved from www.thebmc.co.uk/bmcNews/media/u_content/File/press/factsheets/ParticipationStats03.pdf (accessed 6 November 2014).
Brown, H. (2000). Passengers, participants, partners and practitioners. Working with risk to empower groups. *Horizons*, 12, 37–39.
Brymer, E. and Gray, T. (2010). Dancing with nature: Rhythm and harmony in extreme sport participation. *Journal of Adventure Education and Outdoor Learning*, 9, 135–149.
Chow, J-Y., Davids, K., Button, C., Shuttleworth, R., Renshaw, I. and Araugo, D. (2006). Nonlinear pedagogy: A constraints-led framework to understanding emergence of game play skills. *Nonlinear Dynamics, Psychology and Life Sciences*, 10(1), 71–103.
Claxton, G. (2002). *Building Learning Power: Helping Young People Become Better Leaders*. Bristol: TLO Limited.
Collins, L. and Collins, D. (2012). Contextualising the adventure sport coach. *Journal of Adventure Education and Outdoor Learning*, 12(1), 81–93.
Collins, L. and Collins, D. (2013). Decision-making and risk management in adventure sports coaching. *Quest*, 65(1), 72–82. Collins, H. M. and Evans, R. J. (2002). The Third Wave of Science Studies: Studies of Expertise and Experience. *Social Studies of Sciences*, 32(2), 235–296.
Collins, A., Brown, J. S. and Newman, S. E. (1987). Cognitive apprenticeship: Teaching the craft of reading, writing and mathematics (Technical Report No. 403). BBN Laboratories, Cambridge, MA. Centre for the Study of Reading, University of Illinois.
Collins, L., Collins, D. and Grecic, D. (2014) The epistemological chain in high level adventure sports coaches. *Journal of Adventure Education and Outdoor Learning*, doi.10.1080/14729679.2014.95059
Crum, B. J. (1991). 'Sportification' of Society and internal sports differentiation. *Spel en Sport*, (1), 2–7.
Ferrero, F. (2006). *Whitewater Safety and Rescue*. Caernarfon: Pesda Press.
Hatano, G. and Inagaki, K. (1986). Two courses of expertise. *Child Development and Education in Japan*, 262–272.
Killion, J. and Todenem, G. (1991). A process of personal theory building. *Educational Leadership*, 48(6), 14–16.
Klein, G. (2008). Naturalistic decision making. *Human Factors*, 50, 456–460.
Loynes, C. (1996). Adventure in a bun. *Journal of Adventure Education and Outdoor Learning*, 13, 52–57.
Martin, B., Cashel, C., Wagstaff, M. and Breunig, M. (2006). *Outdoor leadership: Theory and practice*. Champaign, IL: Human Kinetics.
McCammon, I. (2001). Decision making for wilderness leaders: strategies, traps and teaching methods. Proceedings of Wilderness Risk managers Conference, Lake Geneva, WI, 16–29.
McCammon, I. (2004). Heuristic traps in recreational avalanche accidents: Evidence and implications. *Avalanche News*, 68(1), 1–10.
Miller, P. and Kerr, G. (2002). The athletic, academic and social experiences of intercollegiate student-athletes. *Journal of Sport Behavior*, 25, 346–367.
Moon, J. (1999). *Reflection in Learning and Professional Development: Theory and Practice*. Oxon: Routledge.
Perry, W. G. J. (1981). Cognitive and ethical growth: The making of meaning. In: A. W. Chickering (ed.), *The Modern American College*, San Francisco, CA: Jossey-Bass, 76–116.
Priest, S. and Gass, M. A. (2005). *Effective Leadership in Adventure Programming*. Leeds: Human Kinetics.

Renshaw, I., Davids, K., Chow, J-Y. and Hammons, J. (2010). A constraints-led perspective to understanding skill acquisition and game play: A basis for integration of motor learning theory and physical education practice? *P.E. and Sport Pedagogy*, 15(2), 117–131.

Royal Yachting Association (RYA) (2009). *Water-sports and Leisure Participation Survey.* Hampshire. Retrieved from www.britishmarine.co.uk/upload_pub/WatersportsandLeisureOmnibus2009finalpublic.pdf

Saury, J. and Durand, M. (1998). Practical knowledge in expert coaches: On-site study of coaching sailing. *Research Quarterly for Exercise and Sport*, 69(3), 254–266.

Schommer, M. A. (1994). Synthesising epistemological belief of research: Tentative understandings and provocative confusions. *Educational Psychology Review*, 6, 293–319.

Schön, D. (1983). *The Reflective Practitioner: How Professionals Think in Action.* Aldershot: Ashgate.

Schön, D. (1987). *Educating the reflective practitioner.* San Francisco, CA: Jossey-Bass.

Sports Coach UK (2011). *Sports coaching in the UK III: A statistical analysis of coaches and coaching in the UK.* Leeds: Sports Coach UK.

Vallerand, R. J. (2004). *Intrinsic and Extrinsic Motivation in Sport.* Retrieved from http://ess220.files.wordpress.com/2010/12/vallerand-2004-overview.pdf (accessed 6 November 2014).

Vickers, J. N. (2007). *Perception, Cognition, Decision Training: The Quiet Eye in Action.* Champaign, IL: Human Kinetics.

York-barr, J., Sommers, W.A., Ghere, G. S. and Montie, J. (2001). *Reflective Practice to Improve Schools: An Action Guide for Educators.* Thousand Oaks, CA: Corwin.

Young Report (2010). Common Sense, common safety. Retrieved from http://lordyoungreport@dwp.gsi.gov.uk

Zuckerman, M. (1994). *Behavioural Expressions and Biosocial Bases of Sensation Seeking.* Cambridge: Cambridge University Press.

2

UNDERSTANDING THE ROLE OF PEDAGOGY IN ADVENTURE SPORTS COACHING

Matt Berry

Introduction

Adventure sport is a relatively young area of study. Just like all other sport, as it has strived to gain legitimacy and recognition it has aligned itself with various sub-disciplines of more established fields of study such as exercise physiology, sport psychology, physical education, outdoor or adventure education and even environmental science. At some point, however, all these sub-disciplines collide in the real world in adventure sport and in our coaching practice. Continuing work in each of these sub-disciplines has led to a wealth of supporting research evidence that, when used wisely, can inform, support, justify and improve what we do as coaches but it is the skilful *application* of this knowledge base that is pedagogy. Sports science may well provide us with cutting edge empirical research evidence on energy systems or the acquisition of fine motor skills for example; however, if the learners that we work with are to get the best from adventure sport 'someone has to bring these individual disciplines together in meaningful and helpful ways' (Armour, 2013). Effective coaches therefore have more than a wealth of technical knowledge about their adventure sport but they are also knowledgeable about different pedagogical approaches. Effective coaches are not only informed by technical knowledge and theory but are able to use it to bring about learning more effectively.

In this chapter we look at factors that influence our practice from a learning and teaching perspective. Primarily we aim to show the importance of understanding pedagogy and the way that it shapes our coaching practice. To do this we discuss the conceptual parameters of pedagogy and aim to offer a definition suitable to the adventure sports context. Like the other chapters in the book, this chapter does not aim to present the content as a set of idealised principles or best practice. It is intended to provide an insight into pedagogy that should then affirm or challenge ideas historically implicit within adventure sports.

What is pedagogy?

Put simply, pedagogy is the study of learning and teaching. However, like many constructs, pedagogy is a contested term and efforts to give a universally accepted definition can be problematic. Stone (2000), for example, said that pedagogy had become amoeba-like and studying it had become 'as rigorous as a jellyfish' (p. 94). This has led authors to develop more specialised definitions of pedagogy depending on the specific context where the learning takes place, the type of learner and the nature of learning goals intended. For example, a coach employed to address youth disaffection through paddle sports would need to develop a different pedagogy to a mountain guide working to get her clients to the summit of an alpine peak. Both have the same basic goal of facilitating learning for the participants in order to achieve a pre-determined goal. However, each situation demands that the coach is able to expertly prioritise and bring together major elements, such as technical knowledge, tactical skill, motor skill, biomechanics or environmental physiology, in ways that best suit the situation, the goal and the learner. This is no easy task yet it is the task facing every coach taking adults and children into the adventure environment with the goal of coaching them. It is this challenge of manipulating such a variety of environmental, cognitive, social and physical constraints however that make coaching adventure sports so alluring and rewarding.

Adventure sports pedagogy is therefore a unique and complex synthesis, accounting for fundamental aims, motivations, the learners themselves and the contexts in which the learning takes place. Therefore, if we are to gain the recognition we seek as professionals we must strive to continue to develop our knowledge in each of the sub-disciplines as pedagogy has the unique function of assimilating all the other sub-disciplines relevant to it. In this way some authors describe pedagogy as being an art form in that effective coaches need to be able to draw upon their creative impulses in order to pull together each of the sub-disciplines to create meaningful, exciting and engaging coaching sessions. More obvious to many coaches is the relationship between pedagogy and science where effective coaches draw upon sound research evidence and established theory to inform and evaluate their practice. In the field of education, much has been written discussing the artistic and scientific characteristics of pedagogy but these are not addressed in detail here. It is worth noting however that the term pedagogy has its roots in ancient Greece where it referred to the *holistic* development of children rather than simply gaining knowledge where the pedagogue was a well-educated servant responsible for the overall development of the child. The relevant link here for adventure sports coaches is that we have also have overall responsibility for our learners comfort and well-being as we purposefully but carefully expose our learners to increased levels of risk and discomfort.

Why does understanding pedagogy matter?

At this point you may think that the discussion about the roots of pedagogy may seem more suited to the philosophy class but we should bear in mind that the etymological roots for pedagogy and its holistic origins are still relevant. If we are to avoid adventure sports coaching being seen and conducted as a simple process of guiding and instruction/transmission we must recognise not only the complexities of coaching but also our own beliefs about what coaching is for. This is a problem with understanding pedagogy in that there is an insufficient focus on the goals of coaching in the broadest sense. i.e. 'what am I coaching for?' This is a different question from 'what are the learning outcomes for my session?' This distinction is important for adventure sports coaches because our fundamental beliefs about what our coaching is for will shape our pedagogy and in turn shape our coaching practice. To understand this point we can consider the following case studies.

Case study 1

Jas is an experienced and well-qualified ski coach and will often focus on skiers developing more athletic short radius turns or carved turns without skidding. Both are typical and sensible learning outcomes for skiers who are looking to progress through an award scheme or just to improve their skiing. Jas has developed great observational skills through experience. She can correct faults and the skiers that she works with usually make rapid progress and consequently have a great ski holiday.

Case study 2

Jim is an experienced and well-qualified PE teacher in a secondary school who works with a wide age range of students. He is rated as an outstanding teacher and the students he teaches usually make great progress in their lessons. In some lessons, however, there would appear to be little or no progress in visible motor skill improvements. In these lessons students are inventing their own practice drills, working together, discussing and, at times, arguing.

In both case studies the focus quite rightly is on progress and the learners clearly benefit from the interaction. However, the underlying philosophies for each person are shaped by the question 'what are we coaching for?' While the skiers will no doubt derive some personal benefit in health, social and emotional terms, even though changes may be temporary, positive changes to the visible performance elements will most likely remain the top priority for Jas. Jim, on the other hand, works with his students over a much longer time frame and his pedagogical approaches are informed by the belief that PE is charged with developing wider learning and personal development goals, such as a sense of personal responsibility, effective communication or sense of fair play. Jim believes that his students should learn *in* PE as well as *through* PE where PE is a vehicle or approach rather than a subject to be learnt. Jim believes that efforts to continually measure progress in PE have resulted in dull and prescriptive lessons where pupils are involved in only superficial learning.

Although Jas and Jim are merely characters from my imagination created to illustrate the point that our experiences inform and shape our beliefs about what we coach for, there have been real efforts to research the values and beliefs of teachers of PE and sports coaches. Green (2009), for example, asserts that competitive sports values tend to underpin the personal philosophies of PE teachers in England, which has led to PE being taught in very traditional ways. This affects us more than you might think as an adventure sports coach because for the vast majority of us PE lessons were our only exposure to formal coaching so it is difficult to ignore its significance in shaping the way we think about coaching.

That is not to say that competitive sport is necessarily bad. Many thrive on traditional sport and competition but these are often those of higher ability in those respective activities and are those who go on into teaching sport and PE. You might be surprised to learn though that high achievers do not necessarily make the best teachers and coaches. Capel (2007), for example, argues that high achievers in sport tend to take a more conservative view about how we should coach and that those with broader backgrounds may be more open minded and innovative.

Unlike physical education and traditional sports coaching, however, adventure sport coaching specifically has had little research attention in this area but it is possible that we may find a similar picture. I believe that this is where this discussion becomes interesting for the adventure sports coach in particular because the adventure sports coach in many situations needs to be a sufficiently high-level performer in order to even be in same place as the learners. A white water kayak coach for example must be able to accompany the learners on the river and position themselves accordingly to ensure effective observations and safety of the learners. Despite this need for adventure sports coaches to frequently be highly skilled performers, few are likely to be in the position to be able to choose the level of the clients they work with. In this way adventure sports coaches need to be highly adaptable in their pedagogical approaches in order to meet the needs of the learner regardless of ability or background. This is due to the contexts that adventure sports coaches often find regular work. Even the most highly qualified adventure sports coaches find themselves in situations where, for example, they are coaching beginner climbers on the indoor wall one day and then teaching advanced rope techniques in multi-pitch contexts the next. The following quote by Rovegno (2008) warns us of the challenges we face when coaches harbour elitist views, prejudices and preferences:

> Probably the most difficult challenge we face is how to modify the beliefs of those … who take a sexist, racist and homophobic stance; are biased against overweight people and are interested in working with only good athletes
>
> *(Rovegno, 2008, p. 89)*

Much to the dissatisfaction of many of my students, there is no correct answer here in terms of a correct pedagogy. This is frustrating for them as the majority of students at this point in their coaching development have been raised on a diet of 'correct' and 'incorrect' coaching practices as dinghy or ski instructors for example. This is an unfortunate side effect of rigid, albeit necessary, coach assessment criteria. However frustrating as this is for the developing coach, it is essential that we simply acknowledge that the pedagogies we employ and continue to develop over time will be influenced by our own experiences and beliefs about what adventure sport is for.

Other than the work of Collins and Collins (2012) little else has been written to conceptualise the specific roles and pedagogies related to the adventure sports coach. For my preferred definition of pedagogy and one that seems most closely related to what we do in adventure sport I refer to Armour (2013, p. 14) who states that sport pedagogy is 'that conceptual and practical space where knowledge of all the other disciplines of sports sciences programmes comes together in the interests of people and their learning'. Pedagogy therefore is the decision-making process that could be described as similar to that of a DJ in a nightclub. Even though great efforts are made to create an extensive library of good music (the coaches knowledge base) and plan a set (the coaches session plan) the DJ must work with the crowd to judge the mood and make adjustments based on the people present in order to be effective. This does not mean that the adventure sports coach necessarily has to take requests but it does mean that they may have to at times consider songs they do not like!

Learning theories

In other chapters we have looked at learning in relation to the acquisition of pure motor skills such as performing a carve gybe in wind surfing or skiing bumps more quickly. In this way coaching could be seen as simply training and the attainment of physical skills. However, if we look at the role of the coach in its broadest sense we see that there are a wide variety of factors that the effective coach understands and accommodates in their coaching. Interview data from elite coaches reveals that these practitioners viewed themselves more as educators than as 'physical trainers' (Jones, 2006). Other research has also found that good coaches act like good teachers in that they take a broader view of their responsibilities in terms of maintaining positive relationships, communicating effectively, caring for the environment and simply caring for and caring about those who are being taught. This view can be represented quite simply by the maxim 'we coach people not adventure sports'. If then we subscribe to this view, what is learning, what can we learn and what efforts have been made to conceptualise how coaches make it happen?

What is learning?

Various efforts have been made to define learning and each effort pertains to the context in which it takes place. Most definitions include sentiments that refer to changes in an individual that are caused by some kind of experience. In adventure sports, this experience may not involve a coach so this raises the question of the role of the coach if in fact we know that it can happen without us. The role of the adventure sports coach therefore is to first increase the value of this experience by enhancing what the learner will do naturally. Second, the role of the adventure sports coach is to facilitate learning that the learners could not achieve by themselves. For adventure sports coaches this can mean something as simple as selecting the right venue (crag, beach or trail for example) to create the best opportunity for implicit learning.

Therefore, to better appreciate our role as coaches we need to appreciate all facets of learning. In terms of classifying all aspects of learning the most widely recognised efforts belong to Bloom (1956) who created a taxonomy that divided the aims that educators set for learning into three domains: cognitive (knowing), affective (feeling) and psychomotor (doing). Within each of the domains, learning outcomes are set out as hierarchical with the most straightforward outcomes such as knowing a fact, for example, coming before more complex skills such as the ability to analyse a performance. While a full discussion of the value of the taxonomy is beyond the scope of this chapter, Bloom's goal was to motivate educators to focus on *all three* domains. This goal has as much importance now as then. While it is obvious that the main focus of the adventure sports coach is to facilitate the attainment of psychomotor learning outcomes, the truth is that the effective adventure sports coach will appreciate the holistic nature of coaching. Good coaches will be aware that even though our best efforts at any time may be directed towards the development of any one domain they will be aware of learning in the other domains whether this is intentional or otherwise. A good kite surfing coach, for example, will appreciate that their learners may be coping with untold frustration but learning a great deal about themselves (affective) while little visible progress may be seen on the motor skill front (psychomotor).

How does learning happen?

Behaviourist learning theories

Traditionally, two main schools of thought have predominated education and sport settings to explain how learning occurs: *behaviourism* and *constructivism*. Behaviourists such as Pavlov (1849–1836), Thorndike (1874–1949) and Skinner (1904–1990) focused on the connections between a stimulus and a response. Thorndike, for example, stated that if an act is followed by a satisfying change in the environment then it is more likely to be repeated. Similarly, Skinner noted the effect of pleasant or unpleasant consequences in order to control behaviour. Pleasant consequences such as praise are known as 'reinforcers' and are considered to strengthen behaviour and unpleasant consequences are known as 'punishers'. In adventure sports coaching we may see this as simply giving praise or criticism for a performance in front of the rest of the group. Other reinforcers might include badges or certificates and although these are widely used and often valued, the value is based on personal perception. Some performers you work with might shy away from public performance, praise and public recognition while others revel in it.

Behaviourism has formed the basis of the majority of coaching practices for a long time and authors have developed detailed guidance on its application. It is important, for example, that desired behaviours such as effort, improvement or having a positive attitude are communicated clearly and an explanation given as to why they are important. Also, reinforcement should happen straightaway so that the learner can make the connection between the behaviour and he consequence. Reinforcers can be extrinsic (from outside like a reward) and may be used to encourage people to do things they might not want to do (run the rapid or ski the steep section) or intrinsic where the learner completes the task for its inherent reward. This type of reinforcement is common in adventure sports where participants usually self select the level of challenge. Each individual may respond differently to a reinforcer so an effective coach will take this into account. For example, reinforcing the behaviour of children that they would do anyway can undermine intrinsic motivation, which is central to long-term participation in adventure sports.

Behaviourism dominated our view of learning over the twentieth century and still has value today in underpinning pedagogy in all sport, including adventure sports. The advantage of coaching ideas based on behaviourism is that they are easy to replicate and offer a great starting point for the budding coach. The learner coach is concerned with correct technique both in terms of the technical aspects of their sport and the 'correct' way to teach it. Behaviourist coaching often relies on a 'watch and copy' format where praise is given for replicating the ideal performance model. Providing the coach can give a good demonstration and has a sound level of knowledge, the learner usually makes progress, especially at the early stages of learning. In recent years, however, coaching based on behaviourism has been increasingly criticised and there are a number of major factors that present themselves for the adventure sports coach. Behaviourism views learning as a linear and measurable process that can encourage the adventure sports coach to have an unrealistic expectation about progress (or lack of) and type and quality of learning. Pedagogies based on behaviourism tend to see all learners as the same, separate thought from action and see the learners as 'empty' passive recipients of a pre-existing body of knowledge. Critics of coaching that is too rooted in behaviourism argue that it constructs coaches as transmitters of expertise rather than facilitators of critical thought (Denison and Avner, 2011). This criticism should resonate with you as an adventure sports coach if you have felt like you have 'taught' a skill well to find that later the learner cannot repeat it in a new setting. Central to adventure sports is the interaction with a dynamic environment, often moving from place to place and learners having to adapt quickly to the changing demands such as gradient, terrain, wind strength and direction, etc. The effective adventure sports coach therefore is able to equip the learner each with their own set of necessary critical thinking skills to act on their own and make good decisions. How we do this can be explained by an alternative view of how we learn. One such set of ideas are called constructivist learning theories.

Constructivist learning theories

Constructivism draws heavily on the work of Piaget (1896–1980) and Vygotsky (1896–1934). Although, each proposed that learners constructed their own unique knowledge and view of the world each time they encounter novel situations, Vygotsky was more concerned with learning as a more culturally and socially situated process, which required social interaction and group dialogue. Each time we make effort to adjust to a new situation we 'disturb the learning equilibrium' and construct new knowledge through a blend of personal experience and what we already know. Although Vygotsky and Piaget viewed constructivism through slightly different lenses, both have four common principles.

First, learning is developmental where learners need to be free to ask questions, develop hypotheses and test them where mistakes are a natural consequence. This is important for an adventure sports coach as effective coaches can provide opportunities for experimentation for any level of participant but the consequences of any mistakes are minimised through the careful manipulation of task and selection of environment. Research evidence tends to suggest that expert coaches have the ability to allow sessions to develop inductively where participants take more responsibility for their own performances. Despite this, the challenge remains for the coach to encourage the participant to buy into the idea of taking more responsibility for their own learning, particularly if the participant measures value by how hard the coach appears to be working (e.g. lots of shouting, feedback, etc.) In reality, the participant will gain significantly more in the long term by taking more responsibility for their own learning as all adventure sports contexts demand that the learners are more capable to learn through experience. Typical practice structures and feedback mechanisms can rarely be rigidly adhered to due to environmental constraints (e.g. wind/water noise, distance, dynamic nature of environment). This would see adventure sports coaches as facilitators rather than instructors, where greater effort is directed towards the facilitation of knowledge creation and decision-making skills.

The second principle centres of new ways of knowing. Through the use of challenging, open-ended investigations into realistic contexts we aim to challenge the learners' pre-existing ideas in ways that lead to the construction of new ways of knowing. Coaching sessions that encourage experimentation with variables, such as speed and edge in skiing or surf kayak, can challenge the learners' conception and should not be avoided. In this context, it is quite common for the learner to be resistant to challenge information they have been told in the past when this contradicts what they have deduced from their current observations and analysis. This cognitive dissonance is a necessary and healthy indicator of deeper learning. However, as it not only leads to new knowledge but also develops the learners' propensity to learn in this way. This is of particular importance to the adventure sports coach as research evidence indicates that skills learnt implicitly tend to be less susceptible to degradation under stress.

The third principle centres on the learner's ability to reflect. Although we have an inherent ability to reflect, the extent and quality of reflection varies from person to person. Some seem more naturally able to reflect in a critical sense, establishing cause and effect; others tend to merely describe what happened. Fortunately the ability to reflect is a learned skill so we can always improve. Time for reflection is essential and learners should be encouraged to reflect in action (during) as well as on action (after). The adventure sports coach in this case would use questioning that directs the learner's attention so that they are engaged in the present moment and create a state of 'mindfulness'. Learning activities structured around solving problems are a good example of this approach such as investigating the relationship between variables like speed and edge in kayaking or speed and sail setting on a sailing journey.

The final principle rests on the premise that the development of new ideas can be generalised across experiences. Kolb (1984) refers to this as abstract conceptualisation and is a major component of experiential learning. These could be principles of carving for example that are transferrable between skiing and snowboarding. In this way, if the learner has reflected sufficiently they could transfer their understanding of how a centre of mass would change at speed in a turn (see Figure 2.1).

FIGURE 2.1 Coaching ideas based on constructivism ask the learner to experiment with variables and reflect on the outcomes

With specific reference to social constructivism, Vygotsky (1978) proposed that children in particular learn through social interaction with others such as the coach or peers. In this way learners are exposed to the thinking of others and co-operative learning is promoted. This approach fits with reciprocal teaching styles outlined in the next section. Working with others, particularly if they are more capable, has other advantages. Vygotsky argued that learning precedes development and so when we learn a skill with the assistance of those slightly better than ourselves we are initially able to perform the same skill without assistance in the future. The significant implication for the adventure sports coach here is that effective coaches are able to provide a variety of different levels of challenge to accommodate mixed abilities in the group. Mixed ability teaching has historically been much debated but in reality all groups have a variety of skill levels within them as well as a variety of propensities to learn, even if we set groups on ability.

The pedagogy of outdoor and adventure education is heavily influenced by constructivist ideas and those who work in outdoor and adventure education settings have broader educational goals beyond the acquisition of skill in a particular sport. Outdoor and adventure educationalists tend to have goals such as developing connectedness with nature, self-esteem or empathy and are familiar with challenge by choice ideologies. It is common therefore to see those with a dual role in outdoor adventure education and adventure sports coaching embrace aspects of social constructivism in their coaching.

Vygotsky's concept of scaffolding is often also often used in outdoor adventure education settings, but can equally be applied to adventure sports coaching contexts. Scaffolding or mediated learning simply means that the coach provides a great deal of support in the early stages of learning. This could take the form of more structure, such as fixing the number of attempts of an exercise and more frequent interactions with the learners. Over time the coach provides progressively less structure and the learners become more independent managing the intensity and frequency of practice attempts or how much interaction they need for example. This would be consistent with a guided discovery style.

The underlying principle of constructivism is to encourage and create opportunities for thinking rather than telling learners what to do. There are many advantages to approaches that are underpinned by social constructivism. The main advantage for the adventure sports coach however is that the host of environmental constraints, such as the continuing movement of learners in the surf, sea or river and wind noise, as well as limited opportunities for constant observation, can be mitigated for to a large degree. Methods that encourage reciprocal learning through observing each other and in turn create a supportive atmosphere go a long way to support learning safely in challenging situations. In this way, the adventure sports coach as 'mobile consultant' maximises efficiency and as a coach you can give higher quality input but less often. Furthermore, it could be argued that these approaches have long-term benefits for the learner as we have equipped them to learn in a variety of ways that do not always involve the coach.

While there is strong support for coaching practices grounded in constructivism, particularly in adventure sports, both schools of thought have merits and drawbacks. Although there are concerns about the limitations of learning through behaviouristic methods in that they can oversimplify learning, in practice the real advantage is that it is relatively straightforward to structure. Senior coaches can set more novice coaches to work, safe in the knowledge that the novice coach will follow a safe routine of instruction, practice and feedback, a sound level of activity and, as I see it, a relatively narrow bandwidth between good and bad coaching. Also, errors made by the coach are easier to correct as a more senior coach could easily identify weaknesses in demonstrations or inaccuracies in the quality of feedback for example.

By contrast, coaching based on constructivist ideas has enormous potential but in practice is difficult to do well and in my experience has a relatively wide bandwidth of good and bad coaching. Although it is evident that coaching in adventure sports should have much in common with constructivism through development of autonomous, critical thinkers and deeper learning, we must concede that constructing learning is considerably more time consuming. Solving problems and discovering solutions takes time and means that learners will make mistakes and sometimes become frustrated. Typical errors when using ideas based on constructivism involve matters such as setting vague problems to solve, becoming impatient with the learners and instructing them anyway. Providing too loose scaffolding or removing it too early and providing poor instructions for the learners during peer observations are other common problems with coaching based on constructivist principles. The best efforts to conceptualise what teachers and coaches do in relation to learning theories belong to Mosston and Ashworth (1986) who created a conceptual framework for teaching decisions that applies well to the adventure environment.

Putting it all together: How should we coach?

As we pointed stated earlier, pedagogy is the conceptual space where we bring together our coaching knowledge and understanding to maximise opportunities for learning. There are many ways to do this but the most notable efforts to provide a working framework for coaching related decision-making for coaches belong to Mosston and Ashworth (1986) who developed a model based on observations of what physical education teachers did to illicit certain types of learning. The model has faced some criticism regarding the overemphasis on the teacher/coach but has attracted a wealth of research interest (referred to as spectrum research) in sport and education. The greatest value of the model is that it goes some way to also help adventure sports coaches to understand and justify approaches, map learning intentions and link them to practical coaching strategies.

Mosston and Ashworth present the model as a spectrum that is based on the number of decisions made by the learner and teacher or, in this case, coach. At the 'Command' end learners make no decisions for themselves, acting on a given impulse from the coach. At the self-teaching style end of the spectrum, learners have moved beyond the need for a coach and therefore make all the learning decisions themselves. Rather than see a discrete adventure sports coaching process we also propose a spectrum approach to adventure sports coaching along similar lines. As the spectrum progresses, more responsibility is given to the learner through the number of decisions that are needed (such as number of attempts, focus of effort and time dedicated to practice).

Command style

I see this end being used rarely in the adventure context as environmental demands (space to move, variation in terrain, etc.) make it too difficult for all the learners to move at the same time. I do see ski coaches use this approach with higher level skiers in synchronised ski challenges. Trying to synchronise with others is a great way to increase motivation and activity levels (in a warm up for example) and can help refine technique. Being more behaviourist in nature however tends not to allow for the development of complex decision-making skills necessary in the adventure environment.

Practice style

This style is the most widely used form of coaching, particularly when developing fundamental movement skills. The coach will give instructions and a demonstration that the learner attempts to replicate. The coach gives feedback on the performance in terms of how different the performance was from the demonstration. Progress can be quick as research indicates that we are often quite good at copying what we see but through trying to replicate, the learners do not have time to work out the interaction between variables (speed, edge, balance, trim, sail setting, for example) and so learners are unlikely to reproduce the skill without prompts or, more importantly, under pressure. The main disadvantage of practice style in more adventurous situations is the ability for the coach to be watching each learner and give feedback straightaway. In a static session this may be possible but in more dynamic environments, such as off-piste skiing, surfing and white water kayaking, it may be a long time between each attempt and receiving feedback. For this reason, effective adventure sports coaches aim to create more opportunities for the learner to become more aware of intrinsic feedback.

Reciprocal style

This relies on each learner to be responsible for observing and providing the extrinsic feedback to a partner. Multiple sets of feedback can be given simultaneously and can free the coach to then assess the quality of feedback being given. The added advantage is that this will develop social interaction within your group and help in the creation of a supportive atmosphere necessary when learners are working closer to their limits of comfort. The coach must provide clear instructions for the task and a specific focus for observations if this is to work. Despite many long-term benefits, without clear instructions learners will be confused and feel short-changed. This is most likely when learners feel they have a disinterested partner.

Self-check style

The coach will provide the criteria for the task either verbally or visually for learners to assess their own progress. Again, this approach increases the level of responsibility for the learner and can free the coach to concentrate on guiding or a specific individual. Discussion relating to the task can then take place when it is safer or more convenient when the learners will be more receptive. The check list provided by the coach is an example of scaffolding, creating a template for reflection and is commensurate with constructivist approaches.

Inclusion style

How this best fits with adventure sports is the principle of challenge by choice. In a static environment the coach will give several versions of the same challenge such as the number of parallel turns required or different grades of bouldering in the same area. The choice may also be to not undertake the challenge at all such as to portage the rapid. The idea behind inclusion is to allow full participation. Despite being desirable for individual and social reasons, inclusion style in adventure sport can sometimes be very difficult to integrate fully, particularly if the activity is centred on travelling (mountain biking, skiing or a sea kayak crossing) and the variation in fitness and ability is large. This is why we often see groupings based on ability in adventure sports compared with those in adventure education. That said, all groups contain a variation in ability so the effective coach can always provide different levels of challenge.

Guided discovery style

Although the goal is to facilitate discovery through solving a problem, the coach will direct the learners towards the understanding of a specific concept or even singular answer. The advantage of this approach is that through making mistakes, the learner will appreciate the interaction of variables in terms of body position or equipment or both. Research indicates that skills developed implicitly through discovery are more robust when stresses are introduced, such as risk-induced anxiety. Given the centrality of risk in adventure sports, guided discovery (when conducted well) can allow for significant developments in skills that can be reproduced under pressure. The ability for the coach to fully understand the skill being developed and the ability to use questions that move from the general to the specific are crucial here (putting on ski boots or sitting in a kayak the right way round do not need to be discovered). The coach must also make decisions about what needs to be discovered at that particular time versus providing a simple coping strategy for the time being. Put simply, some skills, venues and conditions allow for more experimentation than others.

Divergent style

Similar to discovery style, the coach will rely on a problem to solve but the task will have a variety of 'correct' solutions. This approach is particularly effective when facilitating the ability to develop an appreciation of equipment (the merits of a particular ski or boat design) creativity and expression such as in skiing, wake boarding and freestyle/river play kayaking or to critically evaluate skills, such as tactics and decision-making. This style helps learners explore and challenge what is possible and leads to new knowledge. Applied poorly however when skills actually do have a narrower band of acceptability, learners can feel confused by the fact that 'anything goes'. The coach needs to provide some attempt at closure even if the answer is 'there is no single answer'.

Individual style

This is where the coach acts more as a consultant, with each learner working on an individual programme or project. Typically, in adventure sports, learners would be highly motivated to work on their own for longer periods and accept the fallibility of the coach to be everywhere at once. Learners have developed skills and self reflection but will enjoy periodic feedback and discussion. The coach usually still makes decisions here regarding venue and conditions. The learners are more autonomous here and the coach needs to be adept at using questioning to establish progress. Beginners can benefit from this style at times but it is seldom used as the cognitive demands are such that they often need feedback too often to remain motivated.

Learner-initiated style

The coach is almost redundant here in a classic sense of the coach. The learner has initiated the entire project and simply uses the coach as a sounding board for ideas. The learner appreciates the coach's knowledge and experience and would see the coach's role as more of a mentor. In adventure sports I see this when learners need to discuss complex ideas in terms of planning for a big event like an expedition, hazardous sea crossing or adventure race rather than motor skill acquisition.

Self-teaching style

This has often been seen as the apex of an individual's development with the learner able to make decisions regarding all aspects of learning, having passed through all the other styles in the spectrum and no longer needing a coach. In reality, in adventure sports this is more likely the choice for an enthusiastic and motivated amateur. While there are advantages in making all learning decisions, Mosston and Ashworth contest that aspects of social learning are lost and this style complements others in the spectrum rather than supersedes them (see Figure 2.2).

The relationship between learning theory and teaching styles

At the risk of oversimplification we would *generally* advocate styles more rooted in constructivism, where learners are required to experiment, understand, evaluate and synthesise in order to prepare the learner for complex interactions between themselves, equipment and the environment. However, we must take account of the amount of information the learner can process. We need to be aware of the interaction between the individual's current ability, the inherent challenges presented by the environment and what we ask the learner to do. If the learner's ability is low in relation to the environment then we may justifiably use a more behaviouristic approach (copy and follow) to allow the learner to cope in the short term. Alternatively, an individual with a higher skill level in the same setting may well cope with more experimentation, dispelling the myth that adventure sports are risky and therefore require more autocratic approaches. In terms of spectrum research much exists in sport but there is enormous scope for spectrum research in adventure sports.

FIGURE 2.2 In guided discovery the learner begins to understand the interplay between variables such as the amount of edge and rate of flow

Learning styles

Most adventure sports coaches are familiar with the idea of learning styles, such as the notion of visual or kinaesthetic learners or Honey and Mumford's (1992) Learning Style Inventory. It is also evident that the learning styles theory has been translated to a variety of coach education programmes. However, despite its apparent popularity there has been little to no empirical support for the efficacy of this practice. While it might make sense as coaches that different people seem to learn in different ways there are too few studies that have used an appropriate methodology to test the effectiveness of learning style-based instruction. Furthermore, those studies that are sufficiently rigorous have found that there is no satisfactory way to determine an individual's learning style. The picture for learning styles appears even bleaker when we consider that studies that have aimed to demonstrate that learners who receive coaching specifically tailored to their preferred style also show no significant benefits (Tobias, Ball and MacMahon 2012).

There is still value in the underlying principles, however, and we should not be too quick to dismiss all ideas related to learning style. While there is no evidence to suggest that we should diagnose a learner's preferred mode and prescribe a course of action, an adventure sports coach still needs to understand the nature of a learning goal and create an effective way to achieve it. Visual goals such as analysing performance benefit from doing just that and motor skills benefit most from practical approaches. While this sounds obvious, there is evidence that incongruence exists between coaches declarative and procedural behaviours (Cushion, Armour and Jones 2003). Coaches may say that they provide active learning opportunities but in reality give verbal explanations too often as this is usually easier. The effective adventure sports coach decides on the nature of the skill, deciding on when to focus on practical skills and delivery saving complex discussions for the bar, pub or classroom!

Summary

As we said earlier, pedagogy is a complex synthesis without a singular correct method or approach but I make no apology for pushing a constructivist agenda in adventure sports coaching. This is because, first, this will aid the development of more independent, autonomous learners who are capable of critical reflection. This skill set is essential for learning to occur as we progress into more challenging environments. Second, because adventure sports coaches need to work with a wider range of environmental and technical variables (weather, snow conditions, equipment) that simple transmission of ideas is insufficient to facilitate new behaviours in ourselves as coaches.

Therefore, in conjunction with coach education programmes, most researchers would advocate mentoring as a more likely way to develop our pedagogical practice in adventure sports. Rather than aiming to emulate or replicate other coaches in order to improve, mentoring is inherently constructivist in nature. In this way, developing coaches will identify a focus for a critical friend to observe and facilitate reflection and discussion. As adventure sports coaching as a discipline continues to evolve coaches need to continue to engage in their own development, maintain a growth mind set and complement governing body coach education with additional learning. (Cushion, Armour and Jones 2003). Good coaches will make best use of tried and tested prescribed methods implicit within their coaching schemes, but the best coaches will reflect on their practice, be keen to seek new coaching knowledge and inform their current pedagogy. Effective adventure sports coaches are therefore able to appraise the merits of coach education programmes, but are also motivated to exploit opportunities to develop their own pedagogical approaches.

References

Armour, K. (2013). *Sport Pedagogy. An Introduction for Teaching and Coaching,* Pearson.

Armour, K. (2013). *Sport Pedagogy. An Introduction for Teaching and Coaching,* Oxon: Routledge.

Bloom, B.S. (1956). *Taxonomy of Educational Objectives,* London: Longman Group.

Capel, S. (2007). Moving beyond physical education subject knowledge to develop knowledgeable teachers of the subject, *The Curriculum Journal,* 18(4): 493-507.

Collins, L. and Collins, D. (2012). Contextualising the Adventure Sport Coach. *Journal of Adventure Education and Outdoor Learning,* 12(1): 81–93.

Cushion, C., Armour, K. and Jones R.L. (2003). Coach education and continuing professional development. *Quest,* 55: 215–230.

Denison, J. and Avner, Z. (2011). Positive coaching: Ethical Practices for Athlete Development. *Quest,* 63: 209–227.

Green, K. (2009). Exploring the everyday philosophies of physical education teachers from a sociological perspective. In: R. Bailey and D. Kirk (eds), *The Routledge Physical Education Reader,* London: Routledge.

Honey, P and Mumford, A. (1992). *The Manual of Learning Styles: Revised version.* Maidenhead, Berks: Peter Honey.

Jones, R.L. (2006). How can educational concepts inform sports coaching? In: Jones, R.L. *The Sports Coach as Educator: Reconceptualising Sports Coaching.* London: Routledge.

Kolb, D. (1984). *Experiential Learning: Experience as the Source of Learning and Development,* Englewood Cliffs, NJ: Prentice-Hall.

Mosston, M. and Ashworth, S. (1986). *Teaching Physical Education.* Columbus, OH: Merrell.

Rovegno, I. (2008). Learning and Instruction in Social, Cultural Environments: Promising Research Agendas. *Quest,* 60: 84–104.

Stone, E. (2000). Iconoclastes: poor pedagogy, *Journal of Teaching for Education,* 26(1), 93–5.

Tobias, I. F., Ball, K. and MacMahon, C. (2012). Perspectives on learning styles in motor and sport skills. *Frontiers in Psychology.* Available at: http://journal.frontiersin.org/Journal/10.3389/fpsyg.2012.00069/full (accessed 7 November 2014).

Vygotsky, L.S. (1978). *Mind in Society: The Development of Higher Psychological Processes.* Cambridge, MA: Harvard University Press.

3

OBSERVING AND ANALYZING PERFORMANCE IN ADVENTURE SPORTS

Craig Pulling, Peter Bunyan and Sid Sinfield

Introduction

This chapter will explore ways that coaches can observe and analyze performance within an adventure sports coaching environment. The chapter focuses largely on the area of sports performance analysis, a discipline of sport science that has grown considerably over the past 15 years. It is hoped that by the end of this chapter you will learn about sports performance analysis and how some of the techniques used within sports performance analysis can be utilized within an adventure sports coaching environment to observe and analyze performance. We propose that value of the chapter is twofold for the adventure sports coach. First, we explain and detail techniques that we see currently being used. Second, we make the optimistic assumption that approaches are being used in other sporting contexts may be of benefit to us also.

Sports performance analysis

Sports performance analysis is a term that is used to encompass sports biomechanics and notational analysis. Sports biomechanics is concerned with sporting techniques, primarily with the aim of enhancing the efficiency of a sporting technique and reducing the potential injury risk to a sports performer. Notational analysts focus on the gross movements or movement patterns that are performed within a sports performance environment. Notational analysis is further concerned with tactics and strategies that are applied within sporting situations and focuses less on technical analysis (Bartlett, 2012). Sports performance analysis is focused on the 'actual' performance and attempts to analyze performance within the 'real world' environment of sport. This makes performance analysis markedly different from other sport science disciplines (physiology, psychology), where the focus is usually on the preparation of the sports performer (Hughes and Bartlett, 2008). By analysing sporting performances, performers and coaches will aim to learn from the performance, which may help to inform the planning of future training sessions and help with the development of future strategies and tactics. A large amount of information can be collected when analysing performances and it is important that the coach and performer focus on the main areas of performance or potentially a huge amount of time can be wasted. The use of video within adventure sports performance analysis is usually very important as it provides a record of performance that can be viewed an infinite number of times. Also, if required, the video can be viewed in slow motion, which can be helpful when focusing on technical factors completed at speed, such as mountain biking or important moments within a performance especially if there is no real opportunity to conduct detailed analysis in the field at that time.

Sports performance analysis is concerned with providing objective data for performers and coaches. However, traditional coaching intervention regularly involves subjective observations and conclusions based on the coach's perceptions, biases and own previous experiences (Maslovet and Franks, 2008). Observations by coaches during sporting performances therefore have the potential to be invalid and inaccurate, this could lead to coaching interventions that are unlikely to enhance sporting performance. A research study by Franks and Miller (1986) highlighted that novice soccer coaches were only 42 per cent correct in a post-game assessment of what occurred during a 45-minute match. A further study by Franks (1993) stated that there was little difference in the observations of novice and experienced gymnastic coaches; however, the experienced coaches were more likely to report an error in performance when an error did not exist. As coaches make decisions and judgements based on their observations, there is a major concern that these subjective observations will be harmful to the coaching process. Unintentionally, coaches could be providing incorrect and inadequate feedback to performers as well as designing inappropriate training sessions. Therefore the use of sports performance analysis techniques to collect objective data regarding sporting performance has the potential to enhance the coaching process.

Notational analysis

Notational analysis provides an objective way of recording performance, so that key events from a performance can be quantified in a consistent and reliable manner (Hughes and Bartlett, 2008).

Hand- and computer-based notational analysis systems

Traditionally, notational analysis was undertaken using hand-based systems. Although computer-based notational analysis systems are used predominantly in elite sport, it is important to realize that hand-based notational analysis systems are still extremely useful and can be used to effectively collect objective data on sports performance. With hand-based notational systems, symbols are mostly used to record specific events that are considered important to sporting performance (e.g. the relative proportion of a turn that is 'carved' in skiing or number of strokes used in a canoe). Most hand-based notational systems require simple and basic equipment (e.g. pen and paper), they are inexpensive and they can be extremely accurate. However, it can be very time-consuming to process the data once they have been collected. With technological advancements, there has been an increase in the use and development of computer-based notational analysis systems. A major benefit of using computer-based notational analysis systems is that the processing of the data that has been collected is almost immediate, providing coaches with objective data quickly. Another benefit is that the data output is clearer and much easier to interpret compared with a hand-based notational analysis system, as it is normally integrated with a graphics system. Recent developments have provided data output alongside the video of the sports performance, providing an extremely useful tool for coaches, as they can view the data in combination with the context of the sporting performance (e.g. statistics of the strokes used by a kayaker can be viewed alongside a video of the performance). The main disadvantage for the adventure sports coach is that it can be difficult and time-consuming to record the main events of the performance given the environmental demands. We can remember a situation where it was so cold that it was only possible to operate a camera for about ten seconds in Val d'Isere. Once a coach has 'bought into' the idea however most usually see the benefits for use in specific situations. Also, as technology develops the cost of software and apps is likely to reduce, which is good news for coaches and performers (Dartfish Easytag is a basic computer-based notational analysis app that can be downloaded free of charge). One final comment on hand- and computer-based systems comes from Hughes (2008a) who stated that it does not matter whether the most sophisticated and expensive computerized system is being used, or a simple pen and paper analysis, as long the system produces accurate, reliable results that are easy to understand. One final concern is the motivation for the participants themselves to buy into situations that allow for quality data. As an adventure sports coach you need to make difficult decisions about the extent you want to compromise the quality of the overall experience by interrupting the natural flow of a journey.

Live analysis and post-event analysis

It is important to note that notational analysis can be conducted 'live' (as the event is happening) or post event (after the event has taken place). For post-event notational analysis to be conducted, a video recording of the performance must have taken place. For live notational analysis it is absolutely vital that the person conducting the analysis has an excellent understanding of the system to be used. If errors are made or key events of the performance are not recorded, the analysis could be totally useless. It would be advised that anyone intending to collect performance data using live notational analysis should thoroughly test their system and practice using their system before using it for a performance. The main benefit of live notational analysis is that objective data can be relayed to a performer as they are performing or during natural breaks in performance, such as eddies. This data could have an impact on the strategies and tactics applied by a sports performer during a performance, and hopefully lead to an enhancement in performance.

Post-event notational analysis will usually produce a greater amount of objective data as the system is likely to be more complex. This is because the video of the performance can be viewed numerous times and therefore a large number of actions that take place during a performance can be recorded (some of these actions may have been missed when using a live notational analysis system). The main problem with post-event notational analysis is that the objective data will be collected after the event and therefore will not have any effect on the performance that has taken place. It can only be used to influence future performances; however, the contexts of future performances could be very different, such as changes in environmental conditions. We see coaches solve this in adventure sports by devising a simple notational analysis for use in the field, which is linked to a more complex system of analysis following the event.

Elements of a notational analysis system

Potential elements of a notational analysis system are: performer, position, action and/or time (Hughes, 2008b). Performer refers to the person who conducted the key event of the performance that was being recorded e.g. the handholds used when climbing. Adam used two edges and two pockets when climbing a boulder problem. A number or abbreviations could be used to distinguish a performer e.g. Adam is coded as performer number 3 as he is the third climber to climb that route.

Position refers to the area/zone of the sporting environment that the specific component of performance was performed within. This means that prior to a performance, a coach would see the coaching environment as made up of distinct areas. When dividing a sporting environment into areas there is always a trade-off between precision and accuracy. If the areas are large, then it is likely that the coach would be accurate with the area but not that precise with where the action actually took place. If the areas are small, the coach may not be as accurate with the area but they would be more precise.

Action refers to the specific component of performance that is being recorded e.g. the handholds that were used when climbing a boulder. These components could be given codes to make the analysis easier e.g. E = Edge, Si = Sidepulls, SL = Sloper, Pi = Pinch, Po = Pockets. Codes are particularly useful when conducting live notational analysis. The outcomes of this component of performance could be recorded e.g. whether the handholds were successful (advancement on the boulder route) or unsuccessful (no advancement on the boulder route). Again, a code could be used for the successfulness of a component e.g. I = success, O = unsuccessful. With a more complex notational analysis system, there could be more than one component of performance being recorded e.g. handholds and footholds could be recorded.

Time can refer to many scenarios. It could be used simply to refer to the time that a specific component was performed e.g. Adam used the second sloping hold after 26 seconds of the climb.

It is important to state that not all elements of a notational analysis system would need to be implemented. It may be that the inclusion of the different elements may depend on the type of activity being analyzed. Also, as more of the elements are applied, a more complex analysis is conducted.

Developing a notational analysis system

The key to any successful notational analysis system is that you collect performance data that is useful for analysing performance and that can be used to enhance performance. There is no point collecting a huge amount of data if it is not going to be of any use. Initially, you must decide what are the important components and/or variables for successful performance within the activity you are analysing. It may be helpful to refer to coaching literature, coaching articles and research articles that have discussed and explored the activity as these may state the main components of a successful performance. These may also highlight important components of performance that you may not have considered. Once you have selected the key components that are going to be analyzed, it is important to define these components. Essentially, these are the operational definitions for the key components of the notational analysis system e.g. when analysing a kayak performance, a draw stroke may be defined as a stroke that moves the boat directly sideways. Again, it may be possible to use coaching literature to produce the definitions. It is vital that these definitions are adhered to when conducting the notational analysis. If you do not follow the definitions, the system will lose objectivity. These definitions are also important if you were to discuss the data you collected with the performer or other coaches, as they will need to be aware of the operational definitions to be able to fully interpret the data. What one coach considers to be a draw stroke could be slightly different from another coach. The definitions will help to reduce the level of ambiguity.

The next stage is to decide upon the notational analysis system that will be used. Decisions will need to be made on whether the system will be a hand- or a computer-based notational analysis system; whether the analysis will be conducted live during the performance or after the performance (for post-event analysis a video recording of the performance will be required); and which type of notational analysis system will be utilized (see the next section).

It is important to check the validity and reliability of the notational analysis system that you have developed. To check the validity of the system (the objectivity of the system) you will need to perform an inter-operator reliability assessment. This is where you compare the data you collected when observing a performance using your system to the data collected by another coach who observed the same performance using your system. It is essential to share the operational definitions with the other coach and you may need to provide a training session on how to use the system. If the results collected by both parties are similar than the system has increased validity and is more appropriate for use. However, if the results collected are different, the system may need to be further developed or even re-designed. To check the reliability of the system (measurement repeatability) an intra-operator reliability assessment will need to be conducted. This involves you observing a performance and using the notational analysis system to collect performance data. You then observe the same performance again (a video recording is required) and use the same notational analysis system to collect the performance data for a second time. It would be advisable to leave sufficient time (say two weeks) between the two analyses to reduce the learning effects (i.e. if you did it after one hour, you are likely to remember what you had just recorded). You then compare the results of the data collected on the first occasion to the data collected on the second occasion. If the results are very similar then the system has good reliability.

It is important to note that it is unlikely that you will have perfect agreement but there should be a good level of agreement (around 75%+). Modifications to the notational analysis system should be made if you have concerns over the reliability and validity of your system. However, once the reliability and validity of the notational analysis system are at a good level, the system is ready to be used with performers.

Types of notational analysis systems

There are numerous types of notational analysis systems, however, they normally fall within one of three categories: frequency tables, scatter diagrams and sequential systems (Hughes, 2008b).

Frequency tables

These provide statistical data from a sports performance and usually provide an overview of the noteworthy events that occurred during a performance (see Table 3.1). These frequency tables are commonly seen in newspaper sports reports and on television during half-time or full-time analysis segments (they are particularly common during television coverage of football, rugby and hockey, for example). Frequency tables are usually basic in their design but they are quick and easy to use (this is a good introductory system if you have never conducted notational analysis before). A tally can be used to record the key events of the performance and because frequency tables can be pretty basic they are useful if you want to conduct live notational analysis. Another benefit of using frequency tables is that they provide immediate feedback. The drawbacks of using frequency tables are that they do not provide a sequence of events and they do not display where in the environment the major events took place. Both of these issues can lead to misinterpretation of the data (Bartlett, 2012).

TABLE 3.1 Simple frequency table for climbing handholds

Handhold used	*Frequency*
Edges	I
Slopers	I
Pinches	
Pockets	IIII
Sidepulls	I
Gastons	
Undercling	
Palming	III
Matching hands	

Frequency table example

A frequency table can be very useful when working with novice performers. Let us take the example of working with a novice climber. As a coach you could observe the climber and record the handholds that are being used by the performer to climb a boulder. In this example, the key events you have chosen to focus on are the handholds being utilized by the performer. From conducting this simple notational analysis, you would have objective data on the handholds used by the novice climber. From the data, you may notice that certain handholds are being used more often than other handholds, some handholds may have not been used, etc. This is now where the knowledge of the coach comes to bear. Have the performers used the handholds in the way the coach might expect? Have they not used certain handholds because they did not need to use them or because they did not know how to use them? The coach is central to understanding the context of the climb. The coach should then be able to provide appropriate feedback to the novice climber and aim to enhance the climbing performance.

Scatter diagrams

Scatter diagrams are used to display a diagrammatical representation of the performance environment. The critical events are recorded onto this diagrammatical representation to show where they occurred within the performance environment. Again, you may have seen examples of these when watching sporting performances on television. A common example is seen in football where the touches of the ball by a football player are shown on a diagram of a football pitch. As with frequency tables, scatter diagrams are simple and quick to use. They can provide immediate feedback and can be used easily for live notational analysis (Bartlett, 2012). It is common for scatter diagrams to not provide a sequence of events (i.e. with the football example above, you do not know the location of first touch or the fiftieth touch). However, if designed appropriately, you can produce a scatter diagram system that will display a sequence of events (see example below).

Scatter diagram example

A scatter diagram could be used when working with a group of climbers on an artificial climbing wall. A diagram could be made of a particular route or a photograph taken of the route (a photograph would save time). The photograph could be downloaded onto a computer and copies printed in an appropriate size (A4 should be sufficient). This photograph then provides a diagram of the climbing route and you could have a diagram for each climber. You could then record the handholds that are being used by the climbers at each stage of the route. As mentioned previously, you could use codes for the different handholds that are utilized (e.g. Po = a pocket was used by the climber). To make this system sequential, you could simply just draw an arrow from one handhold to the next and number the arrows to display the sequence.

Sequential systems

Recording the sequence in which major events occur during sporting performance can provide valuable information for coaches and performers. Sequential systems are used occasionally for live notational analysis. However, sequential systems are usually applied post event using a computer-based system, in which time is automatically coded (Bartlett, 2012). Computer-based systems (that use sports performance analysis software, examples include SportsCode and Focus) that link to video footage of the performance are excellent for producing a sequential system because they provide a timeline of the key events.

Sequential system example

A sequential system could be used when coaching a high-level kayaker. You would need to video record the kayak performance and then download the video footage onto a computer. Sports performance analysis software (e.g. SportsCode; Focus) would then be used to record the main events of the performance. These key events will be linked to a timeline where there are a series of video clips of the key events that you have recorded in chronological order. If there was a performance error during the course, you could quickly go to the timeline and view the video of that sequence. You could also go backwards frame-by-frame to observe the strokes leading up to and after the sequence. This would hopefully help you as a coach to highlight why a particular error occurred. Also, statistics of the key events that have been recorded are produced by the software package.

Analysing notational analysis data

Once the key events have been recorded by the notational analysis system, you must then analyze the data and consider whether the data require further processing and analysis. If no further processing is required, you will be able to almost feedback immediately to the performer using the data collected. If further processing is required, think carefully about what needs to be done to make the data relevant for the performer so that they can benefit from the analysis that has been conducted. If the performer does not see the benefit, then the whole process you have gone through may not have been worthwhile.

Conducting notational analysis within an adventure sports environment

It is important to state that an adventure sports coach must think carefully about when to conduct notational analysis. For some activities and for some environments it may not be appropriate or safe to analyze a performance using notational analysis. It is most commonly currently used in an environment where the coaches can position themselves at a suitable observation point, where they are able to view the key aspects of performance and safely conduct a notational analysis. Adventure sports in general have yet to embrace notational analysis in the same way as more traditional sports have but coaches will in time be creative in the way that it is applied. For example, coaches may employ reciprocal techniques, giving participants more responsibility at times where they collect data on each other to be analyzed during the event at a convenient time or at the end of the day. In short, the potential to develop these techniques in adventure sport is vast.

Observation and analysis: A biomechanics approach

Up until now, the emphasis has been on the 'quantitative' measurement of movement. We have concerned ourselves with factors such as 'how often' a particular stroke is used or 'how long' it has taken to ride a particular section of an off-road cycle route. Among other things, this has allowed us to comment on performance, map technique occurrences and monitor training. We now consider analysis through the application of 'sports biomechanics'. This has a much more qualitative flavour to it, where the focus is again on human movement patterns but this time through direct observation. The aim here is to provide the adventure sports coach with some of the tools necessary to analyze movement patterns where they take place rather than in a setting that is temporally or spatially divorced from the performance. We see this more often in adventure sports due to the opportunity for observation to lead to feedback and coaching that is meaningful and timely to their participants.

There is a great benefit to reading some of the sports biomechanics literature in terms of developing a command of the language used to describe movement. It allows you to read technical journals and converse with other coaches more informatively. Rather than filling your head up now and making this chapter over long, we are leaving that part to you. Our intention here is to 'down tune' the language used in order for you to start developing a knowledge insight, that you can enhance at a later date by learning things such as the names of the 'cardinal axes' and the difference between 'speed' and 'velocity'.

The basic principle

Movement analysis centres on making a comparison between an athlete's performance and a theoretical model of expert performance. The differences between the two performances are then prioritized to develop a coaching strategy. For example, a sailing coach will observe a dinghy going downwind. He or she will evaluate this against an ideal performance that draws on his or her knowledge of 'aero' and 'hydro' dynamics. Subsequently feedback is given to the crew about 'sail set', 'dagger board placement', 'balance', 'trim' and the 'course' that is being sailed. The process sounds a simple one, but it requires the careful consideration of a four-stage model (Figure 3.1) put forward by Knudson and Morrison (2002).

In the 'Preparation' stage the coach should have a clear rationale for choosing this aspect of performance, why this downwind leg rather than an upwind or crosswind leg? Again this draws on their ability to prioritize the needs of the learners. It may be that previous competitive performances have indicated that this is an area of concern, or a potential area for enhancement. Consideration at this stage should also be given to the developmental phase that the learners are going through brought about by age, experience and the competitive cycle. The coach may well come to the conclusion that the crew need to spend more time together in the boat becoming acquainted with each other rather than fine-tuning their downwind handling skills. In the 'Observation' stage the coach needs to consider 'how' they will observe (real time, video, etc.), 'how many' occurrences and from 'where'. In Figure 3.2, the coach has decided match boat speeds and film from alongside capturing most of the important detail, a heeling boat might have made this considerably more difficult.

Consider the merits of observing from more than one place, and whether it is important to see the performance in real time rather than slow motion as this might compromise the temporal aspects of the performance. Having chosen the most appropriate thing to observe and captured performance effectively the 'Evaluation/Diagnosis' stage has the potential to unlock performance enhancement. The majority of National Governing Bodies help the adventure sports coach by publishing analysis frameworks. For instance, the Swimming

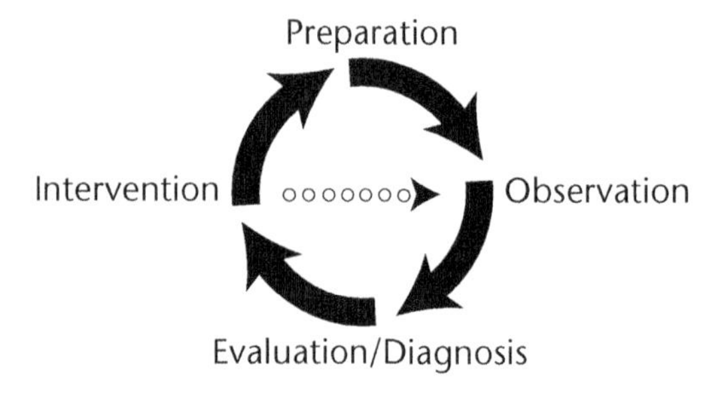

FIGURE 3.1 Knudson and Morrison four-stage coaching model

FIGURE 3.2 Downwind coaching
Source: Photo courtesy of Toby Hamer

Teachers Association champion the BLABT (body position, legs, arms, breathing, timing) framework against which an open water swimming performance can be considered, identifying both the important aspects of performance and their developmental priority. Similarly the British Canoe Union's Body-Boat-Blade and the Royal Yachting Association's Five Essentials approach gives the coach a benchmark on which to evaluate performance. Other approaches have identified 'critical shapes' that the body should pass through to optimize performance success.

For example, if rolling a kayak (Figure 3.3) many consider the 'lay back' as a vital position for successful completion of the roll. Using frameworks such as these the adventure sports coach can make a comparison between the performance they have observed and a theoretical model they are working towards. We will return to technical models later to consider just how much value they are to you as a coach.

During the 'Intervention' phase of the model feedback is given to the performer, matters of timing, amount, language and frequency considered previously in the chapter still apply. This stage is also used to set up further observations, the whole process should become cyclical where appropriately set goals based on identified critical movement features become the stepping stones to enhanced performance.

Technical models

Bartlett (2014) is extremely cautious of the use of technical models stating: 'This approach has nothing to recommend it except, for the lazy analyst' (p. 68), he

FIGURE 3.3 Critical shape in learning the kayak roll

continues further to say that this approach requires little creativity from the coach, and it is based on the false proposition that there is a 'universal optimal performance model' (p. 68). Similarly Hay (1985) comments that the 'copying the champion' (p. 3) approach has major limitations in that many of them have succeeded despite having techniques that are far from optimum. Logically, at best, modelling yourself on a champion results in adopting both desirable and undesirable attributes: if your personal attributes differ at all then the potential for enhancement is considerably compromised. Similar caution has been expressed over the use of 'trial and error' modelling in that it is time-consuming, and potentially physically and psychologically damaging to the performer. So how can the adventure sports coach surmount this difficulty, how can they be of use to the aspiring performer? The answer lies in the understanding of basic movement principles that become the foundations of performance observation, analysis and intervention (coaching).

Basic movement principles

Bartlett (2014, 1999) provides a readily understandable framework in which those principles that apply to every (well very nearly) sporting activity are divided, and those that have speed generation as a significant component. In our world, the latter would include such activities as a climbing 'dyno', or a 'diagonal stride' in cross-country skiing.

The stretch shortening cycle

The first of these general principles is the application of the 'stretch shortening cycle'. This uses the elastic properties of the muscle structure to supplement muscular action. Think of it being similar to stretching a rubber band before letting it go. The elastic properties of the muscle and in particular the tendons add to the muscle output created by its contraction. While there appears to be some disagreement about just how much additional force is derived from this pre-contraction stretching, and how it differs between activities, there is some agreement that unlike an elastic band the muscular stretch needs to be immediately used otherwise it is lost through muscle relaxation. Prior to the 'dyno' move the climber stretches the muscles around the hips, shoulders, knees and ankles to augment the forceful contraction. The stretch shortening cycle is an essential component of movements requiring force or speed. The principle also underpins some of the common coaching points we use – in looking for new water in the kayak turn we initiate pre-tensioning at the hip, trunk and shoulders.

Minimizing energy expenditure

While this might seem obvious, there are numerous examples where adventure participants seem to waste energy needlessly, often because they are unaware of technical inefficacies. Going uphill when mountain biking, riders unnecessarily get out of the saddle, this disengages the powerful hip extensors.

Another common example is not adopting a position during the kayak roll that reduces the 'moments of inertia' (reluctance to move or change state of motion), requiring the performer to expend additional energy when recovering the body. There are associations here with two important performance 'axioms' (a premise or starting point of reasoning): these are the axioms of closure and segmentation. These two axioms provide a link between biomechanically efficient movement and aesthetically pleasing movement. The closure axiom basically comments that when the body shape should be tucked it should be fully tucked, similarly when it should be extended it should really be extended. In situations where the body is between these two extremes it is less aesthetically pleasing to the observer. The axiom of segmentation builds on this be saying the more body segments that are distinguishable in a movement the less aesthetically pleasing the movement is to the observer. For example in freestyle skiing, an open somersault in comparison to a tucked one is more aesthetically pleasing despite placing greater performance demands on the athlete. Intuitively we can understand how aesthetic enhancement and mechanic demands are positively related.

Controlling the degrees of freedom

The majority of movements require the use of multiple muscle groups being used over a series of joints. The general pattern of movements is for movement to start close to the body core and then move outwards (in technical terms, proximal to distal). This allows the larger slower muscle groups to begin the movement, getting the movement started by overcoming inertia. Subsequently, smaller but faster muscle groups are recruited adding to the speed and range of the movement. The contributions of the various muscle groups are summated as the movement progresses. In a high- kneeling position in a canoe, for example, the paddler recruits the larger hip and truck muscles prior to the shoulders, arms and wrists.

Biomechanically efficient movement reduces any unnecessary additions to the movement chain, and any additional movement directions (the degrees of freedom in the movement are optimized). The C1 paddles must therefore reduce additional steering elements from the stroke as these increase the degrees of freedom and reduce 'power' stroke efficiency.

Reducing the moments of inertia

The next mechanical principal that needs coach consideration is the reduction of any unnecessary reluctance in the body to move (reducing the inertia). This generally means moving the body mass towards the axis of motion subsequently allowing rotation to be faster. In an acrobatic 360 degree loop in freestyle kayaking, the paddler optimizes the rotation speed by reducing the moments of inertia as they tuck close to the deck.

Impulse generation

In mechanical terms the maximum 'impulse' is achieved by applying the maximum force for the longest possible time. If we go back to our canoeing example, the paddler needs to apply the maximum force to the blade for the longest stroke length possible. Large impulses result in large changes in momentum. In this case he or she is able to impart the maximum power through the body to the boat.

Increased stability

Finally the adventure sports coach needs to be aware that to effectively achieve the principles above the body needs to be in a balanced stable position such as a mountain biker shifting weight off the back of the seat (see Figure 3.4). Appropriateness being determined by the ability to retain the principles previously outlined.

FIGURE 3.4 The biker shifting weight to achieve optimum stability
Source: Photo courtesy of Dave Giles

Software support

Most compact digital cameras offer some way of recording performance and videos can usually be played back in slow motion. My bombproof digital camera can be thrown into a buoyancy aid or clipped to a climbing harness providing excellent analysis footage when used in conjunction with my desktop computer. 'Ubersense' and 'Coach's Eye' are excellent tablet applications that can give more structure to your analysis. These allow parallel comparisons, reference lines, angles and much more. The adventure sports coach needs to consider the nature of the analysis they are undertaking, with the environment inevitably playing a major part in decision about the use of analysis aids.

Presenting sports performance analysis data

The way you present the data from your analysis is absolutely crucial. You need to ensure that all the data can be clearly interpreted by the performer. The data you present to a performer are a form of extrinsic feedback. The extrinsic feedback delivered by a coach has the potential to impact significantly on the sports performance. Coaches should think carefully about how and when they provide feedback to enhance learning (Maslovet and Franks, 2008).

Statistical performance data can be presented verbally and they can be displayed in tables or graphs. You could link statistical data with video footage of the performance (if a video recording took place). Video editing software could be used to produce video clips of a performance (some sports performance analysis software can do this as well). This could enable annotations and coach comments to be added to the video.

If working with a group of performers, you need to consider when you present the data to them. Do you present information during a performance or do you review the data after the performance? Do you need to allow time for performers to reflect on their performance before you provide any information? Do you share information with all the members of the group or is it more appropriate to provide information on a one-to-one basis? Another key consideration is the amount of information you feedback to the performer. If too much information is presented, the performer may not know what information to attend to. Many performers like to watch video footage of their performance but you may need to observe the video with the performer to provide verbal cues and feedback to help the performer to make sense of the video they are observing. It is advisable to ask the performers how they would like to view information about their performance.

Following the presentation of any data, it is good practice to evaluate the methods used to present information to a performer. This will help you to gain an insight into what the performer found useful.

Using the data to enhance performance

The crux of all sports performance analysis is whether the analysis helped to gain an enhancement in performance. Sometimes one small piece of information gained from an analysis can lead to a positive enhancement in performance immediately. On other occasions, it can take weeks, months or even years for the analysis to have a positive impact on performance.

If working with performers over a longer term, the key to evaluating the effectiveness of the analysis is to keep a database of the performance data, so that the performer can be tracked over time. If an analysis is performed once a month over a period of six months, you have a database of six analyses. The information within this database can be very useful for displaying performance improvements and helping to plan the next cycle of a training programme.

Observation and analysis in action: The coach's eye

Adventure sports coaches will continue to advance their understanding and improve their coaching practice through the adoption of observation and analysis principles developed from mainstream sports science. There are issues however for the adventure sports coach who has developed a sophisticated level of intuition based on years of previous observations and creating future courses of action based upon them. Despite advances in technology and the opportunity for higher volumes of more accurate data about performance there is also more legitimacy being afforded to a coach's intuitive ability to observe holistically, systematically and deductively. This is often referred to as 'the coach's eye'.

A coach's eye narrative

As a practicing sea kayak coach, white water kayak coach and mountaineering instructor I can confidently say that effective observation and analysis underpins all that I do. There are a number of reasons for this, not least because of the way most people access coaching in adventure sports i.e. short intensive periods, such as a weekend or perhaps a five-day or week-long block, followed by time without access to a coach but active in their chosen adventure sport and then further coaching episodes at a later date. In this example, for sea kayaking, it is vital that I am able to profile the requirements of my paddlers such that our time together can be as productive as possible and so that they leave with action points to continue to work on and develop. This profiling isn't only about watching them perform, I need to understand their thinking as well as how they feel during a performance, but that said ultimately it is their performance in the environment that informs much of what I'll do with them. To gain as much information as possible I structure an initial observation in such a way that I'm able to see them execute a range of technical skills. In addition, however, I want to see them having to select from a range of potential solutions and options so that I can start to see their tactical awareness, they may have good technical execution but if it's not the optimal technique for the situation their performance will be limited. How does their mental state affect their performance? And finally is their fitness appropriate to the environmental challenges they want to set themselves. This final component is often a limiting factor but realistically in these short intensive coaching episodes little can be done to improve sport specific fitness and is more often than not a development point for them to work on after our time together.

Writing this narrative raises the question of how this observation would typically be structured. Initially I get the learners to perform an open task where they are free to choose what, where and how they perform. This initial unstructured observation will give me a holistic view of where their starting point is for this session or series of sessions. It will have been preceded by a discussion about what they want to get from our coaching time together so I will have an idea of where they want to be. Hence I can start to compare the starting point to their described objective and start to formulate an outline plan. But being fairly open and holistic in nature it often leaves me with subjective terms that describe their performance. Terms like smooth or clumsy, stable or inconsistent, etc. while giving me an overview of them it doesn't usually give me specifics to start a coaching session(s). To do this I need to start to stress or stretch their performance to identify the gaps. To do this I'll move toward more specific structured tasks, at varied speeds and often linking a number of elements or requiring them to choose from a selection of possible solutions to achieve the tasks. For example, I might ask them to paddle a specific shape or circuit around buoys in winds and waves (see Figure 3.5). This allows me to be more deductive and analytical about what techniques and tactics they are choosing and then how they are executing these. By discussing with them their performance I can start to understand both their decision-making and mental approach to the task specifically if the environment is potentially hazardous.

Finally within this observation period I would attempt to put in some 'measurability' mechanisms that will allow us to compare future performances against their starting point. This will allow them to identify improvements or deterioration in their performance. These measurements can be simple efficiency measures like stroke counting or may use 'rate of perceived exertion' scales, etc.

This observation process will be repeated at various times through our time together usually when faced with new environmental situations for example different water features, a different tide race, stronger winds, etc. This observational process will constantly be adding to the profile I have of them, getting a detailed picture of where they're at and more importantly what's keeping them there.

FIGURE 3.5 Making observations in progressively more challenging situations builds a more accurate picture of performance

Source: Photo by Karl Midlane

So how might we use a notational analysis system in sea kayaking? A sport that's executed in a dynamic environment where no two days are exactly the same due to the weather, tide, etc. the answer is with difficulty! This is because to accurately use a notational system we need to control as many parameters as possible. When I've used notational systems it's been to objectively answer specific questions. The best example I can give is the often ask question "what length paddle should I be using?" To answer this question we need to control as many variables as possible. The first would be their forward paddling action and so our starting point will be on a paddling ergo inside and out of the environment. I'll video their performance from a number of angles and in addition they'll be facing a mirror. The video along with the watt meter on the ergo will objectify the feedback and allow us to improve their technique through accurately informed coaching interventions. The mirror will allow them to develop some useful practical markers and a mental image of their forward paddling which they will need when we move outside. For this example, I'm looking at a sea kayaker so we want to develop a cruising stroke over a longer period of time and not a flat out sprint. To try to objectify this effort we use a 'perceived rate of exertion scale' of around 6 throughout this session.

Once we have an accurate and stable forward paddling action, which the paddler is able to self-gauge via markers within their performance and 'perceived rate of exertion', we move onto the water. Outside I have a measured course on the water 250 m long alongside which we uses a mobile phone app to time runs on this course and calculate an average. The course is paddled three to five times with each of a range of differing paddle lengths but at the same perceived rate of exertion and with the same form forward paddling action. More runs will improve the reliability of the averages but fatigue may start to impact on performance so finding a balance is important. In addition to timings a simple stroke count for each run is counted and recorded. Ideally for this aspect of the testing the environment is as benign as possible i.e. no wind or tide. This will produce some objective data such as Table 3.2.

TABLE 3.2 Using notational analysis to determine ideal paddle length

Athlete name	*Paddle length*	*Stroke rate 1*	*Stroke rate 2*	*Stroke rate 3*	*Average number of strokes taken*	*Average speed from 3 runs*	*Wind speed and direction*
Paddler A	200 cm	85	86	84	**85**	6.7 kmph	0 mph
Paddler A	205 cm	79	82	83	**81**	7.4 kmph	0 mph
Paddler A	210 cm	86	87	88	**87**	6.9 kmph	0 mph
Paddler A	215 cm	87	85	85	**86**	6.5 kmph	0 mph

This table shows quite clearly that the 205 cm paddle gives the paddler the fastest time with the fewest amount of strokes; therefore, both are more efficient and faster.

But these results are only valid for the environmental conditions that the test was in. For a more dynamic environment an increased cadence might be important. Hence these results may not transfer but we have gone some way to objectify feedback for a cruising forward paddling stroke.

Sid Sinfield

Summary

In this chapter we have aimed to present contemporary and more established techniques used in sport to improve the accuracy of our observations, which then lead to a more informed analysis. We hope that through the inclusion of examples that aim to link theory to practice you can see their current value in adventure sports contexts also. Also, by reading the coach's eye narrative we hope that you can appreciate the complex and challenging nature of applying some techniques that were developed in more static and unadventurous contexts. Our own experience as coaches in a variety of contexts both in sport and adventure sport and has resulted in mixed successes based on the specific demands of the activity, the participant and the environment. To this end we hope that you will be able to use and evaluate these approaches in the same way rather than adopting or discarding them in a wholesale way. Ultimately they are all 'grist to the mill' and will ultimately facilitate the development of your own intuitive coaching as seen through your 'coach's eye'.

References

Bartlett, R. (1999). *Sports Biomechanics: Reducing Injury and Improving Performance.* London and New York. E & FN SPON.

Bartlett, R. (2012). Performance analysis. In: R. Bartlett and M. Bussey (eds), *Sports Biomechanics: Reducing Injury Risk and Improving Performance*, Abingdon: Routledge, 177–205.

Bartlett, R. (2014). *Introduction to Sports Biomechanics: Analysing Human Movement Patterns.* London and New York. Routledge.

Franks, I. M. (1993). The effects of experience on the detection and location of performance differences in a gymnastic technique. *Research Quarterly for Exercise and Sport*, 64, 227–231.

Franks, I. M. and Miller, G. (1986). Eyewitness testimony in sport. *Journal of Sport Behavior*, 9, 39-45.

Hay, J. (1985). *The Biomechanics of Sporting Technique.* London: Prentice-Hall.

Hughes, M. (2008a). An overview of the development of notational analysis. In: M. Hughes and I.M. Franks (eds), *The Essentials of Performance Analysis: An Introduction*, Abingdon: Routledge, 51–84.

Hughes, M. (2008b). How do we design simple systems? How to develop a notation system. In: M. Hughes and I.M. Franks (eds), *The Essentials of Performance Analysis: An Introduction,* Abingdon: Routledge, 98–110.

Hughes, M. and Bartlett, R. (2008). What is performance analysis? In: M. Hughes and I. M. Franks (eds), *The Essentials of Performance Analysis: An Introduction*, Abingdon: Routledge, 8–20.

Knudson, D and Morrison, C. (2002) *Qualitative Analysis of Human Movement.* Champlaign, IL: Human Kinetics.

Maslovet, D. and Franks, I. M. (2008). The need for feedback. In: M. Hughes and I.M. Franks (eds), *The Essentials of Performance Analysis: An Introduction*, Abingdon: Routledge, 1–7.

4

THEORIES OF MOTOR LEARNING AND THEIR IMPLICATIONS FOR THE ADVENTURE SPORTS COACH

Ed Christian and Phil Kearney

> He who loves practice without theory is like the sailor who boards ship without a rudder and compass and never knows where he may cast.
>
> *(Leonardo da Vinci)*

Introduction

How do we learn complex movement skills? How do expert climbers gracefully and effortlessly ascend routes that most of us cannot even touch and how do elite skiers move with such fluidity, speed and control through steep mogul fields?

If you are anything like us, you will take great pleasure in watching performances like these and appreciate the countless hours of practice, the trials and tribulations (and yes ... the pain!) that are essential to execute skill at this level, and wonder 'how do they do that?' But it is equally important to ask how a complete novice surfer is able to pop up on their board and ride that unforgettable first wave. For us as coaches and academics, performance at both ends of this skill spectrum is what interests, motivates and pushes us to discover more about how we learn and develop complex movement skills. If this sounds like you too, then read on.

This chapter will begin by considering the role of theory and research in adventure sports coaching before going on to discuss some of the early and more contemporary models of motor control. We hope to convince you that becoming familiar with these models will provide you with some very useful practical coaching guidelines. These models may simply put new names on things that you already do, but we aim to give you a common language so that you can discuss your coaching with others from across the adventure sport world, and even mainstream sport.

The role of theory

The relationship between theory and research is at the heart of science. Research involves gathering information using a variety of methods, such as observation, interviewing or conducting experiments. For example, imagine that you want to find out how efficiently your learners are practicing. You might observe the amount of time that your learners spend practicing skills that they have already mastered, and which should require relatively little time, compared with those skills that they have yet to master, which require a greater share of the practice time. Alternatively, an interview might be used to establish the process that an instructor goes through when attempting to eliminate a 'bad habit', such as throwing the shoulders into the turn, from a skier's technique. Research may also be conducted by carrying out experiments such as providing one group of learners with feedback only when they ask for it, and another group with feedback after every attempt, and evaluating which group learns more quickly.

Regardless of the method used to conduct research, the outcome is to generate new knowledge, which makes us more effective as coaches. For example, Christopher Janelle and colleagues (Janelle, Kim and Singer, 1995) discovered that providing feedback only when the learner requests it accelerates learning compared with other methods of providing feedback. An interesting finding that provides valuable practical advice for adventure sports coaches. However, Janelle's results do not explain *why* providing feedback on request is effective. Theories answer the question why. In essence, research provides facts, and a theory provides an explanation of those facts.

Good theories do more than just explain existing knowledge: they also make predictions about future situations. You may be familiar with the saying that "there is nothing so practical as a good theory". Even though no research may have been conducted on your specific area of interest, a general theory may exist that can provide guidance on how to adapt your practice. For example, while there may be no research on skill failure under pressure when attempting to roll a kayak in white water, an understanding of self-focus and distraction theories (see Chapter 7) will provide a coach with useful ideas to apply to his/her learners.

Theories may also provide clues as to how practices might work even better. For example, Schmidt's (1975) Schema theory explained why practicing many variations of a skill resulted in better performance on novel versions of that skill than practicing only a single version of the skill. Schema theory prompted a group of Italian researchers to explore the benefits of deliberately repeating and exaggerating errors made during skill acquisition, as a means of introducing this variability into practice (Milanese *et al.*, 2008). Their results are described in Case Study 1. The above examples illustrate how a sound understanding of theory should provide the adventure sports coach with guidance in unfamiliar situations, and stimulate novel approaches to learning and coaching.

Case Study 1: Deliberately repeating and exaggerating errors: what was Milanese thinking?!

An experiment by Milanese and colleagues used different methods to teach the horizontal jump to children. Initially, all children performed a set of jumps to give a baseline measurement of their skill level. One group then practiced jumping while receiving feedback on the key aspect of the jump they needed to improve (e.g. bend your knees more). A second group were told to exaggerate their error (e.g. barely bend your knees at all this time). A final group had no practice, and acted as a control group. When the three groups were tested again after practice, the group that had exaggerated their errors had improved the most. Coaches rarely encourage their athletes to practice the wrong thing, but, in this instance, it appears to have been a very successful method to encourage learners to understand and correct the errors they were making. Milanese's idea of exaggerating errors was inspired by the importance that schema theory gave to practicing skill variations. You may be able to identify how you could apply exaggeration of error to enhance learning in your sport.

Before we go on to explore the major theories of how movements are controlled and learned, there is one important point to bear in mind: even though different theories exist, there may be more than one solution to any particular coaching situation. As a result, different coaches might use various approaches with the same learner. Due to the complexity of each learning situation (more of this in other chapters), theoretical underpinnings act as guides rather than as strict rules. It is up to you as the coach to interpret the theories and come to your own conclusions about how you implement them into your coaching. The result of this is that you may often find yourself coaching some learners differently from others and perhaps not in the way that the 'coaching manual' says that you should. If you have a sound theoretical rationale for what you are doing, you are more likely to have confidence in your coaching, and gain the confidence of others.

Early theories of motor control

Up until the late 1970s, sport coaching (and coach education) was dominated by behavioural training (BT) methods. BT has its roots in the behaviourist school of psychology and is more commonly known as conditioning. You may have heard of Pavlov's experiments with dogs, or B. F. Skinner training pigeons to play table tennis and fly missiles into war ships (it's true, look it up on YouTube!) The basis of BT is the relationship between stimulus and response. Pavlov, for example, would ring a bell just prior to bringing out food (the stimulus) and in turn the dogs would salivate (response). Salivation is a normal response to the smell of food, but, eventually, the ringing of the bell alone was sufficient to induce salivating. In this example, successful training required the frequent and repetitive pairing of stimulus and response until behaviour was modified. The success of this stimulus-response technique led to sports coaches adopting methods, which emphasized repetitive practices, starting with simple versions of a task. These repetitive practices require little in the way of thinking from the learner, and may induce little in the way of enjoyment. A good example of this can be seen in my (EC) early experiences of being taught to paddle a kayak where the coach would set out a triangular course and have us paddle round it repeatedly. The first couple of times around, there were problems to solve and so we were engaged by the task. However, by the third time around there were no new problems: performance, motivation and learning start to plateau. You can imagine how I felt on the twentieth time around! This is not to say that there is no value in repeating the basics; rather that the purpose of repeating the basics is simply to get the idea of the movement. Once your learners have a clear idea of what they are supposed to do, it is time to move on.

A further problem with the repetitive practice inspired by the behaviourists is that the ability of the learners to apply what they have learned in new or different situations is not developed. We can relate this back to the example above in that by learning kayaking by paddling round a static and unchanging course, learners will struggle to adapt their skills to meet different and more dynamic environments (which are a unique feature of most adventure sports). The lesson for adventure sports coaches is that if we do not alter the practices that we give learners then we will limit their development and confine them to a limited skill set. We are going to talk much more about variety of practice and why this is important later.

Among psychologists, a major source of dissatisfaction with behaviourist theories was the lack of an explanation for what was happening in the brain when new skills were being learned. Behaviourist theories were frequently described as 'black box' theories, in that while the stimulus and the response could be identified, the mechanisms that linked stimulus to response could not. The desire to 'unpack the black box' led to a significant shift away from the early behavioural theories of Pavlov and Skinner towards cognitive theories that attempted to identify the processes that occur in the brain. In the next section we will meet one of the theories, which attempted to describe the contents of the black box: information processing theory (IPT).

Information processing theory

The cognitive or IPT approach was inspired by the development of computers. Early cognitive psychologists viewed computers accepting input, performing calculations and providing an output, and wondered whether movements might be planned and controlled in a similar way. For example, a rock climber could view a rock face (input), decide upon the next steps to take, and which movements are required to complete these steps (calculate), and start to climb (output). I like to think of cognitive theories literally in terms of cogs in the brain and how they fit and work together to result in skilled movement. Although a bit basic, this analogy highlights the notion that there are several different structures in the brain (i.e. inside the black box) that are responsible for executing movement and that coordination between these structures is vital for successful outcomes. Applying the computer analogy to human learning has produced a number of different models of information processing which share the same basic processes that you can see in Figure 4.1.

The first stage of the model: Perception

The first stage of information processing is perception. Perception may be proactive, as in the case of a climber scanning a boulder for appropriate hand holds, or reactive, as in the case of a mountain biker feeling her front tyre start to slip on loose gravel. Perception is multi-sensory, in that sight, sound and touch all contribute information for the brain to process. Perception also involves contributions from memory. Have you ever looked at a stick and seen a snake, or mistaken a tree stump for an animal? According to information processing theories, mistakes such as these arise because the raw information picked up by your senses is compared with previous patterns stored in memory. Thus, perception is the combination of raw sensory input and previous interpretations of similar input to produce an image of the current situation, which can be passed on to the next stage: decision-making.

How do we develop perception?

Skilful perception is fundamentally important in a wide range of adventure sports. For me (PK), one of the most extraordinary examples of perceptual skill is seen when sailors identify changes in wind direction from the most subtle of environmental cues. A scene, which to me holds no information about wind direction or strength, informs the skilled sailor not only where the wind is coming from, but also when. How is such perceptual skill developed? The obvious answer is through hundreds of hours of sailing, but not just any kind of sailing. Travelling around a

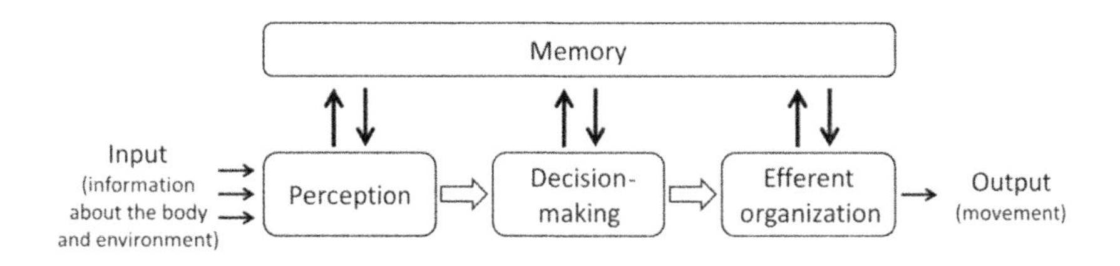

FIGURE 4.1 Information processing theory

Source: Adapted from McMorris (2004)

predetermined course requires minimal perceptual processing from the learner, and therefore will not develop perceptual skill. It is mainly through sailing in natural conditions that perceptual skill may be developed. Let us say that it takes 500 hours of sailing in natural conditions to develop skill in reading changes in the wind. Are there specific activities that a coach and/or learner can engage in to reduce that learning time to 300 or even 200 hours? Although there are many differences between mainstream and adventure sports, mainstream sports may provide valuable ideas on how to develop perceptual expertise in the adventure context. Consider the following quotation from ice hockey legend Wayne Gretzky:

> Who says anticipation can't be taught? It was something [my father] taught me every day … he'd quiz me … Him: 'If you get cut off, what are you gonna do?' Me: 'Peel.' Him: 'Which way?' Me: 'Away from the guy, not towards him.' And on and on for miles. I had them all memorized.
>
> *(Gretzky and Reilly, 1990, p. 88)*

Although eventually a sailor instinctively reads the weather, the development of this 'instinct' is likely accelerated through the asking of key questions. If a novice sailor is not looking in the relevant places, then a coach can ask 'Where are you looking?' and direct the novice to more appropriate cues. If a novice sailor is looking in the relevant places, but not focusing on the key details, then a coach can ask 'What do you see? What will happen next?' A neat illustration of looking but not perceiving important detail can be found in Figure 4.2 of a chessboard (it is the turn of the

FIGURE 4.2 Skilful perception is the detection of subtle patterns

player with the white pieces). If you have played chess, you will notice the precarious position of the black rook. If you have never played chess, and are unfamiliar with the rules, then you will see a collection of objects on a patterned board, and may be wondering why you cannot see the bird that was mentioned in the previous sentence. The point is that perceptual skill comes with experience. Much of this experience will need to be in the natural environment. However, it is possible to accelerate the learning of perceptual skill by guiding the learner at appropriate times.

The second stage of the model: Decision-making

Once perception has determined the current state of the body and environment, this information is passed on to the second stage: decision-making. People tend to think of decision-making as the conscious selection of one of several available options based on their relative merits. In the context of adventure sports, this conceptualization of decision-making appears too slow to accurately account for real-world performances. Indeed, in a range of real-world applications, such as firefighting and emergency room medicine, Gary Klein and colleagues have demonstrated that skilled performers perceive a suitable solution directly, without any weighing of pros and cons (Klein, 1999). Terry McMorris succinctly captures the intuitive nature of expert decision-making, which he describes as "doing the right thing at the right time" (p. 64). For example, surfers will need to perceive information from the waves in a set to decide which is the best one to take-off from. The surfer will consider the shape of the swell, its height and direction, as well as where it is likely to shoulder. Additional relevant information includes the position of other surfers in the line-up and the etiquette that dictates who has the right of way. This is a lot of information! Decision-making is the process of sorting this mass of information from perception and memory to select a course of action: what am I going to do, and how am I going to do it.

How do we improve decision-making?

Basically speaking, the way to improve decision-making is to provide learners with a range of possible alternatives that requires them to select one or another option. This style of coaching requires a 'hands off' approach, which allows the learner the freedom to think and make decisions. This style of coaching is much less prescriptive and more learner-centred than the behavioural approaches discussed earlier. Let us look at an example. When attempting to cross fast currents in white water kayaking, the learner must make decisions regarding the speed, angle and edge of the kayak. The coach may elect to run a short session where the students get the idea of these principles on a small and safe rapid. Once a level of skill is established, the coach may then choose to set challenges on water of increasing complexity. This might take the form of a simple game where the coach asks if the paddler can cross the same current but using fewer power strokes. Say it took 14 paddles strokes to cross the current the first time, could they work out a way (by manipulating the speed, angle and edge of the kayak) to reduce this to ten? The coach might then set a course around a rapid using eddies and jets that encourages different movement solutions to complete. Say the course consists of five different jets to cross, the paddler will have to think about doing the skill in five different ways (see Figure 4.3). The general principle is that the coach has simply set the challenge and allowed the learner the freedom to work out a solution. This encourages cognitive effort (thinking) and decision-making. This is also an example of a practice structure called contextual interference, which we will talk more about in Chapter 6.

FIGURE 4.3 'Where do I go from here?' Decision-making is a central component of many adventure sports

Decision-making can also be trained through reflection and/or observation of others. For example, a climbing coach might discuss with a student the route that they took on a boulder problem, and other possible alternatives that might have been more efficient. By verbalizing their actions the climbers must think about what they did and reflect on the quality of the decisions they made. This reflective process can also be encouraged by having climbers watch others performing on the boulder, and having them predict and justify the route that they should follow.

The third stage of the model: Efferent organization

The final stage in the information-processing model is efferent organization. The term efferent refers to signals that are sent from the brain to the muscles (feedback signals that are sent from muscles to the brain are known as afferent signals). According to the information processing approach, movement patterns result from a stored plan, sometimes referred to as a motor programme. This programme contains instructions for what the movement should look like. Originally it was thought that motor programmes contained specific instructions for each motor unit (set of muscle fibres that are triggered by a single signal), describing the timing and intensity of firing patterns. It was subsequently realized that attempting to control the muscles in this way was far too complicated. Although a definitive explanation of a motor programme has not yet been established, the current understanding emphasizes a general programme, which is modified based on context-specific information. For example, rather than having a specific plan stored in memory for every possible variation of a throwing movement, there exists a single generalized motor programme that can be adapted when throwing different objects (e.g., rope, stone, rucksack) over different distances.

How do we develop efferent organization?

The basic idea of movement programmes stored in memory led to a fundamental misunderstanding of IPT. Coaches emphasized repetition, or 'grooving' of movement patterns, isolated from the context in which the skill was to be performed, with heavy coach involvement in the form of direct instruction and feedback. The logic for this isolated training was as follows: if a programme produces movements, then coaching should emphasize forming that programme. Once the programme was formed, it could be selected and run off when required by the situation, much like selecting a particular song on your iPod to suit your mood. While there is no doubting that the repetitive practice of technique may be useful for helping the novice learner to get the *idea* of a movement pattern, the usefulness of isolated repetition is likely to be limited to short periods at the beginning of practice. As we explained above, motor programmes are *general templates*, not specific sets of instructions. As such, efferent organization involves adapting the template to meet the specific demands of the situation using the information sent on from the perception and decision-making stages. In practice, this means that in order to develop efferent organization, learners must be immersed in the performance context and required to adapt their movements to meet a range of situational demands. Novices may be exposed to a simplified version of the performance context (e.g., an easy grade river), but some requirement to adapt the movement must be present.

When a learner failed to perform a skill adequately in a real-life context coaches would often interpret this as an indication that the skill needed additional practice, with the result that the performer had to endure further repetition of the skill in a simplified context. Ironically, it is likely that the performance was poor because the learner had spent too much time in the simplified context leading to errors in perception, decision-making or adaptation, which no amount of isolated practice would address. Skilful perception, skilful decision-making and skilful adaptation of movement patterns to the context of the skill requires practice in real-life contexts.

A critical evaluation of information processing theory

IPT provides coaches with a logical and intuitive foundation on which to base their coaching. When fully understood and used effectively, IPT permits the coach to evaluate performance and devise appropriate practices to develop perception, decision-making and efferent organization. However, in our experience, coach education programmes have tended to oversimplify IPT. Too much emphasis has been placed on drilling performers to produce specific movements, at the expense of training perception, decision-making and the adaptation of movements to real-life contexts. The simplification of the theory to focus on drilling basic movements is understandable, as it provides the novice coach with a supporting structure to deliver basic sessions. To use an analogy – it provides a few tools for the coaching toolbox. As the developing coach looks to work with more advanced performers and in more challenging environments, there is a need for a shift in emphasis. The priority changes from a coach-centred transmission of information to the learner, to preparing the individual to cope with the demands of the mountain, river or sea.

In reaction to the limitations of the information processing approach, sports science research has taken a different path in trying to understand how movement is learned and performed. This new school of thought, the 'constraints approach', argues that rather than movements being primarily shaped by programmes (albeit general templates) stored in the brain, the most important factors in shaping movements come from the individual themselves, the environment they perform in and the task that they are attempting. This is a completely fresh approach to understanding how we move and learn skills, but stay with us and read on because the constraints approach has profound implications for the adventure sports coach.

The constraints approach

Karl Newell introduced the constraints model (Figure 4.4) in 1986. A constraint is something that permits or restricts movement. The constraints approach starts by

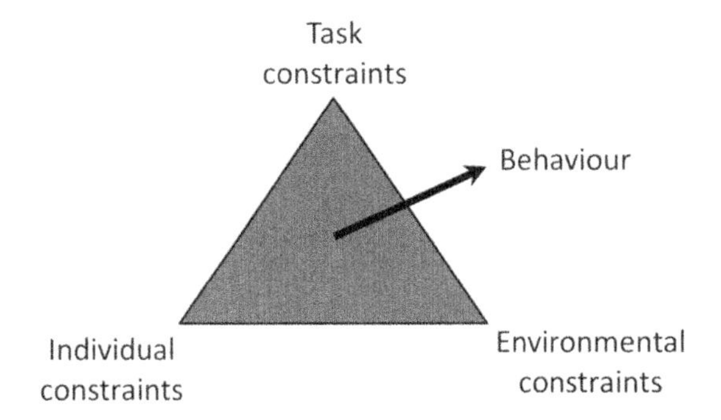

FIGURE 4.4 A model of constraints theory
Source: Adapted from Newell (1986)

asking what the learner is capable of doing. For example, one of the authors of this chapter is 6'3" tall; shorty is a mere 5'8". It follows that when climbing, author A can reach a much greater range of holds than author B. In fact, the movements performed by both authors on the same section of a climbing wall should be distinctly different, determined by differences in build, height, experience or fear. Hypothetically speaking, if both of us took up climbing at the same time, as we improve, our climbing styles will develop differently. For example, it is logical to assume that author A will develop a high-reaching, high-stepping style, whereas author B will develop a style based more around strength and flexibility. The beauty of the constraints model is that it recognizes that everybody is different. This is a really important shift for a theoretical model because it accepts that we cannot impose the same process of learning on all individuals; to put it another way, we cannot programme everyone the same way. In addition to individual differences, Newell also recognized that differences in the environments in which we perform, and differences in the tasks which we are performing, are also likely to shape the movements that we perform.

Individual constraints refer to features of the individual that may influence behaviour. Certain individual constraints are relatively fixed: height, weight, hand size and so forth. Others, such as motivation or confidence, are more flexible. Task constraints relate to the equipment used in an activity, or the rules governing that activity. For example, the length of a ski, specifying the particular holds permitted on an indoor climb. Environmental constraints relate to the environment in which a skill is being performed, such as the steepness of a crag, the condition of a piste or the grade of a river.

For an experienced coach, the constraints model offers more than just an explanation for why a learner is adopting a particular movement pattern. Through the manipulation of constraints, the coach has the opportunity to structure a learning environment to guide a learner to the next step in his or her development. Coaching in this way requires the coach to establish exactly what it is that they want the learner to be able to do, and then to manipulate one or more constraint to lead to the desired movement pattern.

We will now look at the three types of constraints in depth, and how an adventure sports coach might manipulate them to develop a learner's movements.

Example of manipulating task constraints

If a coach is working with a novice climber and decides that the learner would benefit from more accurate footwork, the coach might decide to constrain a traversing task by encouraging the learner to climb with silent feet. This constraint encourages the climber to allocate greater attention to more exact foot placements and discourages feet 'slapping' at the hold. The coach may then decide to constrain the task further by only allowing the individual to use one hand. Now the climber must think even more carefully about how they create a stable base with the feet from which to move. This is a simple but powerful example of how changing the rules under which the learner operates encourages more advanced movement patterns, but also engages the learner in monitoring and evaluating their own performance, and developing alternative strategies. The coach's role has shifted from providing instruction and feedback, to setting carefully designed challenges that will promote the desired response from the individual learner.

Example of manipulating environmental constraints

Manipulating the environment in which learners are practicing is also a useful way of encouraging exploration of different movement patterns. The ability to manoeuvre in and out of confined spaces is an important skill for novice kayakers to master. Such manoeuvring requires a level of boatmanship that involves subtle tweaking of the body, boat and blade rather than specific 'set-piece' strokes. In this instance, the environment could be constrained by setting out an area in which the group have to paddle around each other without touching anyone else. The size of the area depends on the skill of the kayakers: too large an area and the kayakers will be free to move around without experiencing any confined spaces. If the selected area is too small, the task will become impossible. Further, the learners will not have the opportunity to reflect on what they have been trying to do, and devise new ways of moving. The activity can be the teacher, but only if the coach 'rigs' the constraints appropriately to promote the target behaviour.

Example of manipulating individual constraints

Broadly speaking there are two types of individual constraint: structural and functional. Structural constraints relate to the structure of the body (height, weight, muscle mass); functional constraints are behavioural in nature and include things like motivation, fear and attentional focus. Structural constraints are relatively stable and develop slowly over long periods of time, thus they are not so relevant for the coach as they cannot be constrained. We can however manipulate functional constraints. For instance, if a windsurfer is particularly anxious about practicing in high winds and big surf, the coach could seek to reduce this anxiety by using a relaxation technique or staying in close proximity to the learner. This in turn will reduce negative emotions associated with the practice and facilitate greater learning. The same principle could be applied to building motivation or confidence.

We could constrain individuals in more physical ways to enhance learning. A particular favourite of ours is to blindfold kayakers as they practice skills such as edging. By constraining the individual (by removing their vision) we do two things. First, we force them to rely much more heavily on their other senses, particularly proprioception, which is vital for fine kayak control. Second, we make them think much more about what they are doing, increasing the quality of the practice session. There are countless ways of constraining tasks, environments and individuals and the only way to develop your skill at manipulating constraints is to do a lot of playing around and experimenting. Table 4.1 offers a few more ideas.

TABLE 4.1 Examples of how constraints may be manipulated to promote new behaviours

Sport	*Learning outcome/ desired behaviour*	*Possible constraint*	*Type of constraint*
Climbing	Energy conservation	Encourage straight arm climbing (you could tie a scarf around their elbows to stop them bending them)	Individual
	Accurate foot placements	Place bean bags on feet and see if they can keep them on as they climb	Task
	Improving contact on hand holds	Set routes with increasingly difficult hand holds	Environment/ task
Surf kayaking	Efficient take-off on wave	Allow only 3 to 4 paddle strokes to take off on the wave	Task
	Decision-making/ planning in paddle out	Place sand/stones on spray deck, see if learner can make it out back without objects falling/ washing off	Task
	Body management, weight transfer, trim	Surfing without paddles	Individual/ task
Mountain biking	Improving roll-offs	Increase the size and steepness of banks/drops	Environment
	Slow speed manoeuvring in a 360 turn	Width of the track in which they attempt the turn	Environment
	Developing up-hill bike control	Cycle in a low gear while applying a small amount of rear brake	Task

Apply constraints to coaching: 'Games with aims'

Some of you might be reading this and thinking *'hang on a minute all you're doing here is playing games; I've been doing this for years!'* That is the beauty of constraints theory: essentially all we are doing is playing games that encourage new thinking and consequently new movements. It is vital to remember at this point that (as with all forms of teaching and learning) the constraints approach must be governed by establishing the needs of the individual learner at this moment in time and setting appropriate learning outcomes for each session. As such, we need to think about 'games with aims' (i.e., games that lead to a pre-determined learning outcome) as opposed to just games. Pure discovery learning, where a learner is supervised within an environment but not provided with any structure or instruction, may be slow, demotivating and, especially within an adventure context, potentially dangerous. The constraints-based approach operates via guided discovery: identifying that particular set of constraints that will shift the learner towards the next step in his or her development.

Coaching according to a constraints-based approach may appear to involve less work than traditional direct instruction; after all, the coach is much less active during the session. Do not be fooled! Considerable preparation is required to identify suitable manipulations of a range of constraints before a session begins. During a session, the coach's role changes to observing whether the manipulations are having the desired effect, or whether an alternative manipulation is required. A second objection that is occasionally raised is that the constraints-based method is very slow, and that injecting direct instruction into a session accelerates the learning process. The counterargument to this point is derived from the difference between performance and learning (see Chapter 5 for more detail): rapid increases in performance do not necessarily indicate learning. Rather, learning is indicated when changes in performance persist over time, and when performance can adapt to novel contexts. While direct instruction techniques frequently result in rapid boosting of performance, these improvements are rarely maintained. The measure of coaching success is not the speed of acquisition, but the quality of retention and transfer to novel contexts.

So is it all games and no direct coaching? As will be explained in our coaching framework in Chapter 5, what a practice session looks like depends upon the consideration of a number of factors. Sometimes these factors will suggest a hands-off approach, where the coach rigs an appropriate set of constraints. At other times, direct coaching will be required. The main message is that coaches have a number of tools within their coaching toolbox, which can be applied to different problems. The more tools that a coach holds in his or her toolbox, the greater the range of situations that he or she can effectively deal with.

Who is doing the thinking?

As we have already alluded to, one of the overwhelming advantages of the constraints model is that it encourages cognitive effort (thinking) from the learner.

When the student is constrained by the task, the environment or their individual characteristics, they must find a solution to work around the constraint and this involves thinking things through. In the example of our kayakers learning fine manoeuvring this might involve thought patterns along the lines of *'if I do X then Y will happen'*. This is the kind of cause-and-effect thinking that leads to problem solving and ultimately long-term learning. Some of you might be reading this and associating increased cognitive effort from the learner with more student-centred or guided discovery coaching approaches. This is very much the case.

Generally speaking, adventure sports take place in a dynamic environment where it is not always possible to blow a whistle and bring a session to an ordered stop. River currents, ocean swells and mountain slopes will carry on regardless of our wishes. This makes the whole coaching business different for us. It means that we need something a bit different from our learners. It requires our learners to be active in the learning process; that is, to be able to deal with variation, to solve problems, to cognitively engage with the task – to very quickly become 'coach independent'. One of the appeals of the constraints-based approach is that, from the beginning, it encourages this active learning and self-sufficient attitude from the participants. As a result, when a kayaker encounters a challenging rapid for the first time, or a climber ascends a route 'on-sight', they will be better prepared to cope with the complexities of that new situation. Coaching for independence involves us equipping learners with the necessary skills to develop independently of the coach. Philosophically speaking it requires a shift in thinking from viewing the learner as an empty receptacle into which we pour knowledge and skill to seeing them as self-aware movement system that needs nurturing and encouraging to become in tune with its environment (i.e., the river, crag, piste). The constraints approach is ideally suited to this development of independent learners.

Similar to IPT, the constraints model gives us a great foundation for coaching, but it is challenging because it is such a new way of thinking (and coaching). We will next take a look at a model which follows much of the core philosophy of the constraints approach, but provides additional structure that may be of use to the developing coach: decision training (DT).

A practical guide to applying constraints and cognitive Effort: Decision training

DT is a coaching model presented by Vickers (2007), and is based on many years of research. DT places the learner at the centre of the learning process and, as the name implies, involves coaching in a way that incorporates high levels of decision-making from the start of the learning process. To encourage decision-making, a DT approach involves practice within the real-life context of the activity (river running/trail riding/kite surfing) rather than constructing contrived and artificial learning environments, such as triangular courses or lines of cones to navigate through. This philosophy makes DT a close ally of the constraints approach. Where DT has an advantage over the constraints approach, at least for developing coaches, is that it provides a more specific set of guidelines for a coach to follow in the design of sessions. These guidelines include tools such as tactical whole training, random practice and high use of questioning.

The DT process starts with the selection of an appropriate problem for your learner. For a mountain biker who needs to develop his decision-making around downhill route selection (e.g., jumping, riding around or slowing down to manage adverse terrain), this might involve taking the rider to an area that you know will challenge this particular skill because the routes will force the rider to make this type of decision on numerous occasions. The second step in DT is to design an appropriate activity. In this instance, we might run certain sections of a route multiple times, with the instructor calling out to the learner at crucial moments for a decision regarding the upcoming terrain. In response, the rider might call out 'slow', 'jump', 'left' or a similar key word. In this way, the rider is being forced to scan ahead, perceive the terrain and make decisions early. The coach also benefits, in that he/she gains an insight into the accuracy and timing of the rider's decision-making. The final step in the DT process is to apply an appropriate DT tool (see Table 4.2). An appropriate tool to use in this instance might be frequent use of video reviews, using a camera mounted on the rider's helmet. The DT tools can be broken into the three phases of the coaching process: instruction, practice and feedback. We will look at these tools in more detail in later chapters.

In summary, the role of the coach in DT is to (1) identify conditions which the performer's decision-making needs to be improved, (2) design an activity that requires these decisions to be made frequently, and (3) apply relevant DT tools to manage the performer's cognitive effort and thereby ensure optimal learning.

TABLE 4.2 Decision training tools

Decision training
Instruction: • Give the learner tactical problems to solve within naturally occurring contexts • Instruct using an external focus of attention • Use video wherever possible
Practice: • Use whole practice whenever possible • Look to randomize practice as much as you can
Feedback: • Employ a bandwidth feedback approach • Incorporate high levels of question and answer • Review performance using video • Encourage the learner to detect and correct their errors
Overall: Optimize learners cognitive effort

Source: Adapted from Vickers (2007)

Voices from the field: Decision training in action

In my early career I was trained to use a very direct approach to coaching. For example, when teaching climbing I would tell learners exactly which foot and hand holds to use. I would even go as far as chalking up the holds for the climbers to make them more visible. This direct approach gets immediate improvements in performance, but it also made the learner very dependent on me. This dependence becomes really obvious when they are trying something new; my learners would literally wait like robots for me to tell them what to do, because that's what I had taught them to do. Throughout my career I am constantly looking to improve and develop as a coach. Working with other coaches over many years and studying at university has reinforced my belief that direct coaching is limited in its effectiveness. Working in dynamic and unpredictable environments such as the open sea, alpine rivers or remote mountain locations makes it imperative for me to encourage individuals to make their own decisions at an early stage of their learning. To do this I use a technique called DT, which emphasizes increased cognitive effort from the learner through using major tools like questioning, video review and a variety of practice in diverse environments (random practice). So, for example, with new clients I ask a lot of questions to force the learner to rationalize their decisions. As they progress, learners tend to generate and answer their own questions. Although questioning is an ongoing element of my coaching, there is an obvious shift from the questions being generated by me to them asking and answering their own questions. When guiding on advanced alpine water I need people to ask and answer their own questions. Very often in this context I will be protecting the rapid from below in an eddy or on the bank. When the paddler enters the rapid I have virtually no influence on them. If the paddler fails to hit the line they are effectively on their own and will have to make their own decisions about how they are going to rectify the problem. In my experience using DT approaches means that my students are likely to become coach independent more quickly. This reduced reliance on me builds confidence and also, if used early, it allows them to become good at problem solving tactical elements much sooner. This approach has literally transformed my coaching, and I am convinced of its value. Many coach education programmes that I have experienced have limited emphasis on DT, and its application, such approach in my opinion is vital in adventure sports for the development of our performers.

Lee Pooley – British canoe union level 5 coach and national trainer

Summary

This chapter has attempted to explain the role of theory for the adventure sports coach. While research identifies which coaching tool is most effective in a given situation, theory explains why this tool is effective. As such, theories provide general principles that we can use to guide our coaching behaviours in novel or unusual situations. In terms of how we control our movements, two theoretical approaches have developed: the information processing and constraints-based approaches. Both theories have provided valuable lessons for coaches working to enhance the learning process. Information processing has emphasized that errors may result from mistakes in perception, decision-making or efferent organization, and coaches must take care to understand why particular mistakes are being made. However, the information processing approach places too much emphasis on the contribution that programmes stored in memory make to movement form, with the result that coaching practice often neglects the role that the task and environment play in shaping movement. By contrast, according to the constraints-based approach, movements are shaped by the combination of constraints arising from the unique properties of the individual, task and environment. This has pronounced implications for teaching: direct instruction has been relegated to a supporting role where ever possible, with the coach now seeking to guide the individual learner's discovery of new movement patterns and tactics through devising appropriate tasks in carefully selected environments. Given the dynamic environment in which adventure sports take place, the constraints-based approach appears to have additional advantages in terms of promoting learner independence.

The constraints-based approach is exciting, but perhaps overwhelming for the developing coach. DT follows many of the core elements of the constraints-based approach, but also offers additional structure in the form of more precise guidelines. In the next chapter we will attempt to present a more comprehensive framework that you can use to orientate yourself and your learners through the skill development process.

References

Gretzky, W., and Reilly, R. (1990). *Gretzky: An Autobiography*. New York: Harper Collins.

Janelle, C. M., Kim, J. and Singer, R. N. (1995). Subject-controlled performance feedback and learning of a closed motor skill. *Perceptual and Motor Skills, 81*, 627–634.

Klein, G. (1999). *Sources of Power: How People Make Decisions*. Cambridge, MA: MIT Press.

McMorris, T. (2004). *Acquisition and Performance of Sports Skills*. Chichester: Wiley.

Milanese, C., Facci, G., Cesari, P. and Zancanaro, C. (2008). "Amplification of Error": A rapidly effective method for motor performance improvement. *Sport Psychologist*, 22, 164–174.

Newell, K. M. (1986). Constraints on the Development of Coordination. In: M. G. Wade and H. T. A. Whiting (eds), *Motor Development in Children: Aspects of Coordination and Control*. Boston: Martinus Nijhoff Publishers, 341–360.

Schmidt, R. A. (1975). A schema theory of discrete motor skill learning. *Psychological Review*, 82, 225–260.

Vickers, J. N. (2007). *Perception, Cognition and Decision Training: The Quiet Eye in Action*. Champaign, IL: Human Kinetics.
Welford, A.T. (1968). *Fundamentals of Skill*. London: Methuen.

5

SETTING THE SCENE

A framework for coaching practice in adventure sports

Phil Kearney and Ed Christian

Introduction

We are always learning. This important principle underpins our philosophy towards coaching and stimulates the following chapter. We believe that coaches learn to reflect at the same time as they learn the content that they wish to deliver and the soft skills essential to the successful delivery of that content. We believe that it is only through a process of deep reflection and a willingness to learn that we can hope to better ourselves and become more effective coaches.

Coaching is incredibly complex. This is particularly so in the adventure sports context given the dynamic environment in which we are learning and performing. Fundamental coach education addresses this complexity by providing a set of rudimentary tools and techniques that can be used to safely introduce individuals to adventure sports. However, simplifying what the coach does is not likely to lead to successful coaching in the long term because it ignores the variation and complexity of real-world coaching. There is no one size fits all model in coaching. The ability to respond to the complexity inherent in the adventure sports context and deliver a session that is finely tuned to meet the demands of the specific learner, task and environment is the defining characteristic of the more advanced coach.

Over the course of his or her development an adventure sports coach will acquire more and more tools. Eventually, the coach will need to organize their toolbox. The framework that we outline below provides this organization by providing an initial set of questions for the coach to consider, the answers to which suggest what the most effective coaching session will be.

For the student of adventure sports coaching, the working coach or the early career instructor, this may be the first time that you have been presented with an overarching framework of coaching practice. We hope that you recognize its potential to enhance the experience of your learners. For an intermediate coach, who may already have a rudimentary framework in place, we hope that this chapter will provide you with ideas and prompts for further analysis of and reflection on your own coaching. For established coaches, we hope that you will find within this framework affirmation of your current coaching practices. Furthermore, we hope that coaches of all levels of experience will be provoked into thinking more deeply about the practices that you currently employ and continue to improve your coaching by analysing your own performance as much as that of your learners.

Before outlining a framework to promote the acquisition of skill, it is important to clarify a few preliminary matters. First, we will define what is meant by skill in the context of adventure sports. As we are concerned with learning skills, we will next consider how to measure learning. We will then outline the framework, and explain its component parts in detail. As we do so, we will refer to a range of coaching tools and techniques, some of which will be novel to you. These tools will be explained in detail in the next chapter. Finally, we will present a number of case studies so that you can see how the framework may be applied.

What is skill in adventure sport?

Consider your particular sport or activity: can you name an individual who may be considered to have reached the pinnacle of achievement? What are the characteristics of that individual's performances? An obvious characteristic is smooth and efficient movement. For many skills, however, displaying a textbook technique is a secondary concern; rather, it is the matching of technique to the demands of the environment that exemplifies high skill level. A kayaker who executes smooth and beautiful strokes while being pushed off course by the current would not be perceived as highly skilled. A skier may be perfectly balanced and aligned, but is not skilful if he or she is heading for a tree. The primary quality when defining the skilfulness of movements must be effectiveness rather than appearance.

This is not to suggest that all effective movements are equally skilful. Movements must obey the laws of physics. A climber can adopt postures that minimize the load on the muscles and can be easily maintained, or postures that maximize the load on the muscles and rapidly lead to fatigue (Figures 5.1a/b). A climber facing a long and difficult route will benefit on the second half of the climb from energy saved through economical movements over the first half of the climb. Similarly, there are movements that, although they do not impede the effectiveness or efficiency of the mover at the time, if repeated may ultimately lead to an overuse injury, or predispose the performer to a traumatic injury. For example, in bouldering, overemphasis on pulling with the arms as opposed to accurate footwork may place excessive stress on the rotator cuff muscles of the shoulder complex. Such movement patterns must be avoided in the long-term interest of the learner. Crucially, this is not to say that there is only one correct technique when climbing, skiing, kayaking, etc. Rather, the most skilled performer has at his/her disposal a wide range of different movement solutions that could be applied to the problem at hand.

FIGURE 5.1 a/b Examples of economical and uneconomical form – which will tire the climber faster?

In summary, skill can be thought of as finding effective, efficient movement solutions to the problems posed by the situation. For the most advanced performers, skill is also often creative – discovering new ways to master the challenges posed by the constantly changing adventure sports context. Understanding skill in this way will help you to understand a critical component of the framework that we propose below: skills do not simply reside in the mind of the performer to be called up when required, but are shaped by their immediate context. Therefore, any performance or learning situation will be enhanced by consideration of who is performing, what task they are performing, where they are performing the task and the aim of the session.

There is one other adjective that is often applied to definitions of skill: skill is learned. This leads us to perhaps the most important question in skill acquisition: how do you know when a skill has been learned?

How do I know what my students have learned today?

Understanding the difference between performance and learning is an extremely important lesson for coaches at all levels. In the sporting context, learning is defined as a relatively permanent change in the capability to perform a skill (Magill, 2011). Performance, how well we perform a skill on any given attempt, is determined by the interaction of many factors such as weather, mood and fatigue. Just as poor weather may temporarily depress performance of a particular task, practice conditions can be set up to temporarily boost performance. This can be achieved in many ways, such as providing multiple attempts at the same version of a task or frequent feedback. This artificial boost in performance may disguise the fact that no appreciable learning has taken place. To illustrate this point, try the following: multiply 9 × 12 in your head. If you are like us, you felt the cogs whirring as you strained to juggle multiple numbers and complete the necessary multiplications and additions. If we now ask you to repeat that problem, and again multiply 9 × 12, you will likely provide the answer quickly and effortlessly. Your performance is faster, but have you actually learned anything? Is your performance faster because you have learned multiplication skills, or because we have rigged the practice conditions (by introducing repetitive practice) to temporarily boost your performance? The fact that a windsurfer has managed their first water start following 30 minutes of intense coaching does not mean that he or she will be able to return to the beach tomorrow and complete the same skill unassisted. The point is that isolated performance, particularly immediately following a period of practice, is a notoriously poor indicator of learning. Unfortunately, many coaches in both adventure and mainstream sport rely upon performance within a practice session to evaluate whether learning has taken place. So, let me repeat this point, with feeling: isolated performance, immediately following a period of practice, is a notoriously poor indicator of learning! How then do we accurately assess whether learning has taken place?

The most basic method of assessing learning is to wait a period of time and test performance again. This is known as a retention test: how much has the learner retained since the last practice session. By shifting the evaluation to the next session, a coach can start to identify those tools and techniques that enhance long-term retention of the skill rather than those tools that lead to a short-term boost in performance. Particularly among novice coaches, there is often a view that equates effective coaching with changing performance quickly, with the result that coaching tools and techniques that artificially boost performance predominate. Quality coaching involves making permanent changes that are adaptive to changes in environment and robust to pressurized situations. Making such changes involves a set of tools that are distinct from those involved in producing a temporary boost in performance.

An alternative method of assessing learning is to challenge the participant to perform the skill in a novel setting or context. This is known as a transfer task: can the learner transfer the knowledge he/she has learned in the old context to the new (see voice from the field below). Transfer tests are particularly useful in situations where it is not possible to wait for a retention test (e.g. an individual skiing lesson, or session on an indoor climbing wall). The use of transfer tests to assess learning reflects a major component to our definition of learning: in addition to being a permanent change in performance, learning is demonstrated where a learner can produce creative solutions in response to novel demands.

Voice from the field: Transfer as a test of learning

You may have spent the morning on an easy run perfecting your basic skills with me as your ski instructor. At this point, having you perform the same run again will not tell me how much you have learned. A technique I tend to use is to bring learners over to a new area. It could be an area that has been more heavily skied, but it does not have to be harder. The main point is that the conditions are just a little bit different from what they have been practicing on. If you can reproduce the skill under these new conditions, then I know that you have learned. If not, then I know we have more work to do.

Doug Cooper – British Association of Snowsports Instructors Level 2, Mountain Instructor Certificate, Ski Mountain Leader – Glenmore Lodge; National Outdoor Training Centre

There is an important caveat to introduce at this point. Learning for long-term retention and high-level performance is hard! It is effortful, tiring and may not be enjoyable. It is also frequently slow, with many errors along the way, which risks demotivating your learner. It is very reasonable to ask if it is worth the effort. After all, if someone is on a one-week canoeing holiday, what matters is that they can safely execute the basics of canoeing this week. Does it really matter if they have forgotten everything in two weeks? In this context, a temporary boost in performance, and likely confidence, may be the most appropriate fit to the needs of your learner. You as the coach can use tools and techniques that promote rapid but temporary changes in performance, or tools and techniques that promote slower but much resilient changes in performance. You must decide which is most appropriate for the situation you are dealing with.

The important message in this section is that performance does not always accurately reflect learning, and that a true assessment of long-term learning can only be obtained through retention and transfer tests. If a coach evaluates practice methods on the basis of changes in performance within a session, then it is likely that he or she will utilize tools and techniques that produce artificial and short-lived boosts in performance rather than those that promote robust learning. Where the coach's goal is the long-term development of a performer, evaluations of how much is retained at the next session, or on performance on transfer tests, provides a more accurate gauge by which learning may be judged.

A conceptual framework for adventure sports coaches

Many frameworks have been published in the skill acquisition literature (for example, Fairbrother, 2010; Schmidt and Wrisberg, 2004), all with slightly different components and diagrams, but with much the same message: in order to achieve your coaching objectives efficiently and effectively, your coaching must adapt to meet the demands of the situation. Our framework uses four generic questions to guide your thinking in any coaching scenario, and we believe it to be useful for both the developing coach and the advanced skills coach. Considering **Who** you are coaching, **What** you are coaching, **Why** you are coaching it, and **Where** you are coaching it, informs **How** you coach; that is, the content you deliver and the coaching tools and techniques you use to deliver it (see Table 5.1).

Who are you coaching?

Take a moment and think about the last group of individuals that you coached. How did their characteristics compare with the elements outlined in Table 5.1? The complexity resulting from these individual differences provides a considerable challenge to a coach, particularly when working in groups. These attributes may be an advantage (e.g., physical fitness) or a disadvantage depending on the context. An individual who is very strong may take great pride in muscling his way up a climb with no thought for technique; an attitude that he may regret when halfway up a taxing climb. By contrast, a novice who is relatively weak may have no choice but to focus upon technique early on to their long-term benefit. Similarly, previous experience may be a considerable advantage if the experience transfers to the new situation, or a detriment if the experience brings bad habits, which need to be unlearned. The first step in our framework is to map some of these individual differences, and shape our coaching accordingly.

TABLE 5.1 Outline of the coaching framework

Component	*Examples*		*Determines*
Who are you coaching?	• Age • Gender • Skill level • Expectations • Personality • Motivation • Goals	⇨ ⇨	**How** you coach
What are you coaching?	• Technique • Tactics • Safety • Mental skills (confidence, esteem, resilience, etc.) • Environmental understanding • Self-regulation (learning to learn)	⇨ ⇨	Content of the session Duration of the session
Why are you coaching?	• To explore new skills • To embed a skill • To excel in performance • To encourage recreational participation (fun)	⇨	Coaching tools and techniques used to deliver the session
Where are you coaching?	• Man-made versus natural environment • Land versus water based • Predictability • Familiar versus unfamiliar • Weather • Temperature • Altitude • Visibility • Risk • Time pressured (e.g. tidal)	⇨ ⇨	Methods used to evaluate the session

Please note that the examples that we present in this table are a guide and are not meant to be exhaustive.

There is an additional practical consideration to emphasize with regard to who you are coaching: what are your learners' experiences of, and expectations of, coaching? A friend of ours, also a lecturer, introduced a particularly interactive style to his teaching one year. It was a great success with half of the cohort, who were used to this interactive style from a number of similar lecturers. By contrast, the other half of the cohort had no experience of this interactive style, and saw no benefit to interaction with each other when they could have been listening to words of wisdom from their sagely lecturer. The module received decidedly mixed reviews. The lecturer was committed to the interactive style of teaching, and changed only one thing the following year. In the very first session, he explained how he would teach. He acknowledged that this would be different from the style of teaching that they had experienced previously, but presented his arguments and his evidence for the effectiveness of the approach. In effect, he aligned his expectations with those of his students. The module was extremely successful. A similar problem could arise in an adventure sports context. A coach could consider that he is developing learner independence, while his learners feel neglected and unsafe. A coach could consider that she is providing critical technical information, while her learners feel that they do not have an opportunity to think. The fundamental step of explaining how a session will be delivered, and why a session will be delivered in that way, establishes buy in from your learners, and ensures that communication has a prominent place in the coach–athlete relationship from the beginning.

What are you coaching?

Classifications of skill

Skills are classified based on their demands: paddling a kayak on a sheltered lake, and rolling a kayak in rough seas place extremely different demands on the learner in terms of their complexity, muscles required and requirement to match the movements to environmental demands. The differing demands of adventure sport skills define the optimal practice activities that we as coaches should facilitate, thus we should always consider the 'identity' of the skill and how this may affect the way we teach it.

Open and closed skills

The need for movements to adapt to environmental demands varies between skills. For a climber learning to tie a bowline at an indoor wall, there is virtually no variation to consider. Although there are some perceptual demands, these are unchanging and predictable. The climber is in control of when to execute the skill. Such self-paced skills, performed in an unchanging, predictable environment, are known as closed skills. By contrast, skills that are externally paced, and performed in dynamic, unpredictable environments, are known as open skills. Picture a surfer riding an unfamiliar break. The perceptual demands are high, as the surfer constantly tries to position their body and the board at the most efficient part of a constantly changing wave and at the same time scan ahead for dangers, such as rocks or other surfers. In this example, all of the variables in the equation (the rider, the board, the wave and other people) are constantly moving and changing resulting in the skill being unpredictable or 'open'.

The continuum from closed to open skill is particularly useful for practitioners. The differing demands of closed and open skills should lead to different ways of practicing these skills. For the indoor archer practicing a closed skill, the goal is the refinement of one particularly efficient and effective technique. By contrast, the surfer must learn to subtly modify and adapt her technique at each moment, to meet the changing demands of the environment such as the height and steepness of the wave and what they predict it will do in the future. As a result, the surfer must engage in practice activities designed to encourage variations in technique. As we shall see in future chapters, consideration of whether a skill is closed or open is also important in performance under pressure.

It is worth noting that all of the skill classifications operate on a continuum rather than by just being defined as one or the other. In this way a skill is neither entirely open nor closed but is rather '*more open than closed*'. For example, sailing in the open sea is more open than sailing in a tidal estuary, which in turn is more open than sailing on a small sheltered lake (Table 5.2).

TABLE 5.2 The closed-to-open continuum of skill classification

Closed	————————————	———————————→	**Open**
Solo wind surfing on a pond	Wind surfing in a group on a pond	Solo wind surfing in a tidal estuary	Wind surfing in surf among kite boarders

Gross and fine skills

Skills also differ in the size of the muscles used. Rolling a kayak is a gross motor skill, as it uses many of the body's large muscle groups. By contrast, the same kayaker uses much smaller muscle groups when raising the knee to assist a turn on a wave, a fine motor skill. Fine skills are often not particularly demanding, and therefore practice may include many repetitions. An important consideration for the practitioner is how to maintain sufficient challenge on the learner when learning fine skills, as a major source of challenge, fatigue, is not likely to be a concern. Time pressure, additional cognitive tasks, such as doing maths in your head, or the combination of some physically demanding task with the fine motor task may be considered to ensure the learner maintains engagement with the task during later repetitions. Gross motor skills lead to fatigue more quickly, and novices in particular are therefore limited in the number of attempts that they may perform. For gross motor skills, it is important for the coach to consider what additional activities a learner may do before an attempt, or in the gap between attempts, in order to accelerate learning. Mental practice, the rehearsal of a skill in the mind (which will be considered in the next chapter), is one approach that is likely to be of benefit. Research has also pointed to the benefit of learners watching other learners, and listening to their feedback. If video recording is available participants could review and evaluate their own performance. Particularly relevant for gross motor skills is the understanding that learning does not simply occur when you are physically doing the task, but may be accelerated by a range of activities before and after task execution (Table 5.3).

TABLE 5.3 The fine to gross continuum of skill classification

Fine	⟶		Gross
Tying a knot with one hand	Stern rudder in canoe	Short swing turns in skiing	Dynos in bouldering

Discrete, serial and continuous skills

A further continuum that is often used when describing skills is discrete-serial-continuous. Discrete skills have a clear beginning and end, and are typically of short duration. Rising to standing when surfing would be an example of a discrete skill. Continuous skills are cyclical activities, such as running, cycling or paddling on a sheltered lake, where the same movement pattern repeats. Serial skills are best described as a chain of discrete movements that are performed in the same order. Rolling a kayak is a good example of a serial skill, where the performer must adopt a specific sequence of body positions in a specific order to effectively execute the movement.

The relevance of this discrete-serial-continuous continuum for the instructor again relates to the implications for optimal practice. For serial skills, a coach would be advised to explore different ways to use demonstrations (e.g., who demonstrates, timing of demonstration, amount of demonstration), as well as different orders of practicing the elements (e.g., forward chaining, backward chaining, random practice). For continuous skills, the instructor must be particularly aware of how much concurrent feedback is being provided (that is, feedback provided while the learner is executing the skill), and to explore a 'question and answer' approach to coaching to develop a learner's self-awareness. For discrete skills, the challenge often becomes ensuring that the learner remains engaged with the context in which the skill is to be executed (see Table 5.4).

TABLE 5.4 Examples of discrete, serial and continuous skills

Discrete	Serial	Continuous
⟶		
An aerial manoeuvre in kite surfing	Planned routine in freestyle kayaking	Cross country mountain bike ride

Cognitive and motor skills

A final classification for adventure sports coaches to consider is cognitive versus motor tasks. Motor tasks place a high demand on physical movements (i.e., efferent organization from Chapter 4): long distance swimming in a sheltered lake, or sea kayaking in calm conditions are examples of primarily motor tasks where there are minimal cognitive demands. Cognitive tasks place a much higher demand on the perceptual and decision-making processes that we met in Chapter 4, such as route selection in climbing or mountain biking. As you have probably concluded from the examples above, the question is not whether a skill is a cognitive task or a motor task, but whether the task involves a relatively higher cognitive demand, or a relatively higher motor demand. Considering the relative demand placed on cognitive and motor components has implications for the design of coaching sessions.

The most important consideration when dealing with highly cognitive tasks is that the learner is already processing a large amount of information. Therefore, the coach must be careful not to overload the learner, for example, by providing feedback too frequently. In addition, the learner may benefit from being guided towards the desired movement through the use of demonstrations of correct technique, or video review of their own performances. Alternatively, the cognitive demand may potentially be reduced through the use of an appropriate part practice strategy. By contrast, with more motor tasks, encouraging the learner to focus on the outcome of the movement during whole skill practice should prove effective. For example, when practicing throw bag rescues the coach may encourage the learner to focus on the point where he wants the throw bag to land rather than on the technique of the throw.

Summary of skill classifications

Each skill has its own identity in terms of skill classification. For example teaching kayak rolling in a swimming pool is a closed, gross, serial task. For a coach, classifying a skill provides a set of guidelines on how practice should be structured and feedback provided so that the learner gains the most from the session (see Table 5.5). Understanding the unique classification identity of the skill that we are coaching is a characteristic of higher level coaching, and allows the more advanced coach to fine tune his or her delivery to optimize learning.

In the adventure sports context, coaching often addresses other topics, such as tactics, safety, environmental understanding or self-regulation (learning to learn). It is beyond the scope of this chapter to analyze each of these variables in depth. The main message that we are trying to communicate, and which we have hopefully illustrated through the examples on skill classification, is that breaking down and analyzing *what* you are coaching will significantly alter how you coach, and ultimately, the success of your sessions.

TABLE 5.5 Summary of skill classifications

Category	*Implications for coaching*
Closed	Emphasis on refining an efficient technique
Open	Emphasis on developing technique variations
Fine	Increased number of repetitions possible Need to ensure challenge on learner is maintained
Gross	Reduced number of repetitions possible Explore less-fatiguing methods of practice (e.g., observation of self and others; mental practice)
Discrete	Explore methods to ensure the learner remains engaged with the context in which the skill is performed
Serial	Explore the use of demonstrations and the order in which the elements are practiced
Continuous	Take care to avoid providing excess feedback and explore a 'question and answer' approach to coaching
Cognitive	Take care not to overload the learner Consider the use of part practice techniques
Motor	Focus on the outcome of the skill Encourage whole practice

Why are you coaching?

It might seem strange to ask why are you coaching. After all, coaching is about developing individuals, and therefore the aim of all sessions should be to improve some element of performance. In this section, we are encouraging you to think in more detail about what precise element that you are trying to improve. After all, an introductory lesson with a beginner should have a quite different purpose to a lesson with an advanced skier who is preparing to tackle a formidable back country off piste run. This different purpose should have a profound impact on your coaching. The neatest breakdown of the different types of practice that we have seen was presented by Paul Ratcliffe of GB Canoeing, which we have summarized in Table 5.6. Depending on your aim for the athlete, to explore, embed or to excel, the coaching session should look different. Paul's concern was with the developing athlete in a performance context. To meet the goals of the recreational performer, we have also added 'Practice to enjoy' to these types of practice.

Practice to explore

During practice to explore, an athlete experiments with a new way of moving, or searches for a new tactic. For example, a climber who over-relies on reaching for holds may need to develop strategies for using smaller holds to open up more

TABLE 5.6 Types of practice

Type of practice	*Definition*
Practice to **explore**	Practice designed to uncover new ways of executing skills, or to discover the strengths and weakness of existing skills
Practice to **embed**	Practice designed to refine and consolidate a particular skill
Practice to **excel**	Practice designed to prepare the performer for the performance context
Practice to **enjoy**	Practice designed to facilitate immediate enjoyment of the activity and to encourage further participation

movement options. There will inevitably be lots of mistakes during practice to explore, so the learner must be prepared for this, and encouraged to embrace the idea of exploration. Preparation for the session might involve watching the range of solutions that other performers have adopted in response to this problem. It is likely that practice will be quite repetitive, as the novelty of the variations, particularly early on, should provide adequate challenge for the learner. The bulk of the session will likely be spent working on this one skill alone. Particularly if the learner is of a high skill level, then on each trial it is the learner who is likely to have the clearest understanding of what he/she wants to do, how he/she wants to do it and whether he/she has been successful in executing that component of the action. As such, self-selected feedback should be encouraged, whereby feedback is provided when the learner requests it. This does not mean the complete absence of coach-led input, but rather that the coach must be mindful of the possibility of overwhelming the learner who may be working on a different part of the problem. As such, any coach input is likely to be most effective if question and answer is first used to establish what the learner is currently focused on, and aware of. If the coach and learner are observing the same aspect of performance, then the coach may step in. If not, then the coach's observation should be stored for use later in the session, provided there is no immediate need for the information (e.g., safety). An important caveat to add here is that when adopting a practice to explore approach the consequences of failure must be minimal and activities should be structured to accommodate failure as making mistakes is likely to be a natural consequence of performers exploring movements or strategies (e.g. spotters in bouldering/buddy system in kayaking).

Practice to embed

Practice to explore ends when the learner has identified a particular way of moving or a tactic that he/she wishes to develop further. Practice to embed is the process of making the identified movement pattern more efficient, or effective. For example, imagine that you have been working with an intermediate climber who is not particularly strong. You have explored a number of possible techniques that this climber could use to increase their reach, and to allow them to take some pressure off of the arms during the climb. The heel hook technique emerged from your exploratory session as one method that it would be appropriate to develop further. Practice to embed would emphasize learning when the heel hook could be used, and improving the performer's effectiveness and confidence in applying the heel hook. Routes could be set up which allow numerous opportunities to use this skill, with the difficulty of the entire route, and of the specific holds where a heel hook may be used, adjusted as the skill and confidence of the learner improves. Identifying when to use the heel hook could be promoted by reviewing the route, initially standing out from the wall, but later, when the climber is paused at various points in the climb to replicate a more natural search pattern. As practice to embed progresses, the learner's emphasis should shift away from focusing on the specific technique towards completing the route. As such, opportunities for the specific technique should be fewer on later routes, which resemble more natural climbing conditions.

Practice to excel

Perhaps the most intensive practice involves preparing the learner for the performance context. Practice to excel will involve few, high-intensity attempts at the full skill in as realistic an environment as can be produced. Many coaches go further, and attempt to exaggerate the demands of the performance context at this stage, so that the learner is placed under relatively greater demands. For example, rest intervals may be restricted to exaggerate the effect of fatigue. However, it is important to also practice long durations of inactivity or low-level activity if this is an accurate representation of the performance context. For example, a surf kayaker might perform for three 20-minute heats during a six-hour competition. The key skills for this performer include being able to manage arousal, switching in or out as the situation demands. If a performer has never practiced with long intervals, then he or she may not have developed the skills essential to managing arousal. So a coach may want to set up mock competitions, which mimic the time demands, and include details such as the performer signalling when he wants his ride to be judged. Learner- or coach-selected rewards or forfeits depending on the performances produced may enhance mock these competitions.

Successful training requires a careful balance of success and failure. Failure is inevitable when exploring new or alternative methods. During practice to explore, success must be redefined as the discovery of new ways of moving, or the strengths and limitations inherent in existing techniques. During practice to embed, success can be gradually redefined in terms of performance outcome, initially for the specific technique under construction, later for the entire activity. During practice to excel, success is solely defined in terms of outcome. This is an essential but challenging period for the performer, and requires careful planning of both the technical and psychosocial aspects of learning.

Practice to enjoy

Within adventure sports, there is a huge market for introductory or taster sessions to activities. In the UK, this is characterized by companies such as PGL and in the US by Camp America. Many coaches of adventure sport will spend their formative years coaching in this arena, where the aim of the session is orientated around a safe and fun introduction to the sport. In our framework we characterize this kind of coaching as coaching for enjoyment. This is not to suggest that no learning takes place during practice to enjoy, or that all practice to explore, embed or excel are not enjoyable. It is a question of emphasis. Practice to enjoy has a more playful focus, concentrating on performing basic skills in a relatively safe environment (see Figure 5.2). By contrast, practice to explore, embed or excel place a greater focus on the refinement of skills to the level necessary to allow the learner to attempt increasingly adventurous contexts.

Remembering that all coaching should start with establishing the needs of the learner, we might surmise that when coaching for enjoyment, the beginner simply wants to be given the opportunity to play and enjoy himself or herself. The implication of this for coaches is that we need to give minimal technical instruction; in fact, only what is absolutely necessary so that we maximize activity

FIGURE 5.2 For many participants, fun and adventure is the primary motivation for engaging in the session

time. Playing well-designed games, in addition to providing beginners with the fundamentals required to move competently, is a powerful tool in coaching for enjoyment. While in other practice contexts the goal is to promote long-term learning, practice to enjoy is successful when the learner masters the essential skills and is enthused to the point of wishing to return to the sport. Good coaching in this context will lead to children begging their parents to take them back next week.

Where are you coaching?

Adventure sports take place in diverse environments and planning must take this into account. While we have grading schemes for rivers, climbs and ski slopes, which provide a useful guide, grades do not tell the full story and can be open to interpretation; for example, what is the exact point at which a blue piste becomes a red piste? A grade three river located close to a road in South Wales is a quite different prospect from a grade three river in a remote corner of Scotland in mid-winter. Many of you who have experienced lead climbing will recognize the change in an individual from assured and daring on their local indoor climbing wall, to hesitant and jerky on an exposed rock face when placing their own gear, despite the fact that the physical demands of the climb have not changed. The question 'Where are you coaching?' is included within the framework to encourage you to think about how your learners will react to the environment, but also so that you can consider how you can best use the environment to achieve the goals of your session.

While the eventual aim of participating in adventure sports is to perform the skill in challenging natural environments (e.g., sailing in Force 6 on the Solent, or mountain biking a steep single track), introducing the full skill within this context will overwhelm the average beginner. This does not mean that you should not ever introduce someone to an activity in a demanding environment; our point is that the demands of the environment that you choose will shape the delivery of your coaching. For example, attempting to use a guided discovery approach with a large group of novices in big surf that they are not used to is clearly not appropriate.

Coaching involves the careful balancing of psychomotor (i.e., have they learned the movement) and psychosocial (e.g., confidence, motivation) demands. Adventure sports skills are frequently taught in favourable environments that allow the acquisition of the psychomotor aspects of the sport. For example, people are often introduced to wind surfing with the board tethered to a buoy in light wind, or surf schools run introductory sessions in ankle-deep reformed waves. Let us look at an example in more depth. A rite of passage for every budding kayaker is the all-important first white water roll. Many learners will be introduced to the roll in a swimming pool and be taught one-to-one with copious amounts of instruction, manual guidance and feedback. It is not uncommon for kayakers to assume that because they can perform a consistent roll in the calm water of the swimming pool, that they will be able to transfer the skill to moving water. More often than not, this is not the case. Our framework promotes the manipulation of favourable environments in order to establish the foundations of the task as the first step, to be followed by the addition of a series of progressions of increasing complexity (see Voice from the Field below).

Voice from the field: Mimicking the natural environment

Once my learner has mastered the basic sequence of movements involved in a kayak roll, the next step is to get them ready for the real thing. Here are some of the things that I get my learners to do, while still in the relative comfort of a heated swimming pool:

- Have the kayaker paddle up the pool, or perform a sequence of turns, and then roll on command.
- Complete a series of sprints to tire the learner out, and then initiate the roll.
- Push or pull on the kayak, paddle or learner at various points in the manoeuvre.
- Briefly hold the kayak in place to prevent them from righting it.
- Throw a bucket of water into the kayakers face as they come up or just prior to their entering the water.
- Have the kayaker perform multiple rolls in quick succession, and on different sides.
- Have the kayaker perform the roll in close proximity to the side of the pool.
- Randomly and unexpectedly capsize the kayaker.
- Have the kayaker adopt a range of postures to begin the manoeuvre (e.g., leaning forwards, both hands on the wrong side, hands up in the air, leaning back, etc.)

Over the years I have found this to be really effective because it is fun, safe, but also genuinely demands that learner can successfully roll in a wide range of conditions. My aim is eventually to have added such complexity to the manoeuvre in the swimming pool that it potentially exceeds the demands of rolling in moving water. Stress proofing the learner in this way bridges the gap between the simplified, controlled roll in the swimming pool and their first white water roll.

Glyn Brackenbury – British Canoe Union Level 5 Coach – Skern Lodge Outdoor Education Centre

As the complexity of the environment moves through the grades and becomes more dynamic and unpredictable, we often see that the psychomotor aspect of performance (the movement) breaks down. Very often this is due to changes in the psychosocial aspects of performance, such as fear and anxiety. As a result, coaching the mind has a central role for the adventure sports coach. Part of the attraction of adventure sports is that we can often experience emotions of such magnitude that they have a profound impact on our lives. Just think about the endless tall tales of terror you have been subjected to with friends over a pint. Very often these are based on experiences that have had powerful effects on the storyteller (e.g. riding that monster wave, the 20-foot gap between gear placements). The other implication for this is that adventure sports are often used by coaches as methods of promoting behavioural change and discovering new ways of thinking and feeling. Considering and manipulating where you coach is a powerful tool in promoting such changes. Much more of the psychology coaching adventure sports will be covered in Chapter 11.

In summary, within our framework, considering where you are coaching involves asking yourself a series of questions to plan effective sessions:

1. Where am I going to take my learners today?
2. Why am I taking them there?
3. Could I creatively manipulate a controlled environment to prepare them for more advanced conditions?
4. How will I manage them in a testing environment?
5. How will I coach their mind?

Application of the framework: Case studies

We opened this chapter by defining skill within the adventure sport context as effective, efficient and often individual solutions to the problems posed by the task and environment. We followed this by explaining the difference between performance and learning, and highlighted that coaching to create a short-term boost in performance looks different from coaching to promote long-term learning that will transfer to novel situations. We have also emphasized that coaching in adventure sports is highly complex. To cope with this complexity we have presented a framework to help coaches organize their thinking. The answers to the questions '**Who** am I coaching?', '**What** am I coaching?', '**Why** am I coaching?' and '**Where** and I coaching?' will inform **How** your session is delivered. We hope that students of outdoor and adventure education and level two coaches will find this framework useful in structuring their thinking as they plan and evaluate their coaching in greater detail. For the advanced coach, we hope that the framework has provided stimulation to reflect upon your own practice and to evaluate your personal coaching framework.

The final section of this chapter will present a series of case studies illustrating the application of our framework. In each case, we have described the answers to the key questions of our framework, with a further column describing what the coaching session might look like. You may not be familiar with some of the tools mentioned, but these will be covered in detail in the next chapter.

Case study 1: High-level slalom kayaker

Questions	Context	How to coach	Coaching tools
Who?	Frank competes at national level, and has reached a performance plateau. He is very motivated to find a solution to his current difficulties. Having worked successfully with you in the past, he trusts in your advice and has deliberately sought you out	***Question and answer*** will be used throughout, to identify Frank's current understanding of the situation, but also his awareness of his movements	• Question and answer
What?	Frank believes that his method of transitioning to upstream gates is costing him time, and is looking for a way of improving his performance on this specific element. Thus, he will be working on an open skill involving large muscle groups	The skill is physically demanding, and therefore limited attempts will be possible. The session will ***block practice*** on this skill alone, and will minimize exertion on additional activities. Practice will begin on two gates that have been identified as particularly appropriate for exploring this skill. In addition, ***video replays*** will be used as part of a debrief after each trial, and ***mental imagery*** used to help preparation for each trial	• Blocked practice • Video replays
Why?	At present Frank knows that he needs to find a better method, but does not know what that method will look like. The emphasis will be on practice to explore	If possible, Frank will also be encouraged to ***watch other kayakers*** attempting the skill, either live or using video, both before the session and between attempts.	• Mental imagery • Observational learning
Where?	The particular aspect of his performance that Frank is looking to work upon requires realistic practice conditions. Frank knows that this year's championships will be held at Holme Pierrepont. Given Frank's experience and confidence, he is comfortable in these conditions.	As Frank is not sure what the solution to the problem is, the emphasis will be on exploring different methods of completing the task	

Case study 2: Improving climber

Questions	Context	How to coach	Coaching tools
Who?	Alan is a rugby player who has recently become interested in rock climbing. After a few introductory sessions at a local centre he has contacted you as a freelance coach to develop his skill further. He is looking to refine his skills so that he can tackle similar routes as his more advanced girlfriend	***Environmental constraints*** will be manipulated by selecting a series of negative holds that will not allow Alan to rely on his in his habitual manner. To initially reduce the difficulty, a supportive incline will be used, but both the incline and the shape of the holds will become more difficult as skill level progresses ***Random practice*** will be used to equip Alan with a range of movement solutions. As random practice already places a high load on Alan's memory, ***self-selected feedback*** will be used so that overload will be avoided and when Alan is ready for feedback, he can receive it As Alan will be relying on new muscle groups, in addition to the mental fatigue induced by the random practice and the constraints-based learning, the breaks between climbs can be longer than usual, but during these breaks Alan will be encouraged to ***spot other climbers*** with more refined technique, and to ***verbally analyze*** their performance	• Environmental constraints • Random practice • Self-selected feedback • Observational learning • Verbal analysis
What?	Having watched Alan climb, you quickly conclude that he is relying too much on his upper body strength. His focus needs to be on the development of footwork, core management and use of smaller handholds		
Why?	Having chatted through what you have seen with Alan, he knows what he should be doing in terms of footwork and body management, but has not invested the time in practicing these specific elements. Therefore, this will be practice to embed and further refine his existing skills		
Where?	Alan requires an environment that emphasizes the need for accurate footwork and body movement. This environment can be easily constructed on an indoor climbing wall		

Case study 3: Taster session with a surfer

Questions	Context	How to coach	Coaching tools
Who?	Sarah has never surfed before. She is a competent swimmer and an active triathlete. She is on holidays and has seen a surf school on a beach and decided to give it a go	The session will start with a comprehensive safety brief and the setting of boundaries Sarah needs to be able to operate independent of your feedback, as you will be less accessible once in the water. The better you can develop Sarah's awareness on the beach, the more independent she will be, and her practice will be of better quality. As such, beach-based ***games*** will be used initially to develop awareness of the fundamental principles of balance, trim and stability. ***Minimal direct instruction*** will be used. Instead, ***question and answer*** will accompany the games to develop Sarah's ***awareness of intrinsic feedback***, which aid her understanding of body position and weight transfer Once Sarah has mastered the core concepts on the beach, the session will move into the water where further games will be played to see if Sarah can take the lessons she has learned into the more dynamic environment. Depending on her progress, activities will progress from riding lying down, to kneeling, to standing, all the while experimenting with stance and posture Given the complexity of surfing, its novelty to Sarah, and the cognitive demand inherent in coaching through games and ***question and answer***, the activities can be performed using ***blocked practice***	• Games • Minimal instruction • Question and answer • Intrinsic feedback • Blocked practice
What?	By the end of the session, your aim is for Sarah to have experienced riding a wave, either lying, kneeling or standing depending on how well she gets on. The key to this will be to develop her understanding of the concepts of trim and balance Surfing is a complex, gross, open skill, which is demanding both physically and cognitively. The initial movement from lying to standing is a discrete skill. Riding the wave is a continuous skill		
Why?	The aim is for Sarah to have a positive introduction to the sport (both in terms of success and fun), and be inspired to continue with the sport.		
Where?	The lesson will take place on a sandy beach with a gentle gradient. Broken waves in waist high water		

Refeences

Fairbrother, J. T. (2010). *Fundamentals of Motor Behavior*. Champaign, IL: Human Kinetics.

Magill, R. A. (2011). *Motor Learning and Control: Concepts and Applications* (9th ed.). Boston, MA: McGraw-Hill.

Schmidt, R. A. and Wrisberg, C. A. (2004). *Motor Learning and Performance: A Problem-based Learning Approach*. Champaign, IL: Human Kinetics.

6

COACHING TOOLS FOR ADVENTURE SPORTS

Ed Christian and Phil Kearney

Work hard when it's easy, work easy when it's hard.

Introduction

This chapter aims to equip you with knowledge of the major aspects of the coaching process that follow from the theories of motor control presented in Chapter 4 and the framework for coaching presented in Chapter 5. Previously we have alluded to the adventure sports coach possessing a metaphorical 'toolbox'. This chapter aims to display the contents of that toolbox.

A guiding principle in this chapter will be that learning is enhanced when individuals expend the optimal amount of cognitive effort. Cognitive effort is generated by the various mental operations that we engage in; for example, searching, comparing, analyzing, questioning, deciding, remembering or planning. The specific context in which you are coaching demands a certain amount of cognitive effort. The environments in which adventure sports are performed are often dynamic and complex, and as such inherently require high cognitive effort from the learner to learn and perform. For instance, due to its complexity, attempting to roll a kayak places a high intrinsic cognitive load on the learner. By contrast, body boarding in small surf requires far less cognitive effort. In what is sometimes referred to as the 'Goldilocks principle', learning is optimized when coaching adjusts the level of cognitive effort so that it is 'just right' (Guadagnoli, 2009).

The adventure sports coach has a number of methods available to gauge the learner's cognitive effort. The first option is to use performance as an approximate indicator of cognitive effort. Very high levels of performance during practice could imply that the learner is not experiencing a sufficient challenge. Very low levels of performance could imply that the learner is experiencing excessive challenge. A more direct measure of cognitive effort involves using a simple self-report scale, similar to scales used by physiotherapists to assess the magnitude of pain, or by physiologists to evaluate the physical effort required by a task. The learner is asked to respond to the question "How mentally demanding is this task?" on a scale from 0 (not at all demanding) to 10 (very demanding). Finally, there is a range of behaviours that a learner may display that are indicative of high and low cognitive effort. Are your learners pausing in activities to think through their options? Are they asking questions of their coach or of other learners? Are they stopping to watch each other? The advanced coach can effectively monitor cognitive effort by observing performance, by asking learners to report their cognitive effort and by watching for signs of excess or insufficient cognitive effort, and adjust how a session is being delivered accordingly by manipulating instruction, practice and feedback.

By the end of this chapter you should have a better understanding of how learning can be optimized by manipulating cognitive effort. You should also be familiar with a range of coaching tools available to the adventure sports coach and understand the effect they have on cognitive effort.

Instruction

Instruction can be defined as the process of conveying the necessary information about a particular task to a learner. Adventure sports coaches possess a range of methods to convey this information that can be categorized as: verbal, visual or physical. As the name indicates, verbal instruction refers to the words we say to the learner and the tone in which they are expressed. Visual instruction uses demonstrations to communicate information. Finally, physical instruction involves manually guiding the learner to the correct position or through the appropriate movement. The adventure sports coach must decide on the most appropriate method for any given situation.

To highlight the importance of selecting an appropriate mode of instruction, I find the following task very effective. Working in pairs, with one student acting as the coach and the other as the learner, the coach is only allowed to use verbal instructions relating to specific body movements to get the learner to move from a lying down position to standing upright. It's not easy! This task highlights that in certain situations verbal instructions are virtually redundant as demonstrations communicate the necessary information much more effectively. Another exercise that I have found to be extremely effective in promoting reflective practice is to video your coaching session. When you spend some time analyzing what you say, and when you say it, you may be very surprised by the results. Both of these exercises are really useful for getting developing coaches to consider the words that they use and whether they are effective, or even if they are needed at all. The key message is that instruction has the potential to have a profound effect on learning, but the skill is in delivering the most appropriate mode of instruction at the right time.

Visual instruction

Demonstrations provide the leaner with a 'cognitive blueprint' of a desired movement and are an essential asset in the adventure sports coach's toolbox. Recent developments in neuroscience have significantly furthered our understanding of the process of how demonstrations actually work. Although a full-blown foray into neuroscience is a bit out of scope here it is interesting to consider the basics. The brain is made up of approximately 100 billion cells called neurons (give or take a few), and scientists have known for some time that *motor command neurons* located in the front of the brain are responsible for controlling movement. More recently it has come to light that there is a sub-group of command neurons, called mirror neurons, which fire when we observe the actions of others. For example, as I write this I am overlooking a sports field where some students are playing football. As I observe a player taking a shot at goal I know that his command neurons are controlling his movement, but in addition my own mirror neurons are firing and giving my motor system information about how the student just kicked the ball. In this way his neurons are communicating directly with mine; a strange concept but one that provides the basis for understanding how demonstrations work. You can view an excellent introductory video to mirror neurons by V. S. Ramachandran at http://tinyurl.com/rama-neurons. When we give demonstrations to our learners we are providing them with neural information to guide their own attempts at the movement. Understanding how mirror neurons work adds to our knowledge of observational learning theory that was developed by Albert Bandura in the 1980s. Bandura proposed that learning from demonstrations requires four processes: attention retention, reproduction and motivation. We have outlined these four processes in Table 6.1.

The nature of adventure sports presents significant challenges to the successful application of demonstrations. Gathering a group of tennis players in to observe a demonstration is a relatively straightforward affair. In comparison, when a learner is pre-occupied with fear 75 meters up a sheer rock face, ensuring that you have their attention is considerably more complicated. Similarly, in sports like surfing, it is difficult for a coach to ensure attention is being paid to the major elements of a demonstration, or to encourage rehearsal, if he/she is 50 meters away on the water providing the demonstration. In this instance, coaches will often stand on the beach with the learner and look for *ad hoc* demonstrations from unsuspecting surfers in the line-up. The nature of adventure sports is such that you must take the opportunities to demonstrate when they are available. Thus, as you consider the four processes outlined by Bandura, think carefully about the coaching demands of your particular sport and how Bandura's model might be adapted to meet those demands.

The aim of any demonstration is to convey enough information for the learner to establish an accurate mental representation of the task. In order to achieve this representation, there are several important questions for the coach to consider: Do you always have to give a demonstration? Do you need to use an expert as a model?

TABLE 6.1 Bandura's (1986) guidelines for the application of demonstrations

Stage	*Description*	*Implication for the adventure sports coach*
Attention	The learner must be actively attending to the demonstration	• Direct learners towards the main elements of the demonstration (e.g. watch how my thumb moves during the J stroke)
Retention	The learner must be able to encode and retain information from the demonstration	• Minimize the amount of time between the demonstration and learner activity • Use cue words or mental practice to encourage encoding and retention of key information • Minimize other factors that could affect retention (fear, stress, fatigue)
Reproduction	The learner must have the intellectual and physical capability of reproducing the movement	• Are you demonstrating a movement that the learner is physically capable of performing, and confident enough to attempt? • Observe the first attempts carefully. Are any failures to perform the action due to an incomplete understanding of the demonstration, or because of some physical or intellectual deficit?
Motivation	The learner must have the necessary motivation to want to do the task	• Consider the learner's motivational state, level of fatigue, desire to learn • If motivation is low, then poor performance may result despite the learner having a perfect mental representation of the skill. In this instance, the coach must address the motivation, not repeat the demonstration

How many demonstrations are needed, and when should they be given? We shall now look at each of these considerations in turn (see Figure 6.1).

Do you always have to give a demonstration?

There is significant research evidence to suggest that demonstrations are more effective when learning complex motor tasks (McMorris and Hale, 2006); that is, tasks that have several movement components (i.e. serial skills). This not to say that demonstrations are never required in simple skills, but that the adventure sports coach may not use them to the same extent with this type of skill. It seems intuitive that a learner will need more emphasis on demonstrations when learning complex skills, such as belaying, than relatively simple skills, such as the forward sweep stroke in kayaking.

FIGURE 6.1 A dry land demonstration to ensure learners are able to direct their attention to critical points

Do you need to use an expert as a model?

When coaching forward paddling to novices in sit-on-kayaks, do I need to demonstrate my best high-angle racing stroke; exemplifying appropriate core rotation, pushing with the feet, angle of catch and length of stroke (expert model)? Alternatively, do I just need to draw their attention towards the basic technique so that they can manoeuvre the craft around independently (coping model)? Or finally, do you have them observe each other as they attempt to perform the movement (learner model)?

The value of an expert model is that it swiftly guides the learner towards a movement pattern worth exploring. In addition, expert models can also serve as a motivational force in sport. For example, the first time I (EC) saw someone perform a flat water cartwheel, I didn't get out of my kayak for days! However, expert models also contain much information that is irrelevant to the beginner. For a beginner, a coping model may provide a clearer picture of the critical information. As a general rule, if using expert or coping models, the skill level of the model should be scaled to be slightly above that of the learner.

While either an expert or coping demonstration provides a clear picture of what to do, learner models appear to engage the learner in effortful problem solving. For example, a novice kayaker may observe another learner who is paddling well using a high paddle action and a lot of trunk rotation, and then focus on these aspects of her own performance to see if this makes a difference to her own paddling. When using learner models with beginners who have little knowledge of the skill, then the learner will also need to hear the feedback that the model receives about their performance. Once the learner has a better understanding of the skill then he/she should be able to problem solve more independently (Lavallee *et al.*, 2004).

The main message to consider when thinking about the type of demonstration that you give is whether your goal is to fast track the learner to an appropriate movement pattern (coping), to encourage cognitive effort and problem solving (learner model) or to inspire your learner to work towards learning something new (expert model).

How many demonstrations are needed, and when should they be given?

Generally speaking, in those situations where demonstrations are effective (e.g. belaying), multiple demonstrations are better for skill acquisition. Demonstrating from different angles and viewpoints is also beneficial in allowing the learner to assemble an accurate cognitive blueprint. Often we will provide verbal cues to direct the learners' attention to specific key points either before or after a demonstration (generally we avoid talking during the demonstration as this may disrupt their attention). Research carried out by Carroll and Bandura (1990) showed that providing higher numbers of demonstrations was associated with improved movement reproduction and that giving verbal cues, or 'verbal coding' as they called it, was only necessary when a high number of demonstrations was given. The implication for adventure sports coaches is that providing a block of demonstrations before practice, followed by additional demonstrations interspersed throughout practice, as required, is most effective.

Should slow motion demonstrations be used?

Demonstrations given in 'real time' are considered to be more effective than slow motion demonstrations. This is probably because slow motion demonstrations distort important information regarding the relative motion of body segments. So does this mean that there is no place for slow motion demonstrations? Consider our old friend the kayak roll for example. There are subtle nuances of positioning of the body and paddle that may be totally lost on a beginner observing this movement at high speed. In this case, a slow motion demonstration may be particularly useful to allow the learner to build an accurate cognitive blueprint of the skill, or part of the skill. Once this accurate blueprint is established (likely to be within one or two demonstrations), then slow motion demonstrations have no further purpose.

Verbal unstructions

Verbal instructions can be given either before or during attempts at performing a skill. There are numerous considerations for adventure sports coaches when providing verbal instruction.

In this section we will provide an overview of the content of instruction; that is, *what* a coach should say. However, it is worth remembering that the way in which we say things is sometimes more important than what we actually say. Take shouting for example. Being able to raise our voice is useful in conveying urgency in certain situations (e.g. increased background noise from the wind, rain, river). However, from the perspective of the learner, shouting can also be perceived as a sign of danger or a loss of control and can induce panic that, in turn, can break down performance. Generally speaking, learners will respond better to verbal instructions that are presented in a calm, positive but authoritative manner.

What does the learner need to know?

When giving verbal instructions it is helpful to consider this analogy: a sniper rifle, rather than a machine gun, should give instructions. The coach that adopts the machine gun approach will fire continuous information relentlessly at the target (the learner) in the hope that at least one part of it will hit the target and have an effect. By contrast, the coach who uses the sniper rifle approach will carefully identify the one piece of information the learner needs at a given moment that will have the biggest impact on their development. We could think of this as establishing *'the difference that will make the difference'*. Once the coach has identified this vital piece of information, they should wait for an appropriate moment and then deliver the required instruction to the learner. When a coach applies this sniper rifle approach, the learner often describes that as a 'light bulb' moment of clarity. I remember many years ago being told to lead my freestyle kayaking manoeuvres with the head and the rest will follow – for me that was a light bulb moment that changed my kayaking forever. This is a good example of accurate verbal instruction delivered at an appropriate point.

A particular downfall of the machine gun approach to giving instruction is that a lot of the information that is fired at the learner is in fact redundant; that is, information that the learner already knows. One thing that I have learned over many years of coaching is that it is often best to ask myself 'is it actually necessary to say this?' before giving an instruction. It is surprising how often the answer is no. Foundation coaches are often guilty of giving redundant instruction, presumably due to that fact that when we start out on our coaching career we tend to feel that we must be seen to be constantly giving instruction. As a result, much of what we say is not needed, and may actually dilute the useful information. The fact is that sometimes we say it best when we say nothing at all.

When we do instruct our learners, it is better to use five words than fifty to get the message across. Have you ever walked away from a coach's lecture and thought 'Hang on, what do I actually need to do?' Reducing information to salient points takes less time to communicate and is easier for the learner to remember. As a rule of thumb, most adventure sports coaches work to the principle of giving up to three (but rarely more) coaching points. I was taught how to do a bottom turn in a surf kayak by learning and reciting the keywords 'Look, lock, lean'. For the many hours and countless attempts it took for me to acquire a semi-decent bottom turn, my coach would simply give me one or all of the keywords to remember and that formed the basis of the verbal instruction. Keywords used in this way are particularly beneficial for adventure sports coaches as we often coach in an environment that does not allow us to have long and protracted conversations; in this case, in the surf.

In some contexts, even three coaching points are too many. This is especially the case when we add in the effects of anxiety and arousal into the equation. Minimizing the number of coaching points that we give also makes us think about the ones that we choose to give and guides us towards finding the illusive 'difference that makes the difference'.

Giving instructions using analogies

Heuristic instruction, also known as 'analogy learning', is a valuable asset to the adventure sports coach (see Table 6.2). Similar to keywords, analogies allow us to reduce the amount of verbal instruction that we give by clustering multiple task-relevant cues into single metaphor (or analogy). For example, if we are teaching novices the canoe draw stroke, we might say 'hold the paddle vertically, like a lamp post'. By trying to make their paddle resemble a lamppost, learners will invariably hold the paddle vertically, stack their hands and get the hands outside of the canoe – exactly what we want. In this example we have reduced several technical points into one memorable analogy.

We often see coaches using heuristic instruction without knowing what it is or even how effective it is. You might be reading this and thinking: 'I do that all the time'. If so, brilliant! Do more of it.

TABLE 6.2 Examples of coaching through analogies in adventure sports

Sport	*Analogy*	*Effect on performance*
Bouldering	'Climb like a ninja'	Quiet and considered movement of feet and hands
Skiing – carve turns	'Leave train tracks behind you'	Gives feedback to the skier whether their turns are carved or skidded
Mountain biking – negotiating berms	'Bank the corner like an aeroplane'	Brings centre of mass towards the centre of radius of the turn
Canoeing – pry stroke	'Lever the paddle as if you were pulling a pint of bitter'	Promotes deep paddle and weight on the paddle throughout the stroke

Internal and external focus of attention instructions

Focus of attention refers to the thoughts that the learner adopts when attempting a skill. For example, a kayaker might think about dropping their right hip to edge a kayak right. This is an example of an internal focus, as it directs attention to the specific actions of the body. By contrast, an external focus directs a learner's attention to the *effects* that their movement has on the environment. So, rather than thinking about hip movement, we might ask our kayaker to think about the shape of the kayak in the water. Although internal focus instructions are commonly used, a considerable body of research has built up demonstrating that external focus instructions lead to superior performance and learning (for a review, see Wulf, 2013). External focus of attention appears to encourage more automatic control of movement, while an internal focus encourages a disruption of this automatic control: 'paralysis by analysis'. Does this mean that you should never think about your movements when learning? The key to attentional focus is timing: there is a time to think, and a time to act (Lee and Schmidt, 2014). When planning the movement you want to make, then thinking about specific body positions might be helpful. However, when it comes to executing that movement, your attention should shift to the effects of your movement on the environment (see Table 6.3).

A kayaker could focus on the action of their paddle, the trim of their kayak or a point that they are aiming for: all three are external foci, but which one should your learner choose? External foci vary depending on the distance between the movement and the effect. So, focusing on the shape of the paddle motion would

TABLE 6.3 Examples of internal and external focus of attention

Skill	*Internal focus*	*External focus*
Skiing – carving	Controlling edging through position of the knees and legs	Controlling edging by attending to the skis themselves relative to the snow
Windsurfing – water start	The position of the arms	The orientation of the rig
Throw bag rescue	The rotation of the trunk and arm	The desired path of the bag through the air
Mountain biking – entering a corner at high speed	Ensuring pressure on the front wheel by focusing on the position of the shoulders and head	Ensuring pressure on the front wheel by focusing on pushing the tyre into the ground
Control of rotation in kayaking/surfing/skiing/snowboarding/skateboarding	Managing an anticipated body shape by conscious rotation of body segments	Managing an anticipated body shape by disciplined use of gaze control (looking forward throughout the turn)

be a proximal (that is, close to the body) external focus. Focusing on the path you wish the kayak to follow is an example of a distal (that is, far from the body) external focus. For novices, particularly on highly complex skills, it appears that a proximal external focus is most appropriate. As skill level increases, then the optimal focus of attention shifts along the continuum towards an increasingly distal focus.

Physical guidance

The purpose of visual and verbal instruction is to guide the learner towards an improved movement pattern. Occasionally, an even more direct approach is used, where the coach physically manoeuvres the learner into the correct position, or through the correct movement, or simply provides additional physical support. This approach is known as physical guidance (occasionally you will see the term manual guidance used instead). How effective is physical guidance? As with so many other questions in this chapter, the answer is 'it depends'.

When we initially discussed demonstration, we used the metaphor of a 'cognitive blueprint' to convey the message that the learner must initially form a general idea of the to-be-learned movement pattern. There may be times when the learner struggles to form this blueprint, typically due to poor self-awareness of their movements or positioning. In these cases, physical guidance may be used to educate the senses. For example, in ski coaching the instructor may physically manipulate the learner's arms to give them the ideal arm position for the pole plant. A second occasion when physical guidance may be appropriate is to reassure a nervous learner. This is commonly seen when swim teachers physically support a learner who is nervous about floating, or when a kayak coach stands in a pool beside someone learning to roll. Particularly when the consequences of a mistake become more severe, then physical guidance provides an appropriate safety net allowing the learner to more confidently engage in activities, and potentially to progress more quickly than if left to their own devices.

The standard objection to the use of physical guidance is that it stops the learner from thinking for himself or herself. In general, this is correct, and physical guidance should be rarely used in your coaching. However, there are some occasions encountered early in the learning process, as outlined above, when some learners may benefit from brief exposure to physical guidance.

Practice

Adventure sports coaches should always be mindful of the fact that the most important determinant of learning is not what they do, but what the learner does. For this reason we should structure our coaching so that the time taken to transmit instruction is kept minimal and the time given to practice the skill is maximized. In coach education this is often referred to as the talk-to-action ratio, and is one of the most difficult principles for foundation coaches to acquire. However, maximizing the time given to practicing a skill is only effective when the practice is of high quality. The following sections will consider outline a number of coaching tools and techniques that can be used to enhance the quality of practice design.

Part/whole practice

Part practice refers to the isolation and independent practice of an element of a skill, or the practice of a simplified version of a skill. Given the complexity of the environments in which adventure sports are performed, and the demanding nature of many of the core skills that learners are required to master, reducing the demands placed on the learner through some form of part practice is a sensible approach for coaches to adopt. There are four principle methods of part practice, which have been outlined in Table 6.4.

When should you use part practice?

The first question that an adventure sports coach must ask when considering the use of a part practice technique is whether the skill is really too complicated to practice as a whole? It is vital to remember that part practice is a tool for dealing with complexity, and not a method that should be universally applied.

TABLE 6.4 Methods of employing part practice

Method	*Definition*	*Example*
Fractionization	Two or more elements of a skill that normally occur at the same time, are practiced independently	Practicing the paddle placement component of the bow rudder in kayaking
Segmentation	Two or more elements of a skill that occur in sequence are practiced independently	Practicing individual moves on a boulder problem before putting them together
Simplification	The equipment (e.g. size of surf board or skis) or the environment (e.g. indoor climbing wall, calm lake) is manipulated to present a simpler version of the skill	In windsurfing, the learner might initially learn on a very wide board specifically designed for stability to enable faster learning of the fundamental sailing skills
Attentional cueing	The entire skill is practiced, but the learner's attention is drawn to one specific aspect of the skill	While practicing drop offs, a mountain bike rider concentrates on weight distribution through the movement

The traditional guidance on whether to practice a skill in parts or as a whole is based on the concepts of complexity and organization (Naylor and Briggs, 1963). Complexity refers to the number of parts that a movement has. Organization refers to the interdependence of elements of the movement pattern. A kayak roll is a highly complex movement, given the number of distinct actions that comprise it. In addition, it is low in organization because the components are easily isolated (paddle orientation, body movement, recovery). As such, some form of part practice is appropriate (see Table 6.5). By contrast, throwing a rescue bag consists of far fewer movement elements (backswing and forward swing), which lends itself to whole skill practice.

Fractionization

If the decision is made to introduce part practice, then the adventure sports coach must then decide which method to apply. Research has not supported the use of fractionization, however, it should be noted that the majority of research on fractionization has utilized skills such as typing or playing the piano, where there is a requirement to divide attention between two complex elements. In kayaking, the application of the principle body-boat-blade illustrates an alternative method of applying fractionization. Consider coaching the bow rudder, for example. A learner might be asked to leave the paddle on the bank, to use their hands to build up speed and then to use hip and leg movement to edge the boat and achieve a turn. In this way, the early emphasis is placed on exploiting the potential of boat alignment to achieve an efficient turn, rather than relying on brute force on the paddle. Once the learner has mastered an effective turn using the body, the paddle action can be introduced to complete the whole skill. Further research is required to establish whether applying fractionization in this manner is an effective technique.

Segmentation

There are a number of methods of applying segmentation (Christina and Corcos, 1988; see Table 6.6). Part Whole and Progressive Part methods start by practicing individual elements in isolation. In Table 6.6 this is illustrated by the letters A, B and C representing different segments of a skill, which may be practiced

TABLE 6.5 The implications for practice of task complexity and organization

	Low complexity	*High complexity*
Low organization	Whole practice	Part practice (fractionization, segmentation, simplification, attentional cueing)
High organization	Whole practice	Part practice (simplification, attentional cueing)

TABLE 6.6 The different methods of applying segmentation to a skill that may be broken into three parts (A, B and C)

Part Whole	*Progressive Part*	*Repetitive Part (forward chaining)*	*Repetitive Part (backward chaining)*
A	A	A	C
B	A-B	A-B	B-C
C	C	A-B-C	A-B-C
A-B-C	A-B-C		

independently (e.g. A represents practicing part A independently) or in combination with other segments (e.g. A–B represents practicing parts A and B together). As such, they are particularly effective when the segments of the movement are complex, even in isolation. In bouldering, for example, there may be one particular move in the problem that is so complex that it is worth isolating it for a number of attempts until a solution has been found. By contrast, Repetitive Part (or chaining) is more effective when the individual segments of the movement are relatively straightforward. Returning to our bouldering example, if the next move in the sequence that is being practiced is relatively straightforward, then there is no value to isolating it: simply add it on to the chain of moves.

Whole-Part-Whole

A learner may not see the immediate relevance of practicing part of the skill in isolation, particularly when engaging in segmentation. As such, Whole-Part-Whole is often recommended. Whole-Part-Whole involves initially demonstrating, or if possible having the learner attempt, the whole skill, to gain an understanding of how the elements fit together, and the overall purpose of the skill. Whole-Part-Whole is a particularly valuable tool when the goal is to increase a learner's appreciation for some aspect of a movement. Timms (2006) describes a nice example of this in kayaking, when a learner is not utilizing trunk rotation in the forward paddle. The paddler can be asked to grasp the paddle at the neck of the blade, and to paddle forward without bending the arms. The only way to succeed under this set of task constraints is to use an exaggerated trunk rotation. Thus, this exercise should raise the learner's understanding of the feel associated with trunk motion. This modified activity, which emphasizes part of the action (in this case, trunk rotation), can be interspersed throughout practice to encourage the learner to bring the feel of trunk rotation from the modified activity into the whole skill.

Simplification

Simplification is particularly useful for skills that are high in organization (where you want to maintain the whole skill as much as possible) and high in complexity (so you want to reduce the demands on the learner). The main aspects of simplification are that (1) the function of the movement must be maintained, (2) the coach should simplify as much as necessary, but no more, and (3) as the learner improves the scenario should progress towards the natural performance environment. Choosing a surfboard with a large volume for a novice is an example of simplification, as the board will react more slowly, and be more forgiving of slight errors in technique, while preserving the essence of the skill. Alternatively, the environment may be simplified, such as where the principles of lead climbing can be initially taught without actually climbing by using fence posts on a shallow gradient as running belays: the actions required by the learner are the same, but the additional demands that might distract the learner from the core elements of the skill have been removed.

Attentional cueing

The advantage of using attentional cueing is that the organization of parts is preserved. This makes attentional cueing particularly appropriate for situations, which are high in both complexity and organization. Thus, a skier may complete a run while focusing on weight distribution, ankle knee and hip flexion or arm positioning. Once that aspect of the movement improved, attention can shift to the next element. The key to attentional cueing is to prioritize the aspect of performance that is being cued. In terms of skiing, a useful guide is to teach from the snow up (LeMaster, 1999). Thus, attention could initially be focused on weight distribution, followed by lower body inputs, and then upper body inputs.

In summary, part practice is an essential tool for adventure sports coaches. Although adventure sports are often complex, and take place in demanding environments, this does not mean that part practice is always necessary. Rather, part practice allows the coach to manipulate the cognitive effort experienced by his or her learners to an appropriate level.

Scheduling of practice

In mainstream sports, such as tennis, the coach may divide up a session by time spent practicing different techniques; for example, spending 20 minutes on forehand, 20 minutes on backhand and 20 minutes on service. In many adventure sports, it is much more difficult to isolate individual techniques in this way due to the highly contextualized nature of the activity. As such, the adventure sports coach might focus on general principles of the activity rather than individual techniques. For example, a climbing coach may decide to construct a session based around three principles of climbing: balance, flexibility and core strength. The coach has a number of options in terms of how to schedule practice on these three principles. They could, for example, start with 30 minutes setting problems which focus on balance (maintaining stable positions), followed by 30 minutes setting problems based around flexibility (utilizing high steps), and finish with 30 minutes on problems that promote core strength (including overhangs and twist locks). This method is known as blocked practice, as the activities are organized into distinct blocks of one type of problem.

Blocked practice involves a lot of repetition, and as such the feedback from one attempt may still be fresh in the learner's mind. As a result, blocked practice does not encourage additional cognitive effort from the learner. In situations where you have a climber learning new movement patterns, a child, or someone with reduced intellectual capacity, then the problem that you set may already demand considerable cognitive effort. Attempts by the coach to introduce additional cognitive effort would only overwhelm the learner. For intermediate or advanced climbers, however, the same tasks may demand relatively little cognitive effort if practiced in a blocked schedule. In this case, the learners may be more appropriately challenged if the practice was scheduled in a larger number of shorter blocks (e.g. 10 minutes per theme), or using random practice (changing the theme of the problem on every trial). The total number of trials at each skill remains the same; it is only the order (or schedule) in which the problems are attempted that changes.

The frequent switching between movement patterns seen in random practice demands additional cognitive processing from the learner. This additional processing leads to poorer performance during practice, however, superior long-term learning is achieved. Sport scientists have termed this phenomenon the contextual interference (CI) effect. CI is best viewed as a continuum (Landin and Hebert, 1997), where the coach manipulates the cognitive effort demanded of his or her learners so as to provide an optimal mental challenge. Blocked practice introduces low CI (low cognitive effort), random practice results in high CI (high cognitive effort), while small blocks of practice result in moderate CI (moderate cognitive effort).

A useful guide for a coach when attempting to manage the amount of cognitive effort imposed on your learner is to use a Win-shift/Lose-stay strategy (Simon, Lee, and Cullen, 2008). If a task is executed successfully (a win), then the learner changes to an alternative task (shift). If the task is not executed successfully (a loss), then the learner stays to perform an additional attempt at that task (stay). This simple rule allows learners to manage the amount of cognitive effort they experience. A highly skilful climber may experience a lot of success, and therefore will frequently shift between types of problem, which maintains high cognitive effort. A beginner who experiences reduced success will follow a more blocked practice schedule, which reduces cognitive effort and prevents overload. This rule is particularly useful when working with large groups, and has the additional benefit of encouraging the learner to manage their own practice.

Distribution of practice

In our discussion of practice up to this point, we have concerned ourselves with what an adventure sports coach can do within a session to manipulate the cognitive effort experienced by his or her learners. Cognitive effort can also be influenced by the distribution of practice (Lee and Wishart, 2005). For example, a coach may have the option of organizing four separate one-hour sessions, or a single four-hour session. The former is an example of distributed practice, where a coach organizes frequent sessions of short duration. By contrast, massed practice utilizes relatively few sessions that are of long duration. As a general rule, the advice for coaches is to utilize more frequent, shorter sessions where possible (Magill, 2011).

Unfortunately, adventure sports coaches do not always have the luxury of being able to dictate the distribution of practice sessions. In addition, while practices that are short and spaced out may be very *effective* in promoting long term learning, they are also very *inefficient* in terms of total time use. For example, participants may require three one-hour sessions over three days (total learning time three hours) to reach a set level of sailing competence. Attempting to reach the same level of competence in a single session might take five hours, due to the relative ineffectiveness of massed practice. However, the participants will have been brought up to the desired level in a single day, rather than the three days required by distributing practice across sessions. When considering practice distribution, the adventure sports coach must balance the requirements for practice effectiveness and practice efficiency.

Where an adventure sports coach is required to deliver massed practice, the challenge becomes identifying those tools and techniques, which can be used to encourage cognitive effort. While learners may prefer to push through with few breaks, these breaks are an important source of challenge, as the learner must expend effort recalling previous instruction and feedback and getting back up to speed on an activity. The adventure sports coach should also prioritize those activities (such as observing other learners, or using question and answer), which we have already highlighted as increasing cognitive effort.

Mental practice

Mental practice refers to cognitively simulating an activity, such as imaging yourself skiing down a slope or recalling what it feels like to jump a mountain bike (MacIntyre *et al.*, 2013). Mental practice has been covered in detail elsewhere in this book, so this section will present the main information relating to the use of mental practice for skill development. Research has repeatedly indicated that mental practice is more effective than no practice, and that combinations of mental and physical practice may be as effective as physical practice alone (see Magill, 2011 for a review). This fact should be of great interest to adventure sports coaches, given that the environments in which adventure sports are performed, or the fatigue associated with these skills, often limits the number of practice trials that can be performed. Indeed, Singer (e.g. Lidor and Singer, 2005) has proposed that learners may benefit from including mental rehearsals prior to every physical performance of a skill. Mental practice is a technique that has been proved to supplement the effectiveness of physical practice sessions.

Feedback

Feedback is an essential part of the coaching process, and when used effectively, can be one of the most powerful tools available to the adventure sports coach. Over the years, in our capacity as coach educators, we have arrived at the belief that many foundation coaches give too much feedback, much of which is redundant. This is a problem because ill-conceived feedback can leave performers dependent on the coach's guidance. As we have repeatedly stressed, adventure sports take place in dynamic environments, which very often change throughout the day. For a coach to be effective in preparing performers to meet the demands of these environments, they must develop performers who have the ability to think and respond for themselves. The way in which a coach provides feedback is a crucial factor in developing such performers. The theme of promoting 'coach independence' runs through the following section as we explore the many facets of feedback.

What is feedback?

Intrinsic feedback is sensory information that is generated as a natural consequence of a movement. Intrinsic feedback can come from several different sources, which can be further classified as exteroceptive (outside the body) and proprioceptive (inside the body). By far the most dominant exteroceptive source of information available to the learner is vision.

Proprioceptive feedback on the other hand is information that comes from within our body and gives us information about our body position. Proprioceptive (sometimes called kinaesthetic) information comes from various sources within the body, for example, the vestibular apparatus with the ear act as a kind of spirit level and provides us with information about posture and balance, while muscle spindles and Golgi tendon organs provide us with information about the length and position of muscles. It is essential that we coach learners to become aware of the proprioceptive aspects of the movement due to the fact that many adventure sports are characterized by maintaining and making fine adjustments to posture and balance (e.g. surfing, climbing, windsurfing, mountain biking, snow sports). The message here is that adventure sports coaches should take every opportunity to encourage learners to focus on proprioceptive and kinaesthetic sources of feedback. We can do this in several ways including asking learners to describe how the movement felt. For learners who have poor awareness of the feel of their movement, we can heighten their other senses by blindfolding them or having them perform with their eyes closed.

Augmented feedback refers to information from sources that are external to the learner and that supplement (or augment) intrinsic feedback. Augmented feedback can be used to motivate the learner, or to accelerate skill acquisition. When used to promote learning, it is vital that augmented feedback is used to educate the learner to interpret his or her own sources of intrinsic feedback. In adventure sports, there are several ways that a learner can receive augmented feedback, including verbally from the coach, by body language, by video analysis or by scores or times (mainly when competing). In the context of this chapter the primary source of augmented feedback that we are concerned with is what you as the coach verbally feedback to the learner.

When does a performer need augmented feedback?

Generally speaking when a learner wants feedback they will do one of three things; they will either look at you blankly, ask for it or both. For many years I have used the guiding principle that I want my learners to be self-determining, autonomous and cognitively engaged with the task. If then, I bombard them after every trial with excessive augmented feedback, I reduce this autonomy and decrease their cognitive engagement. A coach should only provide augmented feedback under two conditions: (1) when a learner cannot interpret their intrinsic feedback, and (2) when, due to the complexity of the task, the learner cannot attend to the critical intrinsic feedback. Therefore, the primary role of the coach is to assess whether one or both of these situations is present. When the learner has correctly interpreted their intrinsic feedback, then the coach should step back and continue to observe. If the coach determines that the learner requires augmented feedback, then the next question is at what point of the activity this feedback should be provided.

Concurrent, terminal and delayed feedback

The adventure sports coach must decide whether to provide augmented feedback during the activity (concurrent feedback), immediately after the activity (terminal feedback) or following some time delay (delayed feedback). To a certain extent, adventure sports will dictate when we can give feedback. For example, the surf coach positioned on the beach must wait until the surfer returns to the beach to give them feedback. Therefore, generally speaking the beach-based surf coach is restricted to giving delayed feedback. However in many situations, the adventure sports coach will have a range of options available to them. If the coach's goal is simply to get a client safely up a multi-pitch route in climbing, then concurrent feedback is an appropriate tool. In this case the coach might identify specific holds for the client to use and then feedback on the quality of each individual movement. This coach-centred approach will minimize the learners' cognitive effort and is unlikely to lead to long-term learning. By contrast, terminal feedback, where the coach waits until the end of the climb to give feedback encourages greater cognitive effort from the learner, as they are responsible for monitoring their performance during the trial. Performance will be poorer when using terminal feedback, as the learner makes more mistakes and takes longer to figure out what movements to make. However, due to the greater cognitive effort resulting from terminal feedback, long-term learning will be enhanced. Delayed feedback offers the opportunity for even higher levels of cognitive effort, as the learner also has the opportunity to reflect on their performance after a trial. However, the learner may not take this opportunity without prompting. The coach may need to consider whether general or specific questions would be most appropriate to guide the individual learner's thinking.

How much augmented feedback should be given?

The matter of feedback frequency is a major consideration for the adventure sports coach. When given too frequently, feedback can lead to the learners becoming dependent on the coach, and incapable of processing their own intrinsic feedback. When too little feedback is provided, learners may feel neglected, and bad habits may start to form. To maintain learners' confidence, it is good practice to ensure that learners understand how the coach is giving feedback, and why they are giving it in this way. The simplest method to discourage coach dependence is to provide feedback less regularly as skill level improves. For example, a mountain bike coach may provide abundant feedback early on in the day, and then gradually reduce the amount given as the day progresses. Coaches of many adventure sports operate in this way, with the guiding principle that by the end of the day the learner should be able to provide their own feedback. Dependency can also be avoided by providing feedback as a summary after a series of trials, rather than after each individual trial. This is particularly evident in surf sports where a surfer may be asked to ride a certain number of waves before returning to the beach. As with faded feedback, the cognitive effort can be increased by gradually including more trials in the summary (in this case, more waves) as skill level progresses.

A final method of managing feedback frequency is to use a performance bandwidth (see Figure 6.2). When using a 'bandwidth' approach, the frequency of feedback is dictated by a set of criteria predetermined by the coach. These criteria may be quantitative (e.g. distance, time, number of strokes) or qualitative (e.g. at this stage, the movement should look like). If a practice trial of the skill falls within this acceptable boundary of performance then the coach gives no feedback. If, on the other hand, the attempt falls outside of the bandwidth then the coach will give precise information to guide the learner's performance into the acceptable boundary of performance. For bandwidth feedback to work effectively the learner must be made aware that if they receive no feedback after practice that this indicates that the performance was essentially correct (Schmidt and Lee, 2014). A really neat application of bandwidth feedback can be seen when teaching gear placement in lead climbing. The coach might ask the climber to place several pieces of gear on a route while still on a top rope, and then grade each placement on a 10-point scale. The bandwidth might start at 7/10 (i.e. augmented feedback would only be given on placements scoring 6 or less). As with faded and summary feedback, as the learner improves the coach could adjust the performance bandwidth (e.g. to 9/10) to elicit further refinement of gear placement.

FIGURE 6.2 In bandwidth feedback, learners only receive feedback when their performance falls outside a predetermined level

Note: In this example, the surfers are attempting to hold a steady kneeling position. As such, the two surfers in the foreground will not receive feedback on this attempt as their performance is within that bandwidth.

How much detail should your feedback contain?

Knowledge of Results (KR) provides the learner with information about the outcome of a movement. For example, 'you stood up for 15 seconds on that wave', or 'you completed that section in 3 minutes 12 seconds'. Much KR is information that the learners could, or should, be able to generate themselves, and we must be careful that we do not give redundant KR. For example, there is little point in telling a skier that they fell over twice on their last run. Where KR is particularly valuable is in providing targets for advanced learners as they push the boundaries of their performance.

In contrast to KR, Knowledge of Performance (KP) focuses on the process of the movement. KP may be descriptive or prescriptive. Descriptive KP describes the movement that has been performed. Prescriptive feedback explains what needs to be done in future trials to improve the action. For example, a canoe coach might tell a paddler that their paddle shaft was at a 60 degree angle through the power phase of the stroke. In this instance, a complete beginner may have no idea whether this is correct or not, and the feedback would be of limited value. Prescriptive KP, such as 'next time, keep your paddle vertical throughout the stroke' is more useful for the beginner. By contrast, an improving performer who knows that the paddle shaft should be as vertical as possible through the power phase would be able to utilize the descriptive feedback to improve. In addition, the descriptive feedback has the advantage of encouraging the improving performer to think more analytically about their movements. As a general rule, as the skill level develops, KP feedback should shift from being prescriptive to descriptive.

Summary

This chapter has outlined a range of tools and techniques relating to instruction, practice and feedback, which the adventure sports coach can apply to optimize the learning experience. It should be apparent that there is no one 'correct' set of tools which can be applied to any coaching problem. Rather, optimal learning results from optimal cognitive effort. Each activity, from throwing a rescue bag to jibing in windsurfing, demands a certain amount of cognitive effort from the learner. The coach may reduce the cognitive effort required of his or her learners, for example, through the application of blocked practice or high feedback frequencies. Alternatively, the context may demand that the adventure sports coach increases the cognitive effort required of his or her learners, such as through the use of whole skill practice, or learner demonstrations. To determine the most appropriate tools to use, we recommend our framework outlined in Chapter 5: asking who am I coaching, what am I coaching, where am I coaching and why am I coaching will provide the raw data that you need to establish whether your goal is to increase or decrease cognitive effort, and how this might best be achieved. Applying the framework will highlight the range of tools and techniques that should prove effective. The key to learning is to manage cognitive effort, and there are multiple tools available to you to do this. The most important factor is that you have a sound rationale behind your choice of coaching tools and techniques.

References

Bandura, A. (1986). *Social Foundations of Thought and Action: A Social Cognitive Theory*. Englewood Cliffs, NJ: Prentice Hall.

Carroll, W. R. and Bandura, A. (1990). Representational guidance of action production in observational learning: a causal analysis. *Journal of Motor Behavior*, 22, 85–97.

Christina, R. W. and Corcos, D. M. (1988). *Coaches Guide to Teaching Sport Skills*. Champaign, IL: Human Kinetics.

Guadagnoli, M. A. (2009). *Practice to Learn/Play to Win* (2nd ed.). Penryn: Ecademy Press.

Landin, D. and Hebert, E. (1997). A comparison of three practice schedules along the contextual interference continuum. *Research Quarterly for Exercise and Sport*, 68, 357–361.

Lavallee, D., Kremer, J., Moran, A. and Williams, M. (2004). *Sport Psychology: Contemporary Themes*. Basingstoke: Palgrave Macmillan

Lee, T. D. and Schmidt, R. A. (2014). PaR (Plan-act-Review) golf: Motor learning research and improving golf skills. *International Journal of Golf Science*, 3, 2–25.

Le Master, R. (1999). *The Skier's Edge*. Champaign, IL: Human Kinetics.

Lee, T. D. and Wishart, L. R. (2005). Motor learning conundrums (and possible solutions). *Quest*, 57, 67–78.

Lidor, R. and Singer, R. N. (2005). Learning Strategies in Motor Skill Acquisition: From the Laboratory to the Gym. In: D. Hackfort, J. L. Duda and R. Lidor (eds), *Handbook of Research in Applied Sport and Exercise Psychology: International Perspectives*. Morgantown, West Virginia: Fitness Information Technology, 109–126.

MacIntyre, T., Moran, A., Collet, C., Guillot, A., Campbell, M., Matthews, J., Mahony, C. and Lowher, J. (2013). The BASES expert statement on the use of mental imagery in sport, exercise and rehabilitation contexts. *The Sport and Exercise Scientist*, 38, 10–11.

Magill, R. A. (2011). *Motor Learning and Control: Concepts and Applications* (9th ed.). Boston, MA: McGraw-Hill.

McMorris, T. and Hale, T. (2006). *Coaching Science: Theory into Practice*. Chichester: John Wiley and Sons.

Naylor, J. C. and Briggs, G. E. (1963). Effects of task complexity and task organization on the relative efficiency of part and whole training methods. *Journal of Experimental Psychology*, 65, 217–224.

Schmidt, R. A. and Lee, T. D. (2014). *Motor Learning and Performance* (5th ed.). Champaign, IL: Human Kinetics.

Simon, D. A., Lee, T. D. and Cullen, J. D. (2008). Win-shift, Lose-stay: contingent switching and contextual interference in motor learning. *Perceptual and Motor Skills*, 107, 407–418.

Timms, B. (2006). Coaching improvers. In: F. Ferrero (ed.), *British Canoe Union Coaching Handbook* Caernarfon: Pesda Press, 153–168.

Wulf, G. (2013). Attentional focus and motor learning: a review of 15 years. *International Review of Sport and Exercise Psychology*, 1–28.

7

COACHING THE ADVANCED PERFORMER

Phil Kearney and Ed Christian

> If people knew how hard I had to work to gain my mastery, it would not seem so wonderful at all.
>
> *(Michelangelo)*

Introduction

Up to this point, the chapters in this section have discussed learning generically, identifying the changes in coaching techniques that may be useful when working with learners of varying skill levels. The natural progression in adventure sports is to seek out increasingly advanced situations. Indeed, one of the characteristics that distinguishes adventure sports from their mainstream counterparts, and one of their strongest attractions, is the relative accessibility of the highest performance contexts: while there is a limit to how many people can represent England in football in any given year, a Grade V river sets no such restriction. There is a wealth of information available for the developing coach who wishes to learn more about introducing people to adventure sports, but relatively little guidance on their later development. This chapter will address this gap in the literature by focusing more specifically upon the unique challenges involved when working with an advanced performer who is seeking out these high-performance contexts.

While we can characterize an advanced performer based on their achievements in relation to the grading of rivers, crags or pistes, this chapter will also characterize the advanced performer by the behaviours that they exhibit during their development which allow them to successfully negotiate a Grade V river, or a challenging off-piste route. A recreational performer is one who is interested in doing the activity, but not interested in engaging in the extensive, carefully planned and effortful practice of specific elements that is vital to overcoming current performance limitations. An example might be a skier, who returns to the slopes year on year and thoroughly enjoys the activity, but whose skill level has not progressed. By contrast, advanced performers are those who identify and practice the specific elements of their activity that are currently limiting their development, such as a climber who knows he is weak on overhangs, and therefore devises strategies to improve on overhangs, and seeks out and practices overhangs. Consider the following examples of three advanced performers and the challenges they are facing, which are representative of the three topics we shall cover in this chapter:

- Adam is a talented climber who has aspirations of completing extremely difficult rock climbs. His skill development, although rapid for the first five years, has now plateaued. Adam is looking for help to break through this plateau and continue his progression.
- Eve is an experienced kayaker who is about to attempt Grade V rapids for the first time. Her coach, Lucy, believes that Eve has the technical and tactical competence necessary, but is unsure about how well she will execute her skills under pressure. How can Lucy best prepare Eve for performance under pressure?
- Bob has been skiing for seven seasons. When he performs carving turns, he fails to maintain the angle of the edge throughout the turn. This is a problem because it allows his skis to slip, slowing him down and wasting energy. Bob has had a number of lessons attempting to correct his technique, but this has not been effective. What does Bob need to do to change his well-learnt technique?

The first part of this chapter will attempt to help Adam. We will identify the lessons that have been learned from the study of experts at practice, and will consider how these lessons may be applied to enhance the quality of practice of advanced performers. Most importantly, we will also consider at what point in an athlete's development such advanced practice techniques should be introduced. The second part of this chapter will discuss Eve's concern: preparing for performance under pressure. Within adventure sports, there are many factors that can result in a pressurized performance situation, such as a siphon on a rapid, or a left-hand turn on a piste bordered by a 700-metre drop. This chapter will include an explanation of why performance may fail under pressure, as well as what the instructor can do during practice to prepare his/her charges for high-pressure situations. The final section of this chapter will discuss the recommendations contained within the skill acquisition literature for addressing ingrained bad habits such as that which Bob is struggling to overcome. Although an instructor may spend much time teaching motor skills to novices, adventure sports also see many individuals arriving for instruction with well-formed movement habits, as a result of previous sporting experience or practice without sufficient guidance. At the end of this chapter you will have a set of practical guidelines for working with individuals with bad habits.

Problem one: How to practice like an expert

There is a debate about whether expertise results from nature or nurture (Ericsson, 2013; Tucker and Collins, 2012). While we do not yet have a definitive answer to this question, through a careful analysis of experts at practice, researchers and coaches have learned many valuable lessons that can be used to accelerate the development of an aspiring performer. These lessons include how to prepare for practice, how to behave during practice and how to review after practice.

Watching performers at the pinnacle of their sport, it is hard to avoid drawing the conclusion that these individuals are somehow different from everyone else: the lucky beneficiaries of a genetic lottery that has gifted them the raw materials to achieve performances that most people could only dream of. However there are researchers, most notably Anders Ericsson, who contend that there is as yet insufficient evidence to credit genetic inheritance with a significant role in the setting of limits to human performance. Beginning with a seminal paper published in 1993, Ericsson *et al.* argued that researchers should instead focus on the amount, and more importantly the quality, of practice undertaken by experts during their formative years. A definitive answer on the origin of expertise is not currently available, and we suggest that the answer, whatever it may be, will be of more use in chalet bar debates than in the practice of the majority of coaches. However, the lessons that have been learned from the detailed study of the practice behaviours of experts has undoubtedly been of profound importance to instructors across a wide range of disciplines, including sport, medicine and music.

Experts are better are practicing

Experts practice differently. Not just in the quality of their performances in practice, but also in the organization of their practice, the manner in which they prepare and reflect, and their basic behaviour within the practice setting. An adventure sports coach working with a promising athlete can analyze their developing performers' practice habits, and attempt to increase the quality of each hour of practice. An early example of how this can be achieved was provided by an analysis of figure skaters by Deakin and Cobley (2003). Participants were classified as international skaters, national level skaters or recreational skaters, and the researchers measured numerous variables including the time spent in practice, in recovering from activities and in additional rest after they had recovered from activities. The time spent in practice was also broken down to measure the relative time spent rehearsing moves that had already been mastered compared with the time spent practicing those moves that the performer had yet to master. The international skaters were the most efficient in their use of practice time, with a minimum of time wasted in non-essential rest. When the researchers looked at what skills the skaters spent their practice time on, again the international skaters were shown to be the most efficient: while national and recreational skaters spent the most time on skills that they had already mastered (and which therefore needed relatively little practice), the international skaters spent relatively more time practicing the moves that they had yet to master. While an analysis of what practice time is spent on should be of interest to coaches working with all advanced performers, it is particularly worthwhile for the coach who is working with a performer who initially developed quickly, but whose development has more recently slowed. Such a performer may be working enthusiastically, but not focusing his or her energies appropriately. As we shall see, the careful focusing of practice is a major distinguishing characteristic of expert learners.

Voices from the field

The description of the different practice behaviours of intermediate and advanced figure skaters applies very well to skiers. Intermediate skiers often reach a plateau in their performance where, after progressing relatively quickly, they settle into repeating what they already know and see their performance stall. Emotionally, continuing to push beyond 'comfortable' and take on 'challenging', with the risks of failure involved, takes real commitment and desire to improve. Expert learners are not afraid of making mistakes and look to make improvements from making mistakes.

John Hendry – British Association of Snowsports Instructors Level 4 International Ski Teaching Diploma – Parallel Lines Ski and Snowboard School

Anders Ericsson coined the term 'deliberate practice' to refer to practice that was effortful, and focused on making specific improvements. Deliberate practice is present when the learner has determined *what* he/she needs to improve, and, just as importantly, *how* he/she will go about improving it. As such, deliberate practice may apply to technical, tactical, physiological or psychological factors underpinning performance. In the adventure sports context, it is easy for a learner to go through the motions – repeat run after run on a piste or section of a river without working on any one aspect of performance in particular. Contrast this with the expert learner, who chooses one focus for his/her practice, perhaps on a single section of the piste or river, and time and again over the course of the session completes variations of the problem until satisfied with the improvements made. For the novice or recreational athlete, such focused repetition of such a small part of the sport may quickly lose its enjoyment. For the advanced performer, it is precisely this intense practice that is required for further development (see Figure 7.1).

Self-regulation

Experts distinguish themselves by more than their behaviour within a practice session; in preparation for and in review of sessions, experts also demonstrate a

FIGURE 7.1 A strong bottom turn is the foundation of surfing technique

Note: If the bottom turn in surf kayaking is an area in which you are weak, then your practice should identify the reason for your struggles, and design activities to address these specific limitations.

range of behaviours that allow them to gain the most return from the time they have invested. While deliberate practice refers to the specific behaviours of an expert learner *within* a practice session, the term self-regulation is used to describe the broader set of learning behaviours, which includes activities before and after a session (for an excellent introduction to self-regulation in a range of contexts see Zimmerman, 1998). For example, experts set specific goals for each session: not just outcome goals (what I want to achieve), but also process goals (how I am going to achieve it). Thus, a climber who identifies that her energy efficiency in traditional lead climbing could be improved might work on her ability to exploit rest positions to achieve this increased efficiency. Experts identify appropriate environments for practice. For a skier, this may mean practicing on a particular grade piste at a particular time of day. Experts frequently engage in some form of mental rehearsal, both in terms of running through the planned activities of the session in advance, and also reviewing the session after it has finished. Additional examples of expert practice behaviours are provided in Table 7.1, and have been consistently demonstrated in activities as varied as academic study, sport and music (Zimmerman, 1998). Thus, the adventure sports coach who is interested in auditing the practice quality of his or her learners has a range of variables to evaluate, before, during and after practice sessions.

Although much of our understanding of self-regulation has come about from observations of experts at practice, this is not to suggest that all advanced learners

TABLE 7.1 The skills and behaviours of experts that lead to accelerated learning

Pre-practice	*During practice*	*Post practice*
Plan what to practice If your edge control is holding you back from basic playboating skills, then identify and practice activities that will promote good edge control	*Use previews as necessary* When learning to mountain bike down steep trails, get off your bike and take the time to plan your route and your movements	*Record activities* When orienteering, use a diary to keep track of your performances across events. A review of this diary should help you identify your strengths, weaknesses and progress
Plan where to practice When surfing, think about what beach, and at what time, offers you the best conditions to work on your chosen focus	*Use self-talk to maintain focus on the aim of the session* Use key words 'posture' and 'core' to maintain focus on effective paddling in an open water crossing in sea kayaking	*Use imagery to reinforce improvements* Today you landed your first wind surfing frontside 360; you'll review it plenty down the pub, but find some quiet time to replay the sight and feel of it in your mind too
Plan when to practice Look at your calendar before scheduling a day kitesurfing. Are you going to be rested enough to take full advantage?	*Keep track of performance* Use a 0–10 scale to rate your performances, either of the whole skill or of the specific aspect that you are working on. Are you improving or do you need to review how you are practicing?	*Revise goals* After a session on the climbing wall, reflect on how much progress you have made towards your goal. Is an additional session required, or is it time to progress?
Review the session in advance to arrive physically, mentally and emotionally ready to practice On the way to white water kayaking, think about the various sections you will face and how you will plan on tackling each one	*Commit full mental and physical effort to the practice* The time for chat is back at the chalet. When you are on the snow, your time should be spent snowboarding, recovering and reflecting	*Seek advice from coach or another performer* You are not required to come up with all the answers yourself. When you are struggling with long radius high speed turns in skiing, find a coach or expert skier to get some advice

quickly develop the component skills involved in deliberate practice and self-regulation. Some intervention on the part of the coach or senior athletes may be necessary. Indeed, in a series of interviews with highly successful performers in tennis, music, sculpture and other domains, Bloom (1985) identified that performers gradually 'learned how to learn', informed, directly and indirectly, by their teachers and by their peers. Introducing the advanced performer to the concepts of deliberate practice and self-regulation in a structured manner is likely a core ingredient in the practices of successful coaches.

When should you introduce a learner to self-regulation?

At this point, you may be thinking that this is pretty obvious and you can see how to encourage self-regulation (including deliberate practice), and will do so with your learners immediately. Stop! There is one extremely important question yet to consider: are your learners ready for self-regulation? Ericsson originally argued that as deliberate practice was the key to success, it would be sensible to start as early as possible. The early introduction of deliberate practice would allow for the large number of practice hours necessary to reach expertise to be accumulated at a younger age. In addition, individuals who accumulated relatively more deliberate practice at a younger age would be likely to perform at a high level compared with their peers. This early high performance could lead to further advantages, such as selection for additional coaching at representative level; a phenomenon known as the Matthew effect (Merton, 1968). Concerns have been raised, however, about the potential negative impacts of adopting this intensive coaching too early in a performer's development. Côté and colleagues have forcibly argued that the application of deliberate practice and self-regulatory strategies to young participants at too early an age is likely to result in a lack of enjoyment, demotivation and dropout (for a review of the evidence see Côté and Fraser- Thomas, 2008). The question, therefore, is at what point in their development should learners be introduced to the concept of deliberate practice?

Deciding when to introduce deliberate practice requires a brief consideration of the broader learning process. Drawing upon the work of Bloom (1985), and the writings of Whitehead (1922), Côté has proposed that early learning should consist of deliberate play across a range of differing activities. Where deliberate practice is highly organized, focused on improving particular aspects of performance, and may not be enjoyable in itself, deliberate play is typically learner driven, emphasizes performing the whole activity and is focused on the enjoyment of the individuals involved. In mainstream sports, deliberate play is seen in children's impromptu games, such as backyard football, which often involve special rules to allow all children to participate regardless of age or skill level. Such deliberate play may be found in adventure sports such as climbing where children (typically behind their parents' backs) climb up trees, rocky outcrops or whatever the environment allows. This initial period emphasizing deliberate play, which Whitehead (1922) termed the Romance phase, seeks to cultivate interest through enjoyment. For many individuals this phase may be sufficient: a basic mastery and competence of the activity may be all that they desire. Alternatively, the learner may not be willing to invest the intense effort required for further development. For others, the Romance phase will not satisfy them, but will awaken a desire for further development. Whitehead (1922) described this further development as the Precision phase, and our above discussion of deliberate practice is a sound description of the nature and activities of the precision phase. For Whitehead the freedom of the Romance phase and discipline of the Precision phase, or in Côté's contemporary terminology deliberate play and deliberate practice, do not represent distinct stages. Instead the role of the educator, and in our case that of the adventure sports coach is as Whitehead, (1922, p. 35) remarked, "to discover in practice that exact balance between freedom and discipline [i.e. deliberate play and deliberate practice] which will give the greatest rate of progress". The learner determines the point of transition between the Romance and Precision phase, albeit guided by the coach. If the coach perceives that the learner has a desire to further develop his/her skills, then some deliberate practice-type activities may be introduced (see Table 7.1 above). If the athlete responds positively to these activities, then the amount of deliberate practice may progressively increase, with deliberate play decreasing. Deliberate practice may be introduced through the coach delivering workshops, providing appropriate reading or encouraging the developing athlete to work with more advanced performers who are already engaging in the target deliberate practice activities. Introducing deliberate practice and self-regulation therefore proceeds by trial and error, gradually offering the athlete the opportunity to engage in more structured and strategic practice, but always aware of the need to balance practice and play.

A learner's beliefs also shape the learning process

At the start of this section we explained how the question of whether natural ability or practice plays the more important role in shaping expert performance has resulted in a set of guidelines, which coaches can use to enhance the learning process. This debate over nature and nurture has an additional complication. It appears that what you believe is responsible for performance has a strong influence on your perseverance on tasks, your selection of challenges and, ultimately, your learning. Carole Dweck suggested that individuals hold either an entity or an incremental theory, more popularly known as fixed and growth mindsets (see Dweck, 2006 or http://mindsetonline.com/index.html). Individuals with a fixed mindset believe that ability (in the form of motor performance, intelligence, musical aptitude, etc.) is fixed and does not change much with practice. If a task requires high effort levels they see this as an indicator of low ability, and they believe initial performance is strongly related to final potential. By contrast, an individual with a growth mindset considers ability as something that can be developed over time, provided the activity is worked on appropriately. Effort is seen as essential for development. To illustrate her theory, Dweck runs an ingeniously simple experiment. Participants receive a test. According to their score on this test, participants are divided into two groups with equal average scores. Participants in one group are praised for their effort to promote a growth mindset (e.g. 'well done, you must have worked very hard to prepare for this test'). Participants in the other group are praised for their ability, to promote a fixed mindset (e.g. 'Well done. You must be very intelligent to have succeeded on this test'). At this point, participants are offered a choice of two problem sets to work on: one easier than the test; one more difficult. Participants who were praised for their effort tend to choose the more difficult version, seeing it as an opportunity to challenge themselves, and thereby develop. Participants who were praised for their ability tend to choose the easier version, fearing that if they struggle on the difficult test it will reveal that their results on the first test were mistaken, and that they are not talented after all. The experiment ends with both groups receiving an additional test, which is the same level of difficulty as the first test. Participants praised for their effort typically improve their score. Participants praised for their ability typically perform worse. It appears that the fear of performing poorly, and thereby revealing a lack of ability, may impair performance on subsequent tests.

The negative impact of a fixed mindset has been demonstrated in a range of domains and populations. The fixed mindset is an unfortunate and unforeseen consequence of the emphasis placed upon concepts such as innate talent, or natural sporting ability. Belief in these concepts stunts development. The lesson for coaches is to watch what you say! Praise effort. Link improvements in performance with perseverance and hard work. For example, a ski coach may say 'Well done, you have worked really hard on your turns and you are now maintaining appropriate pressure on both edges throughout the carve' instead of 'Well done, you have picked that up really quickly'. Encourage challenges as an opportunity to learn. Educate learners on the impact of mindsets, and have them put it to the test.

Summary of problem one: How to practice like an expert

The precise origin of highly skilled performance remains a mystery. There is no doubt that environmental factors such as practice, access to facilities and luck play a major role. It is also likely that genetic inheritance also plays a part, although the precise contribution of genetics, whether this contribution is independent of the environment or through interaction with the environment, has yet to be conclusively demonstrated. While the debate about the origin of high skill may provide an interesting conversation topic for late evenings, of far more practical use to the majority of coaches are the lessons that have been learned from studying how experts practice. We hope that we have shown how the ways in which experts practice, termed deliberate practice, may be distilled and adapted for advanced learners, accelerating learning and facilitating long-term retention of skills. Crucially, deliberate practice should not be imposed before the learner seeks out some method of further improvement. Finally, coaches should not neglect to address learners' beliefs regarding skill development, and should promote a growth mindset through praise for effort and promoting challenges as an opportunity to learn.

Performance under pressure

The final test of a long-practiced skill is how well it stands up under pressure. For a sportsperson, this pressure is often within the cauldron of competition, observed by thousands, if not millions of spectators. In adventure sports, greater pressure may arise from the absence of observers; a frequent occurrence in sports such as climbing, off-piste skiing and white water rafting. Adventure sports are graded by their consequences. Thus, a Grade V river may pose little greater technical or tactical problems than a Grade IV, but contain far greater consequences for failure. In American sporting parlance, someone who performs to his or her potential in a demanding situation, which has personal importance, has produced a clutch performance. By contrast, someone who fails to reach his/her expected level of performance under such situations is said to have choked. In an adventure sports context, consider an off-piste skier who finds herself high on the mountain late in the day. If there were no consequences, she could expect to make the descent error free and within the available time 99 times out of 100. However, on this occasion there are consequences: one mistake, or a slower than normal descent, and she risks great personal danger. If our skier performs to her potential, and successfully completes a speedy and error-free descent, then she will have produced a clutch performance. If she fails to deliver the performance that under normal circumstances she is capable of, then she will have choked. This section will attempt to explain why choking under pressure occurs, and how you as a coach can prepare an advanced learner to deliver a performance when it matters most.

The role of attention in performance failure under pressure

In an attempt to explain the specific effects of anxiety on movement and decision-making, many researchers have focused on the changes that occur in attention. Attention is often viewed as a resource, required by all cognitive processes such as perception, decision-making and efferent organization. The total available amount of attention is limited. As a result, if you are completing a number of tasks at the same time, cognitive processes must compete for attention. If the demand for attention exceeds supply, then performance on at least one of the tasks must suffer. EC recently had an example of this when driving with a colleague. We were having a conversation when I noticed a number of bicycles ahead of me heading in both directions, an oncoming car overtaking one of the bicycles, and a motorbike gaining quickly on me from behind. My colleague kept talking while I juggled the suddenly increased perceptual and motor demands of managing my speed and steering a safe path. Once through, I apologized to my colleague as I had lost track of the conversation when the demands of driving had increased. I had not had sufficient attention to concentrate on both the conversation and the driving.

Distraction theories

The first group of theories, which attempt to explain performance failure under pressure, are called Distraction theories. Distraction theories propose that in pressure situations attention may be drawn away from task relevant details to irrelevant information, such as worrying about long-term consequences. Thus the skier mentioned at the beginning of the section, attempting to make a quick descent as darkness falls, may worry about falling, breaking a leg and being exposed on the mountain overnight. These are all rational fears, but they are not immediately relevant during the descent. Furthermore, worrying about such consequences requires attention, and if attention is spent on worry, then it cannot be spent elsewhere. A climber whose attention is consumed by worry about falling may miss obvious holds or gear placements or a kayaker worried about getting stuck in a nasty stopper on a challenging white water run may miss an important eddy. Distraction theories explain skill failure under pressure as resulting from the attention necessary for performing the primary task being drawn away by irrelevant distractions.

An important advance in thinking about skill failure under pressure came from Eysenck and Calvo's (1992) Processing Efficiency Theory (PET), which was later updated as Attentional Control Theory (ACT; Eysenck *et al.*, 2007). ACT distinguishes between the effectiveness and the efficiency of cognitive processing. Effectiveness relates to the outcome of an action: did the climber get to the top? Efficiency relates to the mental energy expended to achieve an outcome. The core prediction of ACT is that anxiety will impact efficiency more than effectiveness because while worry uses attention, worry also motivates more effort. As a result, performance outcome can be maintained at low to moderate levels of pressure at the cost of decreased efficiency. However, at a sufficiently high level of pressure, performance cannot be maintained as too much attention is being drawn away by irrelevant information such as worry. Alternatively, skill failure can occur under moderate levels of pressure, which are sustained for a long period. While an anxious climber may perform as well as a non-anxious climber on the first section of a climb, the greater mental effort required to achieve the same level of performance will take its toll, and will place the anxious climber at greater risk of making a mistake on later sections of the climb.

Arne Nieuwenhuys and colleagues provided a nice illustration of ACT with an adventure sports task from Vrije Universiteit, Amsterdam (Nieuwenhuys *et al.*, 2008). Novice climbers were asked to follow identical routes located low down, and high up on a climbing wall. Measures of anxiety revealed that performers were significantly more anxious on the higher route. Measuring the time to complete the route assessed performance effectiveness. The novice climbers took 50 per cent longer to complete the climb when anxious. While some of this additional time was due to more time spent executing movements (e.g. testing hand hold was sufficient), the majority of the extra time was spent holding still, suggesting a decrease in performance efficiency as novices struggled to identify a suitable route. A more direct measure of processing efficiency was obtained by analysing data from an eye tracker, which gave information about where the participants looked, and for how long. The results from the eye tracker indicated that, when more anxious, the novices spent more time looking at the handholds and footholds, and looked at their options more frequently. Thus, when anxiety increased, participants took longer to decide upon their route, presumably because the attention required for route planning was being drawn to other, irrelevant thoughts.

Practical applications of distraction theories

The predictions of ACT regarding effectiveness and efficiency have been supported in numerous research studies. At low levels of anxiety, performance effectiveness is maintained while efficiency decreases. At higher levels of anxiety, both effectiveness and efficiency suffer. Thus it appears that failure under pressure may be due to attention being drawn away from the relevant features of the task, and consumed by worry or focusing on irrelevant features. For the practitioner preparing individuals for pressurized environments, ACT theory has a number of important recommendations. First, if anxiety can be minimized, then the demands on attention from irrelevant sources such as worry will be reduced. Individuals should therefore be trained in methods to reduce or reinterpret feelings associated with anxiety through techniques to interrupt negative thoughts, normalize breathing patterns and/or reduce muscle tension (these techniques will be covered in more detail in Chapter 11). In addition, techniques such as self-talk may be used to maintain focus on task relevant information. These techniques, initially taught and mastered in low-anxiety situations, may then be progressively tested under gradually more stressful situations, sometimes referred to as stress inoculation. For example, a kayaker about to roll a kayak in white water for the first time would be far more confident had they experienced rolling under a variety of controlled but challenging conditions, and not simply within a single session in a warm swimming pool (see Coleman, 2006, for an excellent discussion of this point). While a suitable range of environments can prove difficult to manipulate, pressure could be induced in other ways such as completing a fatiguing exercise protocol prior to performing a roll, or by the instructor unexpectedly pushing or pulling on the learner's kayak at various stages of the roll to simulate the effect of a wave.

Self-focus theories

While Distraction theories such as ACT have received considerable support in the literature, there exists an alternative explanation for performance failure under pressure. Professor Richard Masters, of the University of Hong Kong, proposed that skill failure results not from too little attention being paid to the execution of a skilled movement, but from too much. The Theory of Reinvestment proposed by Masters is an example of a Self-focus theory, reinvestment meaning returning to conscious control. At the very early stages of learning, movements are under conscious control. The conscious control system is limited to controlling only a few elements, hence movements, which are under conscious control, are slow, jerky and executed one step at a time. As learning progresses, elements of the movement are gradually automated until eventually highly learned skills are performed entirely outside of conscious control. Many everyday skills, such as changing gear while driving, or tying shoelaces, are executed similarly without conscious control, at least by those who have acquired the skills through sufficient practice. By contrast, watch the great concentration required by a young child to consciously control his/her disobedient laces. Masters' insight was that the movements of performers who fail under pressure resemble those of novice learners: slow, jerky and demanding attention. Masters suggested that, in pressurized situations, performers have two choices: (1) to trust in the execution of an automatic skill, or (2) to take conscious control of their actions in an attempt to ensure successful execution of the skill in question. However intuitively sensible adopting conscious control may appear, for a well-practiced individual adopting conscious control is precisely the wrong strategy to adopt. The conscious control system is not capable of adequately controlling all of the variables required to ensure successful execution of a complex motor skill. This is the reason why, over the course of practice, skill execution becomes automatic. By adopting conscious control, the performer returns to the skill level of a much more novice performer, and skill failure results.

Practical applications of self-focus theories

Self-focus theories have two important implications for the adventure sports coach. The first relates to preventing skill failure in the performance context itself. Attention should be drawn away from how to perform movements. Attending to the route that the performer wishes to take (what to do), rather than the mechanics of the action (how to do it), should result in superior performance. An important step for the adventure sports coach would be to discuss attentional focusing strategies with a client, to ensure that appropriate cues are being utilized. In addition, if possible, a variety of scenarios could be set up to test the client's attentional focus under increasingly stressful, but safely managed scenarios. Where a client demonstrates a tendency towards self-control of actions under pressure, alternative attentional foci could be explored, along with psychological techniques to maintain focus on appropriate cues (e.g., self-talk).

The second implication of the theory of reinvestment is not for the performer in the pressurized situation, but for the coach who is working with the novice performer. Masters argues that the problems faced by the advanced performer in a situation may have their origin in the format of their early learning experiences. According to the Theory of Reinvestment, skill failure under pressure is due to the existence of detailed knowledge of the mechanics of skill execution. Detailed mechanics of the action are typically taught during early lessons. For example, a ski instructor may work on a range of specific body positions such as flexion at the ankles, knees and hips; pelvic tilt; hand position; diverging ski poles; and horizontal eye line. Remove this detailed knowledge, Masters argues, and the potential for skill failure through self-focus will also be removed. So how is it that skills can be mastered without developing a knowledge of the technical detail, or rules, underpinning their performance?

Attentional focus strategies

When a white water kayaker 'boofs' a drop there are a lot of factors that could attract attention. These include relevant cues, such as the position of the kayak, the position of rocks, the speed of the water. Unfortunately, many irrelevant cues, such as fear of injury, or the arm position required on the final big stroke, may also be present. Developing a self-talk script may be a particularly useful way of maintaining focus on relevant information, and a kayaker may be encouraged to develop a script such as the following:

'Ready' (the kayak is on line, moving at a good speed)
'Steady' (minor adjustments are made to keep the kayak on line and at an appropriate speed)
'Go' (the final big stroke and lifting of the bow of the kayak)

This strategy could be incorporated with mental imagery in the preparation for an attempt. An attentional focus strategy provides guidance in terms of the main areas to focus on, and the key elements to execute, to maintain the performer's concentration on appropriate information. The ingredients of a successful strategy include reducing the information to a few command words, and reference to *what* to do rather than how to do it.

Implicit learning

Learning without the formation of consciously accessible technical rules is termed implicit learning. The first point to make is that discovery learning, where a learner is left to figure a task out on their own, does *not* lead to implicit learning. Under discovery learning conditions novices engage in what Masters refers to as 'hypothesis testing'. For example, a surfer struggling with balance may think about widening his base of support by placing his feet further apart. If this adjustment (the hypothesis) leads to success, then 'feet wide apart' will be remembered as a technical rule. Left to their own devices, learners will frequently attempt different variations of an action and develop their own set of technical rules.

In order to prevent rule formation, it is necessary to occupy the learner's conscious memory. Initially, Masters achieved this by having learners perform the main task (e.g. standing on a surfboard) and a simultaneous secondary task (e.g. counting backwards from 997 in threes). Secondary tasks were effective in preventing rule formation; however, they suffered from two limitations. First, coaches and athletes who were used to direct coaching found it difficult to trust in this alternative method. This is understandable, given that the direct coaching is likely to have featured prominently in the qualifications that these coaches completed, and how they themselves were coached. The second limitation was that performance improved more slowly using dual tasks than when using direct instruction or exploration, as coaches have long associated faster learning as being evidence of better coaching. Implicit learning teaches us that it may be beneficial to learn more slowly early on, to perform more successfully when it really matters. More recently, research has started to use analogies to promote implicit learning. (Analogies are statements that summarize the main technical points required for the basic execution of a skill.) For example, when teaching parallel turns in skiing we may refer leaving parallel lines 'like train tracks' to encourage consistent and equidistant leg spacing through the turn. Analogies appear to prevent rule formation without slowing down the rate of learning. In other words, the skill is learned as quickly as when using direct instruction, but with the added benefit of being 'pressure proofed' along the way.

While it is likely impossible to prevent the acquisition of all conscious knowledge about the mechanics of a skill, recent research has suggested that even a brief, initial stage of implicit learning may be of benefit in later performance in the types of pressure situations that we have met throughout this chapter (Poolton, Masters and Maxwell, 2005). Although theoretically sound, the long-term feasibility of implicit learning in real-world learning environments remains to be seen. Expert performers are frequently students of their events, and use their detailed knowledge to modify and enhance their performance. However, there appears to be merit in at least limiting the information, which a novice learner is asked to consciously process, in the early stages of skill learning.

Voices from the field: Using implicit learning

You so often see people making great progress, and then in a high-pressure situation, they just freeze up. You know that they can do the skills, but when there is a consequence, they start to overthink. I really do think that giving people too much technical information when you are coaching sets them up to try and apply all that technical information when the pressure is on. When you are paddling hard rapids, you need to be doing, not thinking. That's why I like the simplicity of using analogies: presenting learners with clear images that summarize the important technical points. Some of the analogies I use are:

- 'Use your paddle to draw a big half pizza' (sweep stroke)
- 'If the paddle is an ice cream scoop, then get it deep to get the most ice cream' (power stroke)
- 'Imagine you're cycling down a street and you grab hold of a lamp post – that's how the boat needs to turn around the paddle' (bow rudder)

This is a big departure from the way I was taught to coach, where it was all about how much technical knowledge you can communicate to the learner.

Now, I think much more about what the learner can handle, not just in the current session, but also in the future when they find themselves under pressure.

Ian Coleman – British Canoe Union Level 5 Coach, Mountaineering Instructor Award

Summary of problem two: Performance under pressure

Theories that explain performance under pressure may be classified into two camps: Distraction theories and Self-focus theories (Table 7.2). Both camps emphasize what the individual is attending to as the major explanatory factor. For Distraction theories, performers fail when their attention is drawn away from the task at hand to other internal (e.g. worry) or external (e.g. irrelevant information) factors. Choking comes from not paying enough attention to the task at hand. By contrast, Self-Focus theories suggest that performers fail when their attention is drawn to the small details of how to perform a task. Choking comes from paying too much attention to the task at hand. Although the theories appear on first reading to be contradictory, it is important to consider the context. When performing open skills, such as paddling to an eddy in turbulent white water, where there are multiple external demands on performance, skill failure is likely to result from attention being distracted away from critical task information. Importantly, this critical task information refers to the perceptual information, which informs decision-making (what to do), and not to information relating to the execution of well-learned skills (how to do it). By contrast, in closed skills such as indoor archery

TABLE 7.2 A comparison of theories of skill failure under pressure

Attentional control theory	*The theory of reinvestment*
Proposed by Eysenck *et al.* (2007)	Proposed by Masters (1992)
Distraction theory	Self-focus theory
Failure under pressure is due to paying too little attention to the execution of the skill	Failure under pressure is due to paying too much attention to the execution of the skill
Emphasis on perceptual and decision-making processes	Emphasis on efferent organization
Implications for practitioners:	Implications for practitioners:
Reduce or reinterpret symptoms of anxiety Develop attentional focusing strategies Simulation practice	Reduce rule formation during initial skill learning (e.g. analogy learning) Develop attentional focusing strategies

where there is no decision to be made, skill failure is likely to be due to the attention being turned inwards to the control of a skill that can be more effectively executed automatically. Knowledge of both theories provides detailed guidance for the coach who is tasked with preparing learners for performance under pressurized situations.

Problem three: Fixing bad habits

For many coaches, teaching a new movement pattern to novices is much easier than changing a bad habit in an experienced performer (Dick, 2002). Unfortunately, dealing with bad habits is a common problem faced by high-level coaches. In adventure sports such as skiing, the problem of bad habits may arise at much lower skill levels due to the fact that much skiing practice is irregular and unguided. Unguided practice typically develops *consistent* movement patterns, but these movement patterns may be problematic for a number of reasons. For example, a particular technique may predispose the individual involved to an overuse injury, such as lower back problems in kayakers. The technique used by a performer may be reasonably effective, but may limit the potential effectiveness or efficiency of the performer due to deviations from core principles of biomechanics (McGinnis, 1999). An example of this problem is often seen in snowboarding where the boarder uses too much arm and upper body movement in initiating the turn. This section will consider the advice that the literature holds for adventure sports coaches who are working on changing bad habits?

It is first important to establish that unusual movement patterns may emerge for many reasons. Ackland, Bloomfield and Elliott (2009) presented the Assessment and Modification Model that identified the potential for improving athletic performance across physical (e.g. strength, flexibility), physiological (e.g. lactic threshold, aerobic capacity), tactical (e.g. anticipation, decision-making), psychological (e.g. attentional focus, self-efficacy) and technical (e.g. energy efficiency, injury risk) domains. This holistic model emphasizes the inter-relatedness of the various factors underpinning the expression of skill. For example, a particular technical flaw may result from a basic muscular weakness, or to a lack of time due to poor tactical nous, rather than any deficiency in the learned motor pattern. In such cases, interventions targeting technical modification would be treating the symptom rather than the underlying performance limiter. Although designed with mainstream sporting performance in mind, the model is equally valuable for practitioners in adventure sports. Regardless of the population one is working with, the main message remains the same: before undertaking a process of technique refinement, it is vital to establish the underlying cause of the bad habit.

Why are bad habits so difficult to change?

There are occasions where the modification of the learned movement pattern (labelled technical refinement by Carson and Collins, 2011) is the necessary and appropriate step to take to improve performance. Such technical change is notoriously difficult to accomplish, due to what Dick (2002) referred to as "the basic inertia of an entrenched pattern" (p. 195). In essence, the presence of an existing movement pattern will interfere with attempts to learn a new, similar pattern. In cognitive psychology, this is termed proactive inhibition. A common experience of proactive inhibition occurs when you have recently changed your computer's password: when prompted for the password you find yourself typing the old password. Proactive inhibition is particularly strong when a stimulus (e.g. prompt for password) that required a particular response (old password) is paired with an alternative response (new password). Thus we may expect considerable difficulty in changing a pattern when a specific situation (e.g. a snowboarder approaching a turn) that the learner has traditionally responded to with one movement pattern (e.g. initiate the turn with arm and trunk movement) requires a different movement pattern (e.g. steering with the knees and feet).

The distinction between learning a new action and modifying an existing action has received little attention in motor learning textbooks (e.g. Fairbrother, 2010; Magill, 2011; Schmidt and Lee, 2011). A survey of adventure sports coaching texts similarly revealed a lack of information on how bad habits could be eradicated. In general, a 'back to basics' approach appears to be adopted, whereby the new technique is built up from an initially simplified state and gradually loaded until it can be performed in the performance context (e.g. Grade V river). The difficulty with this approach is that it ignores what we call the 'elephant in the technique': the learner already has a movement pattern in place to achieve the goal in question. The end product of the back to basics approach is that your learner now has two patterns to choose from. Is it any surprise that performers frequently relapse to their old pattern in a high-pressure context? A good example of this is seen when rolling a kayak. Performers who were initially taught the Pawlata roll, but subsequently adopted the sweep technique, often revert back to the Pawlata technique when they are unexpectedly overturned.

Five steps to effective technical refinement

Step one: Analysis

A small number of case studies have addressed technical refinement in javelin throwing (Collins *et al.*, 1999), speed skating (Godbout and Boyd, 2010), sprinting (Hanin *et al.*, 2002) and swimming (Hanin *et al.*, 2004). Reviewing these case studies, Carson and Collins (2011) proposed the Five-A Model to provide a practical guide for practitioners seeking to implement technique refinement in high-level performers (see Table 7.3). In the first stage of the model, Analysis, the technical flaw is first identified and scrutinized under a range of conditions. In mainstream sport this might involve assessing the performer in both practice and competition contexts. In an adventure sport such as climbing, this assessment might involve observing the performer on a number of routes of differing grades. As we

TABLE 7.3 An overview of the five-a model of technique refinement

Stage	*Description*
Analysis	Prolonged assessment under a range of conditions Detailed evaluation of what the change process would involve Securing of buy in from all relevant parties
Awareness	Bringing the existing pattern into conscious awareness Establishing a clear distinction between existing and target movement patterns
Adjustment	Gradually modifying the technique towards the desired pattern Practice under initially simplified conditions, which are gradually progressed to resemble the performance conditions
(Re)-Automation	Continue progress towards the performance conditions Change to an holistic attentional focus Add physical or mental challenges to increase need for automatic performance
Assurance	Proactive planning of pressurized situations to test the technique and develop confidence in its application

met earlier when discussing Ackland *et al.*'s (2009) Assessment and Modification Model, this prolonged assessment is vital for ensuring that the technique error is indeed the root of the problem, and not a symptom of some other problem (e.g. failure to concentrate under pressure). If it is confirmed that a technical change would be of benefit to the athlete, the next step is to investigate what that technical change would involve (e.g. time required; short-term impact on performance) and to decide whether the investment is appropriate at this moment in time. With the rationale for making a change clearly established, the final step in this first stage is to secure commitment from all relevant parties. This includes not just the client and coach, but also any other major sources of support (e.g. parent). One of the ways in which commitment is secured is through detailed discussions with the client regarding the process. With experienced clients, this process is likely to involve the client shaping the intervention by virtue of his/her past experiences (i.e. what coaching tools has the client experienced previously, and what is the client's evaluation of these tools?) Although it may appear drawn out, ensuring a full understanding of and commitment to the process from all parties is vital to the success of technique refinement.

Step two: Awareness

The second stage of the Five-A Model is Awareness. The goal of this stage is to bring the currently automatic pattern into conscious awareness. By doing so, the athlete learns to distinguish between the current and desired movements. The task may be simplified, and the athlete encouraged to produce both correct and incorrect movements in order to learn to distinguish between them. Practice with the eyes closed may be appropriate to encourage the athlete to concentrate on the feel of the movement. The athlete is also encouraged to provide self-ratings of his/her performance, indicating deviation from the desired movement (e.g. a rating of 0 indicates the old technique was performed; 10 indicates that the new technique was performed). Although the temptation may be to push quickly through this stage and move on to making changes, the Five-A Model suggests that only when the athlete can accurately discriminate between the two movements, and this discrimination is retained after a period of no practice, should the athlete progress to the next stage.

Step three: Adjustment

During the third stage, Adjustment, the technique is gradually modified in the intended direction. The Old-Way/New Way (Hanin *et al.*, 2002; Hanin *et al.*, 2004) technique may be used, along with video review and mental practice. Both the video and mental practice should emphasize progression. Video recording is particularly useful at this point, both to measure progress towards the desired technique and also to calibrate the athlete's understanding of his/her movement. As the movement changes towards the desired pattern, the kinaesthetic cues that the learner uses to describe the movement may also change. These changing cues should be incorporated into any self-talk or imagery script that the athlete uses. The technique is to be practiced in conditions that are progressively closer to the performance conditions (e.g. for a skier, at progressively higher speeds). Towards the end of the adjustment phase, the athlete can perform the movement consistently, but only when directing conscious attention towards the main elements of the action. For open skills, this conscious control may distract attention from important environmental cues. For closed skills, this conscious control may disrupt the smoothness of the performed movements. It is therefore necessary to begin to shift to a more automatic mode of movement control.

Step four: (Re)-Automation

(Re)-Automation actively promotes a more unconscious mode of control while maintaining the desired movement pattern. Rhythm-based attentional strategies may be used to encourage the athlete's attention away from the specific mechanics of the technique. For example, calling out 1-2-3 or humming a waltz can provide a rhythmic cue for short radius turns in skiing. In addition, the learner could be asked to perform under varying physical (e.g. following fatiguing exercise) or mental challenges (e.g. while following an obscure route, or completing arithmetic problems). Re-Automation will also be encouraged by a gradual transition back to representative conditions (e.g. full speed, slope, white water), provided the transition is appropriately paced. The use of holistic cues, and physical or mental challenges, will accelerate this process, or facilitate a gradual transition to representative conditions where natural variations (e.g. river grades) are not readily accessible.

Step five: Assurance

Howie Carson (Carson and Collins, 2011) uses a black box analogy to summarize the Five-A model. Analysis is assessing the box, Awareness is opening the box, Adjustment is tinkering with the contents, (Re)-Automation is closing the box. The final stage, Assurance, involves locking the box and throwing away the key. Assurance sees the gradual and progressive exposure of the new technique to physical and psychological stress to ensure its resilience. This exposure has a psychosocial as well as a psychomotor rationale. The successful application of the refined technique in a range of differing challenges builds confidence in the technique, ensuring that in the eventual high-pressure performance context, the performer trusts the refined technique to deliver the performance. For example, a mountain biker could attempt to execute the new technique version after a challenging ride when fatigue adds an additional challenge. Consequences for failure could be set: for younger athletes the suggestion that poor performance will result in a ban on access to Facebook for a period of time is typically met with abject horror. However pressure is achieved, the coach should be proactive in planning when and how increased pressure will be applied to confirm that the skill refinement has been adequately learned.

Summary of problem three: Fixing bad habits

It is important to stress that research into the efficacy of the Five-A Model in differing sporting domains is still developing. However, the model does provide a structured guide that a coach can take and explore within his/her own practice. Within each of the five stages, the model describes a range of tools from which the practitioner may select to achieve the specific goal of each stage. This flexibility in implementation is likely to be important in meeting the distinctive needs of individuals undergoing technique refinement in the broad range of environments encountered by adventure sports coaches.

Dealing with technical bad habits is a frequent and difficult problem for adventure sports coaches. Recent research has seen the emergence of detailed, theoretically underpinned guidance on the process of technique refinement: the Five-A Model. This section has introduced the model, and provided suggestions as to how it may be applied in the adventure sports domain.

Summary

Many skill acquisition and coaching texts provide detailed guidance on how to enhance the learning of relatively novice performers. Advanced performers face different demands. The present chapter presented three areas of relevance to a coach working with advanced performers:

- Coaches may enhance the quality of an athlete's performance by monitoring the efficiency of practice, and introducing the principles of deliberate practice and self-regulation. Critically, deliberate practice and self-regulation should not be introduced until the athlete is ready or dissatisfaction with the sport and burnout are likely to result.
- High-level performance, whether in sporting competition or in extreme environments, brings pressure to bear on performers. An understanding of Distraction and Self-focus theories of skill failure under pressure provide the adventure sports coach with specific guidance on how to prepare their learners for performance under pressure.
- Technical bad habits are a common concern in high-level coaching, increasing the risk of injury, or limiting the performance potential of an athlete. An understanding of the Five-A Model provides the adventure sports coach with a framework for successfully modifying technique in advanced performers.

References

Ackland, T. R., Bloomfield, J. and Elliott, B. C. (2009). The assessment and modification model. In: T. R. Ackland, J. Bloomfield and B. C. Elliott (eds), *Applied Anatomy and Biomechanics in Sport*. Champaign, IL: Human Kinetics, 3–9.

Bloom, B. S. (1985). *Developing Talent in Young People*. New York: Ballantine Books.

Carson, H. J., and Collins, D. (2011). Refining and regaining skills in fixation/diversification stage performers: The Five-A Model. *International Review of Sport and Exercise Psychology*, 4, 146–167.

Coleman, I. (2006). Rolling. In: F. Ferrero (ed.), *British Canoe Union Coaching Handbook*. Caernarfon: Pesda Press.

Collins, D., Morris, C. and Trower, J. (1999). Getting it back: A case study of skill recovery in an elite athlete. *Sport Psychologist*, 13, 288–298. Retrieved from http://journals.humankinetics.com/tsp

Côté, J. and Fraser-Thomas, J. (2008). Play, practice, and athlete development. In: D. Farrow, J. Baker and C. MacMahon (eds), *Developing Sport Expertise: Researchers and Coaches Put Theory into Practice*. London: Routledge, 17–24.

Deakin, J. M. and Cobley, S. (2003). A search for deliberate practice: An examination of the practice environments in figure skating and volleyball. In: J. Starkes and K. A. Ericsson (eds), *Expert Performance in Sports*. Champaign, IL: Human Kinetics, 115–135.

Dick, F. W. (2002). *Sports Training Principles* (4th ed.). London: A&C Black.

Dweck, C. S. (2006). *Mindset: How you can Fulfil your Potential*. London: Constable & Robinson Ltd.

Ericsson, K. A. (2013). Training history, deliberate practice and elite sports performance: An analysis in response to Tucker and Collins review – what makes champions? *British Journal of Sports Medicine*, 47, 533–535.

Ericsson, K. A., Krampe, R. T. and Teschromer, C. (1993). The role of deliberate practice in the acquisition of expert performance. *Psychological Review*, 100, 363–406.

Eysenck, M. W. and Calvo, M. G. (1992). Anxiety and Performance: The Processing Efficiency Theory. *Cognition and Emotion*, 6, 409–434.
Eysenck, M. W., Derakshan, N., Santos, R. and Calvo, M. G. (2007). Anxiety and cognitive performance: Attentional control theory. *Emotion*, 7, 336–353.
Fairbrother, J. T. (2010). *Fundamentals of Motor Behavior*. Champaign, IL: Human Kinetics.
Godbout, A. and Boyd, J. E. (2010, June). *Corrective Sonic Feedback for Speed Skating: A Case Study*. Paper presented at the 16th International Conference on Auditory Display, Washington.
Hanin, Y., Korjus, T., Jouste, P. and Baxter, P. (2002). Rapid technique correction using old way/new way: two case studies with Olympic athletes. *Sport Psychologist*, 16(1), 79–99.
Hanin, Y., Malvela, M. and Hanina, M. (2004). Rapid correction of start technique in an Olympic-level swimmer: A case study using old way/new way. *J Swimming Research*, 16, 11–17.
Magill, R. A. (2011). *Motor Learning and Control: Concepts and Applications* (9th ed.). Boston: McGraw-Hill.
Masters, R. S. W. (1992). Knowledge, knerves and know-how: The role of explicit versus implicit knowledge in the breakdown of a complex motor skill under pressure. *British Journal of Psychology*, 83, 343–358.
McGinnis, P. M. (1999). *Biomechanics of sport and exercise*. Champaign, IL: Human Kinetics.
Merton, R. K. (1968). The Matthew effect in science. *Science*, 159, 56–63.
Nieuwenhuys, A., Pijpers, J. R., Oudejans, R. R. and Bakker, F. C. (2008). The influence of anxiety on visual attention in climbing. *Journal of Sport and Exercise Psychology*, 30, 171–185.
Poolton, J. M., Masters, R. S. W. and Maxwell, J. P. (2005). The relationship between initial errorless learning conditions and subsequent performance. *Human Movement Science*, 24, 362–378.
Schmidt, R. A. and Lee, T. D. (2011). *Motor Control and Learning: A Behavioral Emphasis* (5th ed.). Champaign, IL: Human Kinetics.
Tucker, R. and Collins, M. (2012). What makes champions? A review of the relative contribution of genes and training to sporting success. *British Journal of Sports Medicine*, 46, 555–61.
Whitehead, A. N. (1922). *The Rhythm of Education*. London: Christophers.
Zimmerman, B. J. (1998). Academic studying and the development of personal skill: A self-regulatory perspective. *Educational Psychologist*, 33, 73–86.

8

PLANNING FOR PROGRESSION

Jane Lomax

Introduction

Working within the adventure sector can present coaches with a range of contexts to plan for and deliver in. At one end of the spectrum coaches might find themselves delivering one-off sessions or working over a short time frame to prepare participants for a holiday or trip. At the other end of the spectrum, coaches could be working with participants for a number of years, preparing a group for an expedition, a round-the-world sailing challenge or even for competition. As a result, the flexibility required from the adventure sports coach for planning skills is extensive. The support network around the adventure sports coach is also varied from the large team of support workers found at the top end of sailing to the one person 'coach does all' at the other end. Some contexts may be very commercial and others more about continuing participation as long as possible within an individual's lifespan.

Adventure sports participation has a longer lifespan than most traditional sports and coaches may find themselves working with different generations on the same activity. For example, in one morning working on a dry ski slope in England I found myself working with a four-year-old who was learning to ski in order to go on a family holiday in one session, whereas the following session included a 62-year-old lady who just fancied learning how to ski, having never had the opportunity to do so till then. I have also skied with over 70-year-olds and cannot help admire skiers of this age who want to improve their control on the black runs! These might be extreme examples but if we consider the range of activities within the remit of adventure sports coaching, working with older participants is becoming a more regular occurrence.

There are many texts that cover the planning process in sports coaching generally (Pankhurst, 2007; Robinson, 2010) that focus on the planning and delivery of a single coaching session, a group of linked sessions or even developing a periodized training programme for the higher level of performer. This chapter aims to draw on that pedagogical and sport coaching science knowledge to examine the applicability of these ideas to the different adventure sports contexts. Coaching in adventure sports will never be a 'one size fits all' approach and there will be times when ideas from other literature sources can easily be transferred and used; there will be times when the fit is not so good. It is down to the skill of the coach to know when to borrow and apply those ideas and how to adapt them. We hope this chapter will help the thought process behind this challenge that all adventure sports coaches will be faced with at some stage in their career.

The planning process

What we actually mean by 'planning' is worth considering as what lies within 'the planning process' can be quite an exhaustive list given the logistical matters that many of the practical venues used in adventure sports coaching can present. Similar to Pankhurst (2007) we define planning as putting together a programme of support that will address all elements of performance improvements. Knowing where your participants are now and where they want to be is an important part of that process as is the time frame participants are working to. Here we will consider the planning process both in the short and the long term and explore how coaches can plan to ensure progression. This will relate to their participants but will also draw examples from progression factors relating to the adventure sports coach as a developing professional too.

For a long time now coaches in many sports have been introduced to the 'plan-conduct-evaluate' or 'plan-do-review' cycle, which is the rubric of good coaching. Coaches are generally encouraged to plan structured sessions, deliver them and then utilize their review and evaluation to inform the preparation of the next session so that progression for the participants is ensured. The planning process thus considers the task progressions within a session as well as between sessions. Here we would like to extend this thinking to assist the adventure sports coach as follows (see Figure 8.1):

1. Identify motivations, goals and expectations

Given the diverse nature of coaching within an adventure activity one of the major elements of planning for the adventure sports coach is the identification of participant(s) motivations, aspirations and expectations (see Figure 8.1). This is an important dialogue within the planning process and is part of what differentiates the coaching environment from that of instruction. There will be times when the commercial side of adventure sports coaching might require the delivery of a somewhat prescribed session, often instructor led, but coaches will need to balance this with the need to meet participants' aspirations and work in a more client-centred approach.

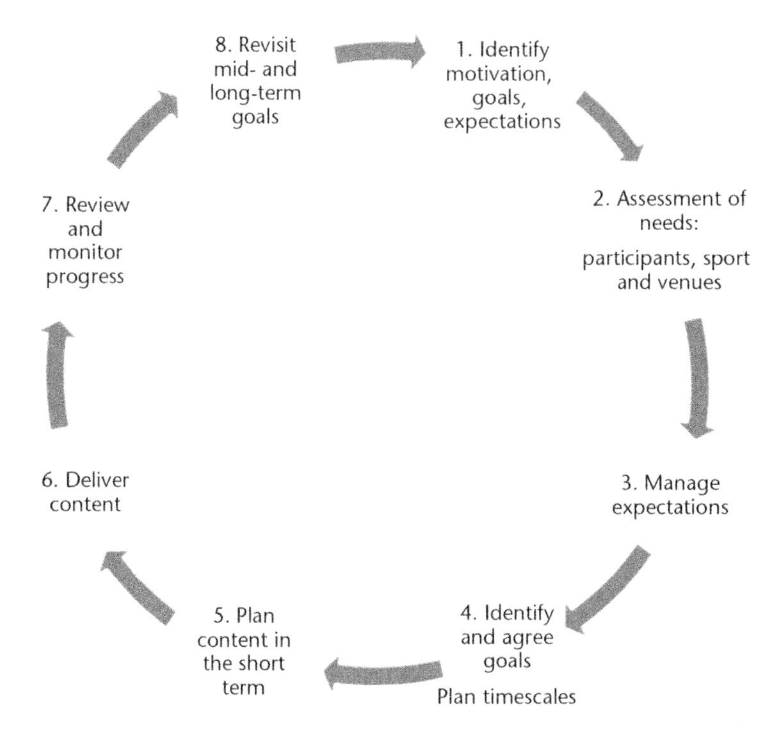

FIGURE 8.1 The adventure sports planning cycle

Identifying the motivations of participants

The reasons bringing participants to adventure sports are multifaceted and individuals can be involved within their adventure sport from childhood or can often be introduced to the activity later in life. Many wish to try something different; some are serious competitors. In their research into motives for participating in adventure sports, Navin and Houge MacKenzie (2012) identified that many participants shared some common motives that ranged from goal achievement, risk taking, social motivation, to escape from boredom, pushing personal boundaries and overcoming fear, in addition to connecting with nature, the environment and the enjoyment of kinaesthetic bodily sensations from moving in the water or air. Kerr and Houge MacKenzie suggest that further research is necessary to gain a better understanding of these motives for participation, highlighting the need to recognize they go beyond excitement and thrill-seeking behaviour. They also recognize that the relative importance of these commonly held motives varies between individuals. So adventure sports coaches would benefit from an early dialogue with performers to gain an insight into the balance of motives within individuals or across the group so that the planning can then cater for their needs from a more informed platform.

When examining how these motives change within the older populations of participants, Sugerman (2002) explored the relationship between skill development and motivation for over 40-year-olds ranging from beginner day hikers to advanced wilderness trips. The motives rated most important were nature, physical fitness and social security though these motivations were more significant for women than for men and for participants younger than 65 years of age. Those who were not retired rated the motives of escaping personal and physical pressure, nature and physical rest higher than those who were retired, whereas for those who were retired introspection and nostalgia were a more important driving force. When it came to differences in skill level, Sugerman reported that those in the beginner level of participation were more focused on meeting new people whereas the more advanced participant enjoyed the risk taking, nature, learning and escaping pressures more. Adventure coaches may also need to consider gender differences as well as age, skill level and retirement status when working with adult populations.

Identifying goals and expectations

Just as performers can be motivated by a plethora of reasons, their goals can be diverse and some very aspirational. It will be down to the skill of the coach to discern those that are realistic and achievable and those that would require more of a magic wand than a coaching session to achieve. These goals need to be explored and prioritized. For example, to return to our over 70-year-olds who would like to improve their control on a black run it may be that they are also wanting to continue to ski for as long as possible in which case the coach will need to ascertain whether practicing on a black run is indeed a sensible choice of environment to plan for, given the increased injury risk here in comparison to other slopes, or whether other goals might be more important to focus on to facilitate longer term participation. An individual's goals and aspirations will have a direct effect on the planning needs and progression opportunities as illustrated below where the message is clear – time spent getting to know our participants will be invaluable in informing our planning.

Voices from the field

When working with public service personnel each cohort presents a different concentration of aspirations ranging widely in employment and career destinations: from police officers to army infantry. Whilst producing an individualized and appropriate scheme of work before the start of the course is good practice – it is in tension with the fact that students aiming for navy officer training demand different coaching to students aiming to become fire fighters.

Tim Parker, Lecturer in Adventure Education

2. Assessment of needs: The participants

If a coach is going to plan to improve all elements of performance and work out whether the goals and expectations of performers are realistic then it behoves coaches to spend time gathering information about the needs of the individuals – where they are now and where they want to get to. Then the coach will be faced with decisions about whether they are able to make that journey with the participants either some of the way or all of the way. This may involve looking at the match between performer desires and the coach's knowledge base or even the coach's philosophical standpoint to help the coach decide who is best placed to support participant progression.

Consequently, gathering information about the participant's current level of experience and capabilities needs to involve all areas influencing performance, i.e. technical, tactical, physical and psychological. Other considerations for longer-term planning might include:

- The developmental stage of performers.
  Many texts will give guidance on children's stages of development and encourage coaches to be aware of the loss of coordination and strength that can often happen as youngsters go through growth spurts, where patience is often needed while those changes in strength and co-ordination catch up with increased limb length. Within adventure activities, though, the ageing process also needs consideration and coaches need an understanding of any limitations that health, injuries or disabilities might be placing on individual participation within an activity.

- The impact of life events.
  Planning within the long term needs to take note of times in the year when there are specific pressures on participants. Where the participants are young adults this pressure will probably come from academic sources – examinations within school or assessment points at university. Older adults could have numerous other life and financial pressures that can impact on their commitment and availability to practice. Those in retirement may have newly found time to enjoy greater involvement within activities.

- Support personnel available to help.
  When coaches work in higher levels of performance they will find themselves as part of a team rather than being 'jack of all trades'. This will require a more co-ordinated approach to planning and can challenge the communication skills of the coach.

- Financial support available.
  Always helpful when it is present but coaches may have to balance sponsor requirements with their own needs so even a generous sponsorship deal may not be without its difficulties.

Where the coach has the chance to observe and analyze participants before agreeing and setting goals that will clearly be helpful to gain a feel for the participant's starting point and thus what is realistic to achieve.

Performance profiling

Performance profiling is a popular method of gathering information about the participant's perceptions of what is important to them and where they feel they are now, performance wise, in relation to where they would like to be in order to achieve a given goal. Performance profiling is a technique largely introduced into sport by Richard Butler in the 1990s, which is based on Personal Construct theory and has gained popularity through its simplicity and use of a visual display. Nowadays, performance profiling is used quite extensively not just by sports psychologists but by coaches too (Butler, 1999; Gray *et al.*, 2011).

Performance profiling asks the participants to identify the qualities, or constructs, they believe to be important within their activity to achieve either top-level performance or the goals the participants themselves are after. Performers can be encouraged to list many qualities and include all four elements of performance i.e. technical, tactical, mental and physical. There may be other factors that are important to the performer that do not fit neatly into these categories, for example, finance or access to training venues, which could also be included, but, generally speaking, it is easier to focus on the performance elements directly as these tend to be more under the participant's control. Performers are then encouraged to fill in the most important qualities, or constructs, around the edge of a target and score themselves for where they are now (see Figure 8.2). Performers need to be encouraged to be as specific as possible in the constructs they use as scoring yourself on a very general statement is much more difficult than a specific one. However, this level of specificity often develops with time and familiarity with the profiling process. Figure 8.2 represents a first effort at the profiling process, which can then be refined and developed over time.

This racer's goal was to make the British team in three years, the England squad in two and for the next 12 months finish in the top 15 on the dry ski slope race circuit. The score of 10 was the level perceived necessary to perform at to achieve these goals. It is important to give the profile context by focusing on the participants' goals and clarifying what a score of 10 means. It needs to be pointed out that some individuals will be hard on themselves with the scoring, while others may be generous and coaches will need to manage each of these situations effectively.

What you do with the scores now is important to inform the planning process. Interpreting the scores accurately is easier if the coach has the time to speak with the participant about what exactly each construct means to them. For example, 'self-confidence' could mean confidence in physical capabilities or confidence in abilities to control emotions in difficult circumstance. The first interpretation might lead a coach to load the planning in favour of physical elements of training and the latter would encourage more of a psychological emphasis, so clarification of construct meaning is worth some investment of time wherever possible. In this

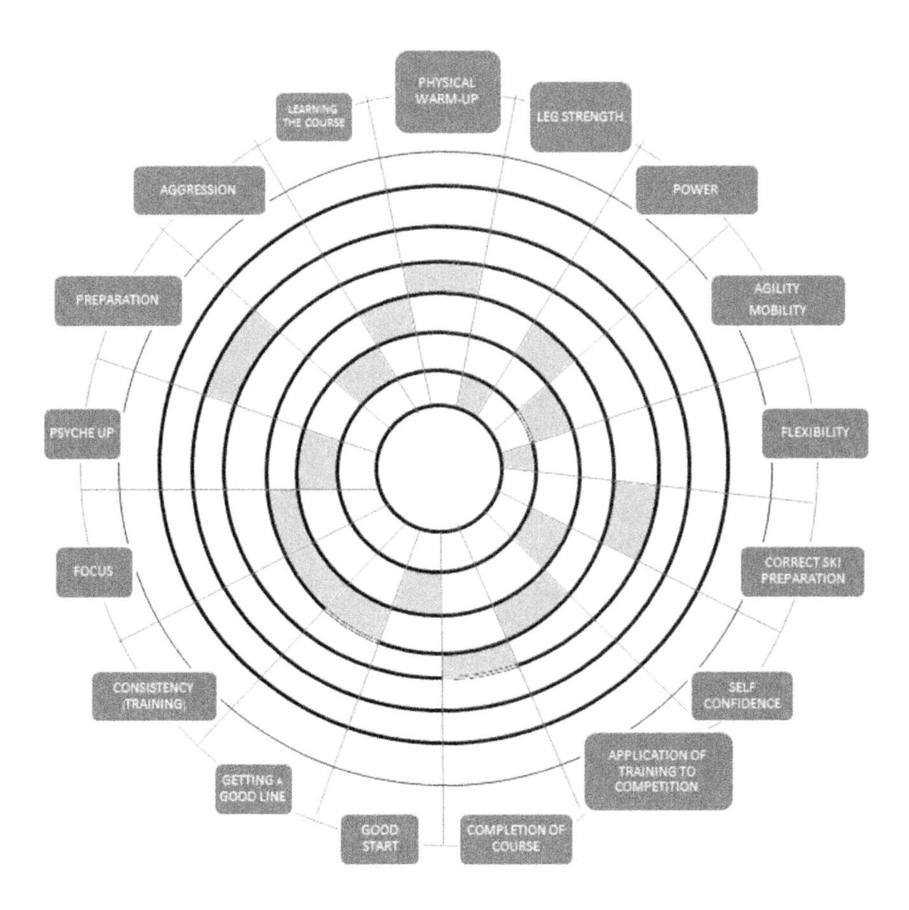

FIGURE 8.2 Example of a completed profile from a teenage ski slalom racer

Note: The shaded sectors are the skier's perception of where they are now

case, the skier felt their confidence relating to performance on the day of competition dropped to 6 while in training tended to be higher, so planning help with the mental side of performance was a more useful direction to take.

In the case of our skier, we asked the coach to complete a profile on the racer where the constructs were available around the outside but not the skier's own scores. This can be a useful way to analyze similarities and differences between coach and participant perceptions of performance levels and can facilitate discussion between the two parties, which should help prevent talking at cross purposes. In many cases this can provide an opportunity to:

- confirm participant perceptions of current performance where scores are well matched;
- provide opportunities to lift confidence where the coach scores are higher; and

- stimulate discussion about the direction of training where the coaches' scores are lower than the participants.

In this example the match on most constructs was a very close one, the only differences were slightly higher scores from the coach on leg strength, agility, starts and psyching up. Such a close match was indicative of a healthy and productive coach–athlete relationship. A word of warning – where there is a difference of scores between coach and participant in 'anger management' take care with the way you approach that conversation!

Performance profiling to help coach progression

Adventure coaches who are aiming to improve their own performance to reach the next level of qualification could use a performance-profiling approach to help structure their preparation for the next level of training and assessment. The constructs could be generated from contents of the syllabus they are looking to achieve. Equally a more-experienced member of staff could profile their leadership and management in a similar manner and perhaps ask their workers to score them. Both can provide help to plan for progression of professional skills as well as performance ones.

Team profiling

Where activities involve working as part of a team, profiles can also be constructed for the team following a similar process. A particularly valuable part of this process is the discussion that surrounds what is important to the team as a whole and the development of agreed team goals. Where individuals offer differing perspectives this is an ideal opportunity to raise awareness to those differences and look for compromises where necessary. This can lead to greater empathy between team members and all of this discussion can contribute positively to both task and social cohesion within the group. Providing, of course, the coach is able to keep those discussions positive as not all individuals make that process as easy as it could be!

Where coaches want more detailed objective measurement to support their assessment of needs they can turn to performance analysis data, fitness tests or questionnaires that can assess psychological aspects – be it mental toughness, use of different performance strategies or current abilities in specific mental skills. These are available in most mainstream sports science texts.

3. Assessment of needs: The sport or activity

What are the demands of the sport?

To plan a programme that improves all elements of performance will require coaches to look at the sport and identify what is required to improve performance.

Many texts, for example Pankhurst (2007), encourage coaches to identify the physical, mental, technical and tactical elements of the sport and then give them an order of priority of importance to balance the focus of training support. All elements are important but it may be that some are more important than others in different activities, for example, the physical demands may be of paramount importance to a cross-country skier but a ski jumper may find the technical, or, indeed, the mental aspects of performance a higher priority. Coaches need to recognize these priorities are likely to change at different times of the year and use this information to structure training in both the short and the long term to ensure progression from one phase of training to the next.

Coaches need to know the developmental stages their performers are. This is not just chronological age but also the development and training ages as these will impact on the coach's planning. For example, a 15-year-old surfer who has been training at their sport for four years with the emotional maturity of a 17-year-old would need a different approach from a 15-year-old who has only just joined the sport, so zero training age, with a developmental age of 13.

When working with youngsters many coaches now follow the guidance given in Istvan Bayli's Long Term Athlete Development (LTAD) model. Balyi suggests it takes 10,000 hours of practice to reach the top in any activity and LTAD aims to give guidance for how the balance between training and competition might be developed through different ages. The aim is to maximize the number of participants being prepared for long-term participation within an activity or sport and minimize the drop out caused by burnout, injury or disaffection when the training does not match the individual's needs and stages of development. LTAD also recognizes the need to retain participants within a sport or activity across the lifespan and recognizes the need to adapt the planning to accommodate the needs of the mature participant too.

LTAD focuses largely on physiological elements of training and the British Canoe Union (BCU) has adopted this approach in its Long Term Paddler Development model (BCU, 2006). LTPD provides paddlesport-specific guidance for appropriate activities and focuses of work as youngsters move through the different stages of performance. It identifies windows of opportunities for developing speed, strength and ability, which can help the coach balance the demands of the sport with the needs of the participants through adaptations to the planned training programme. Further information on training physiological elements of performance can be found elsewhere in this book.

Psychological elements of training are perhaps more serviced by guidance on when to progress participants from deliberate play to deliberate practice and when we are coaching younger participants it is worth considering the following suggestions from Jean Côté's Developmental Model of Sport Participation (DMSP) (Stafford, 2011):

- Sampling years – 6–12-year-olds should be sampling a range of sports and developing a range of fundamental skills. Coaches need to emphasize 'fun' within session delivery at this age and provide the opportunity for deliberate play.

- Specializing phase – 13–15-year-olds start to make decisions about which activities they will focus their energies on and begin to specialize and dedicate more time to training. Coaches can gradually increase more deliberate practice while maintaining the fun and enjoyment so vital to keeping youngsters involved in the sport.
- Investment phase – 16 plus years. Here participants become increasingly committed to the sport and coaches need to ensure deliberate practice and will need to adopt a more strategic approach to planning.

Adventure sports coaches need to consider such suggestions to underpin their philosophical approach to working with these age groups. However, the competitive side of sports may be at odds with some of these suggestions as some sports will require earlier specialization than others and coaches may find themselves having to balance what LTAD and DMSP suggests with pressure from the sport to identify talented youngsters with potential as early as possible.

Where the sport or activity involves preparation for a trip or expedition, coaches will need to consider logistics of travel, equipment, risk management and the specifics of the venue that the trip is planned to visit. For example, the Grand Canyon rafting and kayaking trip outlined later in this chapter required an application for a permit from the National Park before the detailed planning was possible. As developing professionals, the adventure sports coach might consider the reflections of Dr Peter Bunyan, Head of the Adventure Education department at the University of Chichester, who suggests that aspiring adventure sports coaches who want to take groups out on residential trips need to plan for progression themselves. For example, where the coaches intend to take parties of school children on a residential, his suggestion was to start with a school-based residential, progress to one based in a different school and only then take children into the outdoors completely. Not just for the benefits of the participants but also the leaders and coaches so no one is thrown in at the deep end. At a higher level, the demands of the aforementioned trip to the Grand Canyon cannot be taken lightly and coaches need to progress both themselves and their group to cope with that level of paddling both physically and emotionally as well as ensuring they have built up sufficient expertise over the years to lead the group.

4. Manage expectations

Having established the needs and desires of the participants, coaches need to check their expectations and assess the level of realism behind these goals and aspirations in order to finalize the goals with the participants and plan the programme of coaching. For example, participants can arrive at a kayaking session expecting to master new techniques and hit the white water within the first session. There may well be people involved in other sports and thus very competent physically but for some reason they expect their adventure experiences to produce instant results. They may need reminding how many years they have trained at their current sport and just how long it takes to master new techniques and gain proficiency in a new activity. If they are a games player for example they may well be training once or twice a week with a match each week throughout a season, which gives plenty of time for practice and skill development. Swimmers and gymnasts will train more frequently than that. Contrast that with kayaking – or even surfing or snow sport activities – where the individual might buy into a week's course and then not participate at all from one year to the next. Yet some participants still expect to make similar levels of performance improvements to those experienced at home where access to the practice environment is much more achievable on a regular basis.

So, expectations may need to be managed to a greater degree within adventure activities as performers may only be accessing the activity itself for a limited time period in a year rather than more regular involvement. Even when time does permit practice for the participant(s) the surf might not be up or the weather not appropriate so the amount of time physical practice can be accessed is another element of adventure sports coaching that needs taking into consideration within the planning process.

Where a team of participants needs to be brought together to plan an expedition, the management of expectations may be an important part of the selection process. Coaches leading groups need to be sure that the individuals within the group are capable of succeeding at the challenge facing them. Some coaches may well implement a formal selection process involving fitness tests, assessment of technical and tactical prowess and even some kind of psychological assessment to check participants are able to cope emotionally with the challenges they face.

5. Identify and agree goals and plan timescales

Once the motivations are understood, the needs assessed and the expectations managed the real planning can start. The performance profile can provide the basis for goal setting and assists in a coaches desire to share that process. There may be many goals possible but these need to be prioritized and timescales agreed. Goal setting is an essential component to support the planning process and is discussed in more depth in Chapter 11 of this book. A model of SMARTERP is suggested to help the clear identification of session goals as follows:

S Specific
M Measureable
A Agreed
R Recorded
T Time-phased
E Evaluated
R Recorded
P Positively phrased

Some goals may relate to what coaches and participants aim to achieve in a one-off session. Some may relate to a short series of sessions where a coach needs to consider progressions from one session to the next. Others may require planning over a longer timescale across months or even years. Where this is the case, adventure sports coaches can often borrow from the coaching and sports science literature to help structure training over a longer timeframe. Here the long-term goals will need to be broken down into mid and short-term ones and regular review points built into any training programme to monitor progress and make adaptations to the training as appropriate. The recording of goals is invaluable to keep track of where we have come from and where we are heading.

The outcome goals are often the goals that are easiest to agree in the first instance. Then these need to be underpinned by performance goals that are the measurable stepping stones en route to the outcome and the process goals which are the day-to-day focus during practice sessions. It is the process goals that provide the opportunity for coaches to direct the performers' attention to specific elements of their performance development and also can be really useful in involving the performers and differentiating the tasks to meet individual needs more effectively.

Where coaches are working with teams the same can apply for agreeing team goals. Where team members have an input into the team goals coaches are more likely to get 'buy-in' from team members. However there may still be a conflict in the minds of some participants between what the team or group is aiming to achieve and what the individual wants to achieve themselves. To minimize the risk of individuals ditching the team goals in favour of their own individual ones it might be an idea to break the overall team goals down into unit ones (smaller groups) and then encourage participants to '**Perform with PRIDE**'. Here, the individuals identify how they will contribute to the achievement of the unit and thus their team goal, and that this will be their

Personal **R**esponsibility **I**n **D**elivering **E**xcellence

Adopting the use of PRIDE in this way encourages a specific focus for each person within the framework of the group goal. This helps the group as a whole to work cohesively but gives each member of that group a sense of ownership and achievement on completion of the task. If others in the unit are involved in the encouragement and achievement of these goals and their evaluation then this can provide a supportive, cohesive and motivational climate to the practice sessions.

6. Plan content in the short term

Adventure sports coaches deliver many one-off sessions where participants just want to get better or they may plan and deliver a short series of sessions, perhaps within a week. The use of goal setting is crucial here to identify clearly the desired focus of the session or the series of sessions. I refer the reader to Chapter 11, which gives some questions for the adventure sports coach to pose to him or herself when planning the delivery of a single session to help specificity of focus and make the decisions about the practice type and coaching methods easier.

As coaches work through governing body qualifications they will be encouraged to plan the delivery of both a single session and a series of sessions on session planners. These provide the ideal opportunity to think through the goals of the session as well as the practice structure, task progressions and major coaching points. Formats of session planners will vary between sports but most will nowadays encourage coaches to identify clearly the goals of the session for the participants but also which elements of the coaching process are being focused on too. This helps develop good reflective practitioners as coaches can review their own performance as well as that of the participants.

The planning concerns in the short term that an adventure sports coach might also need to consider include:

- Logistical factors surrounding the session delivery – how, when and where instructions, demonstrations and feedback will be given.
- Transportation of participants and equipment.
- Choice of venue and environment for practice.
- Awareness of weather forecast, regular reviews as necessary to monitor changes in weather and thus activities to match.
- The need for contingency plans, or 'what-ifs'.
- The reaction of parents and their interpretation of your actions – often not what we would expect and worth clarifying early!
- Where the activities run over a number of days, ensuring the participants are well rested, fed and watered is a crucial part of the planning process to ensure they can maintain their levels of physical involvement without injury or undue tiredness.
- When under canvas – consider how participants stay warm and dry.
- How to maximize activity and practice time and keep interventions and task transitions to a minimum.
- Where, how and when to bring the group together for a brief intervention and when a more determined break is necessary.
- Any injuries, illnesses or disabilities in the group.

The list can be quite an extensive one, but this should not put off coaches starting out. They need to recognize that you can never plan for every eventuality. Covering the main health and safety aspects is clearly a must and thinking through as many 'what-ifs' as possible will develop confidence in coaches. Nevertheless, adventure sports coaches need to realize that flexibility will always be necessary and adaptations to even the best-laid plans can often be required. So coaches should be confident to take trips, even if every last permutation of possibilities has not been completely tied down before going and be ready to be adaptable and think on their feet to manage any unexpected occurrences.

7. Deliver content

Many adventure sports coaches will be working in an environment where the focus is commercial rather than educational and the coach can find him or herself torn between loyalties. Some companies based in outdoor centres may be selling a product that has specific outcomes in mind within its marketing literature and there may be times when the coach finds themselves compromised as the 'product' on sale may not be the best fit for the participants in front of them. Here the coach needs to utilize their skill to meet the commercial demands on them as well as give a good match of the content of the session to the individuals within it. Coaches may also find themselves becoming master of many trades and expected to fulfil a number of roles behind the scenes in addition to the coaching itself. It is always worth asking questions of the employer just how far your expertise will be expected to stretch!

The delivery of the session is where the coach brings the plans to life. Chapter 5 in this book explores the use of practice types, instruction, demonstration and feedback as the basics of good practice in coaching pedagogy and readers are referred to this chapter for a more detailed insight into such elements of session delivery. Coaches will need to make appropriate choices of communication and coaching styles to ensure the best match between the goals for the session and the needs of the performers. This will include a balance of coach-led elements of the session with performer-led ones. Coach-led sessions would follow a more traditional model where the coach is the provider of information and will tend to use demonstrations and instructions and give the performers feedback. A performer-led approach is likely to include elements of problem solving and decision-making and encourages the performers to have an input into the focus of practices through skilful use of questioning. Effective questioning is an art form of its own. Many teachers and coaches are accomplished at using questioning to check for knowledge and understanding or recap learning within a session, but here we are looking to asks questions to encourage the performers to:

- Reinforce goals for each session particularly the progression of learning and performance changes evident from the task progressions throughout the session.
- Identify which elements of practice are going well and which they would like to focus on next to improve.
- Read the environment to identify which elements of technique are most suitable to practice on a given speed of river or incline of slope.
- Report back on progress and pick up on feelings of movements as the techniques change and develop.
- Highlight the decisions they are making within practice and identify the options available.

Working with the performers in this manner and utilizing the shared goal setting suggested earlier is a different approach from some of the more traditional instruction sessions, but has the benefits of developing dialogue with performers. Giving the performers responsibilities and involving them in the decision-making process has the added benefits of helping them transfer their learning from the coaching sessions to when they are working independently. If they are confident in making decisions within a coaching session they are more likely to be confident when the coach is not there, hence the use of a questioning approach reduces the chance of performers being dependent on coaches for guidance.

Whatever the level of planning, the coach will still be required to adapt the plans to suit the individuals in front of them and should be confident in their ability to do this. Hence a coach faced with a session that is not working as expected, or indeed is working better than expected, can be flexible and think on his or her feet to make appropriate changes to the session delivery. There may be adaptations required for individuals within the group who are developing at variable rates, to differentiate the task. For example, snowboarders working on the sensitivity of their use of edge control will often be seen practicing a falling leaf down the slopes. Coaches will not need to change the task organisation necessarily, but they will need to provide individualized feedback to support those who are picking up the edge control quickly and those that are finding it a challenge. Occasionally, coaches may need a more general rethink on their feet if the initial plan is clearly not working, for whatever reason, on the day. Within adventure sports this degree of flexibility can often be predicated by sudden changes in weather or environmental conditions.

Where this shorter-term work comes to a natural end as holidaymakers go home or residential trips finish, this may well be the end of contact between the coach and participants. In some cases, though, the coach may resume contact with participants at a later date, perhaps when they come back the following year. Where the short-term work is ongoing and part of longer-term goals, coaches will need to have prioritized the short-term goals within the context of the long-term ones and ensure long-term goals are not sacrificed for a 'quick fix' in the short term.

8. Review and monitor progress

Reviewing is an invaluable part of both learning and performance for both the participants and the adventure sports coach. The nature of adventure sports themselves offers several opportunities to review progress during the activity itself, perhaps in natural breaks within the day where small discussion groups can easily be organized over a drink, lunch or at the end of the day if a more formal review is desired. Smaller, less-formal opportunities are also available as equipment is being loaded or unloaded, on ski lifts or while waiting for others in the group to assemble.

Whatever the context and length of time the coach is working in there is always the opportunity to take a few moments out to reflect on progress to date. In its shortest time frame this can be carried out during a session to allow the coach to recognize if the session context, pace and delivery are working as hoped with enough time to adapt the session. As already mentioned the end of session is a really useful time to reflect and use those thoughts to inform the planning of the next session so performance is progressed from one session to the next rather than delivering a series of 'one-offs'.

Where coaches wish to empower the performers and involve them in the direction their training is taking then reviewing and adjusting the goals set becomes a shared process. Reviewing can happen at a number of levels – performers themselves, shared conversations, coaches themselves or between coaches. With children and young people, parents may become involved in the process and even partners or families with adult learners. The review needs to reflect back against the goals set and consider the process and performance goals as well as the outcome ones. Where progress is on target then maintaining the current goals is straightforward unless anything else changes. Where performance is not as expected then goals need reviewing and adjusting. Often this can happen when performers progress at a different rate from that expected or when life events have an impact through work commitments or injury and illness. The R – Recorded – of the SMARTERP given earlier is important to keep track over the months or even years of training and can be a useful top up for confidence when revisited at a review point to remind participants of how far they have come.

9. Revisit goals in the mid and long term

Once sessions have been planned and delivered in the short term, coaches will need to reflect on where they are planning to progress to next. This would normally involve the coach revisiting the short-term goals set for the session first, but then revisiting the mid and longer-term goals to reflect on progress to date. Coaches who deliver a series of sessions in the short term may finish their contact with the client group at that point in time. In this case the coach reflections can be taken forward to next time they find themselves in a similar situation and consider what would they do the same and what would they do differently next time.

Where the goals set relate to a longer timescale and the delivery of a series of sessions within the short term is only part of the picture, coaches need to relate progress back to the goals set in the mid and long term. Such a reviewing process can happen on any number of occasions to check whether progress is still on target to achieve the longer-term goals. Then the whole Adventure Sports Planning Cycle (Figure 8.1) can be revisited any number of times on the way to achieving long-term ambitions. Within longer timescales coaches can schedule review points into the overall time scales, perhaps as training in one phase comes to an end and the next phase approaches. The performance profile can be revisited as well as scheduling fitness testing if required and the context is appropriate.

Planning in the longer term

Adventure sport coaches faced with longer-term planning can draw heavily on much of the literature already available for planning training programmes from sports coaching science (Navin, 2011; Pankhurst, 2007; Pyke, 2012; Robinson, 2010). The use of periodization (Bompa, 1999) is particularly useful to break down the longer timescale of the planning into smaller more manageable chunks of time. Many of the examples found in the literature will relate to competitive sport and encourage coaches to use annual training plans to organize the different elements of training across the year. The competitive season is clearly identified in the first instance and the training programme planned to prepare for this. The most important stages of competitions are normally identified so that coaches know when the performers will need to peak to achieve their best at these points. The relative importance of the psychological, physiological, technical and tactical elements of performance are considered across the different phases of the year and training elements clearly identified to suit the needs of the participants and the sport at that point in time. Opportunities to rest and recover are also identified and the year is generally broken down into the following sections:

- Competitive season – competitions are entered into the calendar with the importance of each part of the competitive calendar clearly prioritized (sometimes called a Peaking Index).
- Where the competitive season lasts over a number of months this can be broken down into early, mid and late season and coaches would normally have different expectations for each of these.
- Off season, or transition time, can be identified to give participants a rest from the sport or activity itself but to encourage involvement in other activities to maintain fitness levels before returning to training suitably refreshed.
- Pre-season preparation. This often starts with general physical preparation before becoming more specific to the activity or sport as the beginning of the competitive phase approaches.

Planning decisions revolve around where to place the emphasis of training at different points of the year from a physical, technical, tactical and mental perspective and how this emphasis will change over time. Coaches are encouraged to follow sound training principles and sequence their activities so that progression from one section of the training programme to the next is planned for. Often the terms macrocycle, mesocycle and microcycle are used to identify different time spans relating to months, weeks or a specific week, respectively, though some texts will extend the use of the term macrocycle as far as a year.

Sequencing of training, particularly the physical elements, needs planning to ensure that the participants are capable of the next stage of training. For example, working on power or speed would normally be underpinned with work on strength and conditioning and increased aerobic capacity to avoid injury. A good coach will ensure the building blocks are in place before extending the participants to the next level of training and guidance is available on which type of activities are advisable with what intensity and volume at which stage in the year in Chapter 10. Some adventure sports coaches will be working in an environment that is a competitive sport one, which means the notion of periodization and compartmentalizing training over an annual period may well be directly relevant.

For those coaches of adventure sports that are not working within a competitive sport environment, there is much information that can be transferred to support the planning of training programmes. Where the longer-term planning relates to preparation for a trip, trek, specific climb or attendance at training or assessment then this could be substituted for the competition as the start point within the planning process and the coach can work back from there, see Figure 8.3 and Voices from the Field below. Time scales may be different from an annual training programme but the notion of breaking down the time available into smaller more manageable phases and planning for each of these to be progressive is directly relevant. Consider the following example where a periodized plan was not followed in its totality but preparation was broken down into sections and review points introduced to monitor progress towards the target trip.

FIGURE 8.3 Chris Heaney's group rafting down the Grand Canyon.

Note: The three week trip involved five rafts and a number of kayaks.

Voices from the field

The planning for our 2012 descent of the Grand Canyon began in earnest in February 2011 when we received confirmation that we had been successful in securing a permit in the National Parks Service Lottery, arguably however the preparation began many years earlier. The main challenge faced by anyone planning an adventurous expedition (once the destination has been set) is the group make-up. The primary question considers whether each individual has the skills to safely complete the challenge? Where some individuals may lack certain skills it is possible others are able to balance that.

During the 11 years since first applying for the permit many experienced and trusted paddlers had expressed an interest to be part of the expedition – so the decisions were more about who to leave out than who to bring in. The decision was made to include some highly experienced paddlers, as well as some less-experienced family members, whose expertise and abilities would permit safe guidance by others down the river. The aim was to provide a healthy mix of individuals to assist positive group dynamics, given some of the strong characters involved.

Rafting down the Grand Canyon would involve large powerful rapids and whirlpools, air temperatures in the high forties, water temperatures barely above freezing, jagged rocky landscapes and shorelines, arduous daily routines of physical activity and, of course, the possibility of several of these components blending together if a raft were to flip and the rafters ended up taking extended swims. So planning for the trip needed to facilitate the monitoring of capabilities towards managing the physical, technical and psychological elements of this challenge. With many participants working, bringing the group together was difficult and two key dates were planned – October 2011 at Lee Valley Olympic slalom course for two days to get to know one another more fully, plan the details of the trip and of course assist the less experienced to become familiar with a white water environment. White water swimming, self-rescue and peer-rescue skills developed well over the balmy weekend and a second date was scheduled for May 2012 as a trip warm-up, at the River Oetz in Austria, for oar rig training/refresher and cold water acclimatization for the less experienced. An oar rig (as seen in Figure 8.3) is the kit carrier of choice for a canyon descent allowing one person to control the boat from a centralized frame and seat with long wooden oars to manoeuvre and power the boat down the rapids.

Chris Heaney, Senior Lecturer in Adventure Education at the University of Chichester and Team Leader and Coach for the Grand Canyon rafting trip 2012.

In the example pictured here, the team leader and coach had spent years developing his own personal expertise to be in a position to attempt such an expedition having developed his advanced white water expertise in various countries in the world and put together a team of paddlers with appropriate expertise. His reflections at the end of the Grand Canyon expedition provide interesting learning opportunities for others considering planning a similar trip. Chris reports he had envisaged the most significant challenges would have been in the preparation of the less-experienced group members. But, in fact, Chris reports his biggest challenge was group dynamics – an area that he had assumed would present few problems! If organizing a similar trip in the future Chris would now spend more time exploring the motivations of each individual rather than making assumptions about what is driving each individual to be part of this challenge. A lesson that could valuably be applied to many adventure sports coaching situations.

Where the goals of performers are continued participation and recreationally based without a competitive element then much of the detail outlined within a periodized training programme may not be relevant. However, coaches wishing to sustain motivation and develop performance should still be planning progression within the goals utilized. There is still plenty of opportunity to attach timescales to long-term goals and use mid- and short-term goals as stepping stones towards this. The emphasis may not be outcome goals here but are more likely to be performance and process based. Indeed, this is central to managing the motivational climate within sessions and encouraging long-term participation within the activity concerned.

Concluding comments

This chapter aimed to highlight some of the planning concerns that will be faced by the adventure sports coach whether working within a short-term situation or over a longer time span. It did not seek to be prescriptive but hoped to raise questions that will assist adventure sports coaches in their quest to plan effectively. All sports coaches need to consider planning for all elements of performance but for the adventure sports coach that is exacerbated by the variety of individuals and contexts they work in. We hope this chapter has given ideas to help address those needs.

References

British Canoe Union (2006). *Preparing for a Life in Sport: A Guide to Good Practice for all People Involved in Paddlesport*. Bangor, Wales: The National Coaching Foundation and The British Canoe Union, Pesda Press.

Bompa, T. O. (1999). *Periodization Theory and Methodology of Training*. Champaign, Illinois: Human Kinetics.

Butler, R. (1999). *Performance Profiling*. Leeds: National Coaching Foundation

Gray, P., Hodgson, C. and Heaney, C. (2011). Enhancing professional development for the adventure educator. In: M. Berry and C. Hodgson (ed.), *Adventure Education An Introduction*. Abingdon: Routledge Press.

Kerr, J. H. and Houge MacKenzie, S. (2012). Multiple motives for participating in adventure sports. *Psychology of Sport and Exercise*, 13(5), 649.

Navin, A. (2011). *Sports Coaching: A Reference Guide for Students Coaches and Competitors.* Ramsbury: The Crowood Press Ltd.

Pankhurst, A. (2007). *Planning and Periodisation.* Leeds: Coachwise Business Solutions.

Robinson, P. E. (2010). *Foundations of Sports Coaching.* Oxon, Routledge.

Stafford, I. (ed.) (2011). *Coaching Children in Sport.* Oxon, Routledge.

Sugerman, D. (2002) The relationship of age to motivation and skill development level in outdoor adventure programmes for older adults. *Society and Leisure,* Autumn, 25(2), 351–376.

9

TACTICS

The missing link in performance

Chris Hodgson, Paul Gray and David Pears

Introduction

Adventure sports performance is a complicated business. There is a popular story about Wolfgang Gullich, the first climber to climb the sport grade of 9a, who after a winter of hard physical training failed on one of his test pieces and exclaimed, "Climbing is so complex!" Wolfgang had trained extremely hard and even created new training protocols that would be adopted by elite climbers across the sport, but he had trained in something that he was already strong in and neglected things that may have helped his performance more. You might be thinking: well how do I avoid the same mistake? How can I know that I have considered all of the factors that might affect my athlete's performance? The answer might lie in completing some kind of activity demands profile for your activity before evaluating training needs. A framework that helps consider the elements that contribute to performance might also help. A number of sports, for example skiing and paddlesport, (see the BASI Alpine manual, 2014 and BCU Coaching Handbook, 2006) have adopted a framework that breaks performance into four main areas as part of their coach training syllabus. The physical, physiological, technical, tactical (PPTT) model (Figure 9.1) is a starting point for the coach to consider limitations on current performance levels and also to ensure that an athlete is developing in a rounded and holistic manner. We need to ask: where are this learner's priority needs? Do they need to be fitter, more accurate, more mentally robust, or do they need a smarter approach to the task?

Collins and Collins (2012) describe the adventure sports coach as: 'coach, captain and manager all while playing in the game'. It would be unthinkable in most traditional sports that a coach might take part in the activity with their performer during anything but basic practice but a sea kayak coach may well do exactly that: providing feedback and guidance during a high-performance activity

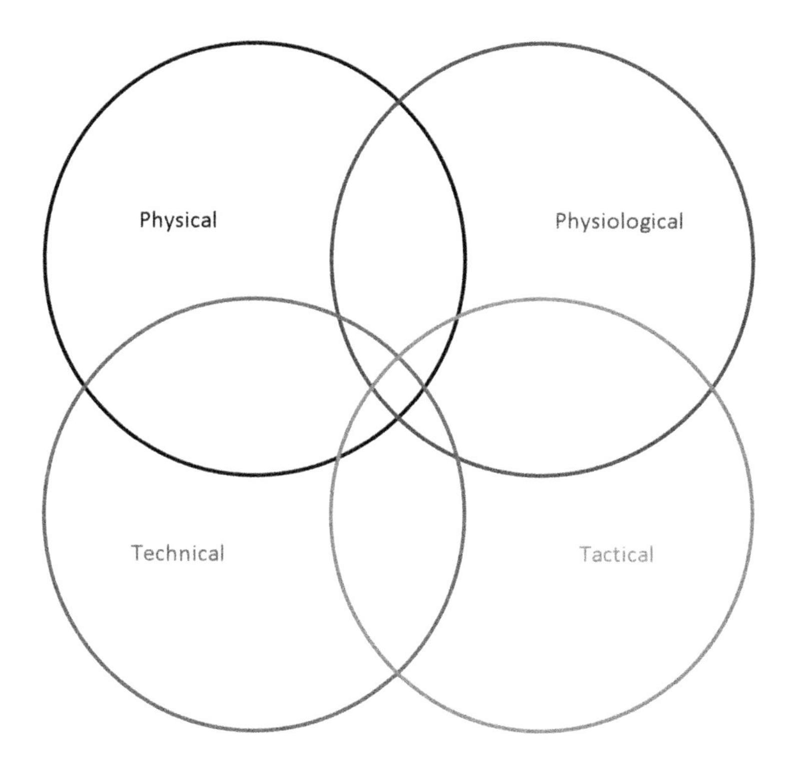

FIGURE 9.1 The physical, physiological, technical, tactical (PPTT) model of sports performance

in difficult conditions. They may even be contemplating at what point they may need to step into a leadership role or offer a physical intervention. This can create a role ambiguity between the coach and the learner and it can lead to the coach taking control of the decision-making aspects to maximize the chances of achieving performance outcomes for the activity. For example, a skiing coach may make the decision about line choice so the performer can concentrate on improved technical performance. Perhaps this explains to some extent why sometimes it is difficult to ensure that we cover all aspects contributing to performance and sometimes coaching the tactical aspect is not fully explored.

This chapter is about the tactical and strategic part of adventure sports performance and by implication its role as a key variable within coaching. In a traditional team sport like football it seems obvious that tactics are a huge part of the game. In fact, football managers are employed mainly for their abilities to make tactical choices that maximize their team's chances of success and organize training and team selections to address this component. In activities, such as triathlon or tennis, the coaching of tactics may be somewhat less obvious. However, tactics for these activities clearly exist and the coach will address tactics in the form of race plans or match strategy. The difference is that this will be part of the coach's role rather than requiring a specialist. Our position is that many adventure sports coaches, particularly in non-competitive disciplines, miss the opportunities for tactics to improve performance in our activities and that this can often inhibit the potential of our participants. Of course there are many adventure sports coaches who consider tactics and tactical decision-making part of their remit but there are also many who have either not considered it at all or have not really thought of how they can actively incorporate tactical choices into the way they work with learners. They provide the technical models and expect the performer to be able to apply these when appropriate. They forget to explore tactical decision-making with learners, such as where and when to rest during an activity or set up camp on a multi-day adventure. Decisions such as when to be well prepared with spare equipment and resources and when to be light and agile are crucial aspects of performance in mountaineering. In this chapter we want to help address this and send out a strong message that adventure sports coaches should be examining where tactics can impact on performance and making real choices about how they can incorporate tactics into their coaching plans for athletes. We will discuss the place of tactics in adventure sport and explore what tactics might look like as well as why a coach should consider coaching tactics explicitly and how they might go about it.

Tactics

So what are tactics? Well, tactics are generally considered to be a game plan that exploits the weakness of opponents and plays to your own strengths. Some commentators differentiate between a strategy, made before the start of play, and tactical decisions made during the activity (Grehaigne and Godbout, 1995). However, we would be inclined to see this as a continuum rather than a dichotomy. There are two separate but related elements to every tactical choice: an effective sport-specific knowledge base and the ability to make good decisions. Grehaigne and Godbout called the first element 'tactical knowledge'. They identify that this kind of knowledge is at the declarative level whereby performers can explain a set of rules or principles that they can employ to solve a particular problem. Having performers talk through the way they understand the sporting situation, its demands and the potential responses can test this knowledge. For example, a learner might identify different lines down a rapid along with the benefits and disadvantages of each.

If we do not have a human opponent to outwit does that mean that tactics have no real role in terms of our success or failure? Not at all: we can look at the environment as providing a challenge to overcome or we might view bettering our previous performances as a benchmark. If we are sailing a yacht upwind on a day trip then there are a multitude of ways we could achieve the same aim. We could stay close to shore and make a lot of tacks as we work upwind or we could sail out to sea on one enormous run, make a single tack and then sail one more enormous run to arrive at our target. And of course we could make any number of runs and tacks in between depending on how far from land we were prepared to go and how many turns we were prepared to make. If we take this situation apart we need to understand two things when we decide how to tackle this problem. First, we need to understand how the different options impact on the technical, physical and psychological demands to our crew and craft. Second, we need to consider how each route exposes us to a different set of environmental conditions that may be more or less favourable. We then need to be able to weigh up the consequences of each option and then choose between them so tactics are about understanding alternative courses of action and their likely outcomes and then making appropriate choices. The psychological consequences of an approach should not be underestimated, particularly in adventure sports, because these can easily be the difference between a traumatic experience and success.

Of course, knowing what the options are is not the same as picking, or constructing, a good solution. That is where decision-making comes in when we need to make a choice over our approach to the problem. For example, in winter mountaineering, knowing that we can either put our crampons on or cut steps with our axe to cross ice on a path is not the same as making the choice of which course of action to take. The tactical process moves from an evaluation of the environment to responses that are both deliberate and automatic or even unconscious adaptations, a process outlined in Figure 9.2. First, we have to recognize the icy conditions ahead, then we work out what options we have. Once we make our choice and put our crampons on then hopefully we automatically

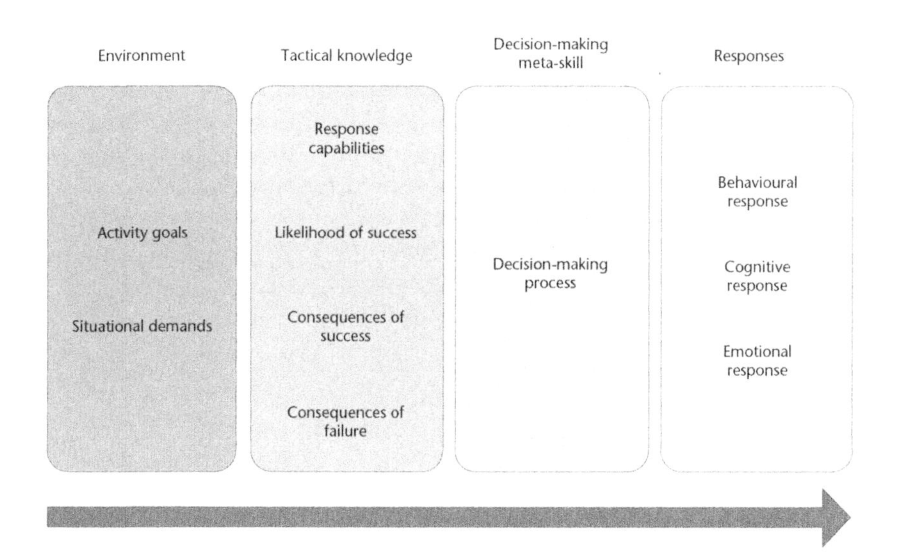

FIGURE 9.2 The tactical process from situational demands to behavioural, cognitive and emotional responses

adapt our motor pattern (behaviour) to walk in them on a variable surface. We will also think differently and our confidence will be improved (or not!) as we move in our crampons.

We hope you will agree that tactics actually play a major role in all of our activities even if we have not previously considered that process as tactics. So maybe we have two kinds of coach who could benefit from making tactics more of what they consider: one who has not really considered strategic decision-making and has focused on physical abilities or technical knowledge; another who has thought about coaching the choices that athletes make but has not before considered this as a job in its own right. Let us start by examining where tactical decisions come into adventure sport.

What are tactics in adventure sports?

It may seem initially that with no physical opponent the necessity of a game plan is much lower for an adventure sport than for a team game, or at least simpler to execute. However, often one approach will provide a far greater chance of a successful outcome than another 'solution' however technically well executed that other solution is. More often than not there may be a number of technically accurate solutions to an adventure challenge but some may differ greatly in the degree of effort required, or energy that would be expended. Maybe the difference in one approach over another will simply come down to aesthetics or feelings of satisfaction in the performer themselves. The choice between alternative courses of action can be difficult because often the challenge that adventure sports present us with is not entirely stable: as our environment changes so too do the demands and the costs and benefits of differing approaches. More often than not we are trying to predict events in an uncertain future. There is a real interaction between the dynamic environmental demands and the individual participant, their attributes and desires. If we want to maximize the performance and enjoyment of our adventure athletes then it makes a lot of sense to invest time in making sure that they will pick the most productive response, or at least not pick from the least productive ones.

Often coaches do not discuss tactics in adventure sport because they have not worked out exactly what they are. In adventure sports the distinction between technical competence and tactical competence can be 'woolly'. A quick search of the sports section of a decent library will unearth books on tactics for traditional sports such as football, tennis and netball. Triathlon or running magazines will contain articles about race strategy for your fastest marathon or Olympic distance event. The Tour de France a few years ago was a complete mystery to most non-competitive cyclists with its different jersey components within the event for sprinting, climbing and the coveted yellow jersey of the 'Général Classement' category. Now that it has become a televised event with a greater following it is more common that non-cyclists understand the principles behind the peloton, the breakaway, the lead out trains of the sprinters and the dogged determination and consistency of the Général Classement riders. How many skiers would consider their speed through the snow when skiing off-piste a tactical choice and that actually moving too slowly might have negative consequences? Another problem is that adventure sports coaches can easily become fixated on the outcome of tactical choices rather than viewing the tactical process as important. If we are concerned with coaching for independence then it is vital that we consider the process of tactical choices with our learners rather than just examine outcomes and hope that improvements in the process follow. We need to remember that sometimes even the best tactical decision might not lead to a successful outcome and that we can sometimes perceive the outcome of a poor choice as successful.

What is a tactic in an adventure sport?

The answer is that lots of choices we can make when or before we start performing should be considered tactical choices. Another way of looking at tactics is that we should have a strategic plan for the activity. It may be a simple plan with a single set of tactical choices or it may be a plan with several steps … each of these steps having tactical choices within them. We are also very likely to make further tactical choices in terms of dynamic decisions about our approach during an activity. This is an area that adventure sports coaches actually have an advantage in. As we can undertake the physical journey with the learner we can discuss decision-making in real time, something few other coaches can really do. A non-participant coach can only frontload tactic choices and then review decision-making during an activity after the performance is completed. One of the most basic but also most common strategic choices will revolve around pacing an activity. Other choices might involve considering the motivation behind participation (see Chapter 11) and trying to match tactical decisions to realize them: some people want to maximize performance; others want to feel safe and in control.

Tactics in practice

Pacing

As we have already said a critical aspect of strategy and tactics often involves choices about pacing. In an endurance activity, pacing is generally about energy economy. This can even be true on a long single pitch rock climb or an extended white water rapid. If the intensity of an activity is higher then it could be about power or strength economy. The performer is making judgements about where to spend their valuable but ultimately limited physical resources. Expend them too quickly and we risk failure to complete the task or at least a sub-optimal performance. Too conservative and we might end up with too much left in the tank and a correspondingly sub-optimal performance. In an intermittent activity we need to be working at a level that gets the job done but allows us to temporarily step up to the greater demand. A technical climb on a mountain bike might be like

I regularly coach a junior competition climbing team who have benefited hugely from understanding competition tactics. A few examples include: learning from the previous performances of fellow competitors, when and for how long to rest, what and when to eat and how to ensure you push hard enough to qualify into the finals but reserve enough energy for later. The tactical options in a climbing competition are endless and it is often the key to beating an opponent who may be a stronger, better climber in any other situation.

The same theory applies to achieving a long-term project or on-sighting a route. A recent client of mine wanted to on-sight a route he had had his eye on for a while. Prior to this ascent we developed a pre-climb ritual. This was a tactical way of maximizing his chance of success. It included a visualization of how he predicted he would perform the moves but especially clipping and potential rest positions.

Belinda Fuller – Performance Coach and Nutritionist – Founder and Director of Be Climbing
www.beclimbing.co.uk

this with a steady output but places where we need to work very hard followed by 'riding recoveries'.

Eric Horst has argued for a number of years that pacing is a main skill in rock climbing and that often climbers climb too slowly on steeper ground. He argues that too much time spent on hard sections can lead to higher levels of fatigue than a less-than-perfect performance that gets the difficult section over with more quickly. He suggests practicing climbing the same route at different speeds and attending to the balance between time efficiency and accuracy.

Make the easy bit hard to make the hard bit easier

This approach works when the demands of the hardest part of the endeavour mean we are actually better off making the surrounding tasks a little harder if we can make the hard part easier. Years ago, Chris Hodgson found himself stuck on a ledge on an ice route with a really difficult exit. The irony was that I could have avoided the exit entirely by not climbing onto the ledge at all. I had climbed the easiest path to the harder ice but if I had just climbed the slightly steeper ice to the right I would have avoided the steepest ice on the pitch and the awkward transition. I learned my lesson and two weeks later I climbed the route again and ensured that I took the more consistent line with a harder start but no obvious transitions. I easily climbed the route that day.

Emotional economy

Adventure sports often have a significant emotional demand and managing this can be a major aspect of strategy and tactics. Following a defined feature on a mountain walk can ease the navigational load but might also reduce the level of perceived uncertainty and therefore ease the emotional load. We do have to be careful though because paddling too close to the shore in rough conditions can actually make the task harder and scarier. Emotional economy can be important because stressors are cumulative and there is a mental energy cost associated with uncertainty and anxiety. Adventure activities can create high levels of anxiety. Overcoming this anxiety and managing acceptable doses can be rewarding but we might need to manage the overall volume of exposure if we want to be successful or even just have a good experience.

Doug Cooper highlights psychology and in particular the emotional control aspect of open crossings in his book on sea kayaking: *Rough Water Handling*. Doug suggests a number of approaches to open crossing including increasing trust in equipment through familiarity and picking a team that you will be at ease with. Having an alternative strategy in terms of escape plans and the equipment needed to make choices can also be reassuring. One problem though can be when the additional equipment need for options like bivouacking mean that the bivouac can become a certainty rather than a plan B. Sometimes we need to be strong enough to ensure that we do not undermine our own plan A.

Technique economy

This strategy might mean deliberately picking a physically or mentally tougher solution because it minimizes the technical demands of the situation. For example, on an off-piste tour we might pick a longer line that includes more traversing or even some uphill work to avoid the most demanding descent. This approach makes sense if we feel that we do not have the technical skills to tackle the more direct line with enough certainty, but feel we do have the physical resources necessary for hiking. It may be a good strategy for a physically strong performer who also has technical limitations on a day where performance is important. However, there is a danger here that this becomes a strategy during training and it is really important that the adventure sports coach can recognize this and make a distinction between performance days and training days.

Dale Goddard and Udo Neumann discussed the weakest link principle in their book *Performance Rockclimbing* and argued that we need to ensure that in training we avoid playing to our strengths and instead focus on the things holding us back. It can be tempting for a performer to practice their strengths. It can be equally tempting for a coach to focus on the things that they are strong in when coaching others. We need to ensure that we do not fall into that trap with our clients.

In a white water rafting event, the choice of route to successfully negotiate a set of gates is always a challenging one. A typical, although technically complex combination, may include a tight left turn, rapid acceleration, tight right turn with minimal sideways displacement and conclude with a powerful drive up an eddy: a manoeuvre known as an S-turn. Alternatively a less technical but more physically demanding solution would be a simple power drive across the current. The outcome of each choice would ultimately produce a similar position on the water. This decision and question of whether the team is physically and/or technically competent would be considered when planning every sequence of slalom gates. Now Paul Gray's rafting team have always been strong in short power strokes and concentrated on this within training. However, their technique skills are not as strong and they had avoided this in training. Following recent performances they are now focusing more on the technical side of slalom within their training.

Coincidence timing

Coincidence timing happens in a situation where everything depends on arriving at the right place at the right time. An example of this would be a sea kayaking trip through the Gulf of Corryvreckan in the Inner Hebrides. At peak flow the Corryvreckan is the third largest whirlpool in the world. Clearly it is unlikely you want to be there in a sea kayak at such times and so the day revolves around timing your paddle to arrive when the gulf is in a condition that you are going to approve of. At a smaller scale paddling out through surf may require similar but more dynamic timing judgements. Other examples of coincidence timing might be planning a mountain tour to cross a dangerous slope at the safest time or even when to paddle out through the waves on a surf board.

Some judgements about timing may be harder for example trying to be in a position to make the most of a weather window for a summit bid or open crossing. In these situations you are working with incomplete information and so it is much harder to know that you made the best decision. There is always an element of chance when making a call you hope is your best; however; you may be unlucky or make a mistake, but it may work out (see Figure 9.3). Mark Twight, the American alpinist and author of *Extreme Alpinism*, describes the idea that you can control a situation in the mountains as vanity and argues that you have to learn to accept that you are acting in a chaotic and uncertain environment. This acceptance of the limits in terms of the control you have is an essential skill for these sorts of scenarios, but also makes unpicking decisions retrospectively much harder.

Strategic decision-making

Choosing between alternatives is an important aspect of the tactical component of performance but this is probably more neglected than consideration of the options available. Decision-making is a complicated area and there are a number of approaches that have attempted to answer the question as to how exactly human beings make choices. Another problem is that coaches themselves often are not aware of the mechanism or process behind their own decision-making. In fact,

FIGURE 9.3 A successful outcome but what about the process?

according to Nash and Collins (2006) the more experienced a coach is then the greater the impression that decision-making is intuitive or a result of 'gut reaction' and therefore cannot be taught.

If the situation is familiar then we would expect the performer to retrieve a well-known solution from long-term memory. However, when this is not possible then we adopt an approach that uses a set of cognitive rules or principles to guide our choices. The evidence is that experts are much more likely to apply a rules or principles approach. However, it seems that there may be two kinds of expert performer: routine and adaptive. Adaptive experts are much more able to cope with varied demands and changing or dynamic situations. Adventure sports are likely to favour the adaptive expert model and so we need to ensure that we are helping our leaners become adaptive experts rather than routine experts.

Behaviourist

Possibly the most simple approach to decision-making is the one taken by the behaviourist school of psychology. Psychologists like John Watson, Burrhus Skinner, Edward Thorndike and Ivan Pavlov examined how outcomes affect the likelihood of behaviour being repeated. Behaviourists essentially believe that the decisions we make are all routed in our past experience and that to a great extent we choose a solution because in the past it has been associated with a pleasurable outcome. If this is not possible then we will choose to avoid a solution that in the past has been associated with a negative or painful outcome. Problem solving to behaviourists is a trial-and-error process with accidental success being rewarded and reinforced and failure being punished. Sometimes we do not even know that our behaviour is being reinforced.

There is a story that a class of students decided to train their professor as a prank and they all agreed to behave in a disinterested manner whenever he moved away from a waste basket and to behave in a very attentive way when he approached the basket. Unfortunately it seems that the story is simply an urban legend but it has stuck because the principles are valid. It is quite possible to learn to behave in a certain manner because we get a reward without realizing what we are doing. Behaviourists argue that complicated responses just have had more layers of subtle training. However our human experience about decision-making is often at odds with the stimuli–response pairing model of behaviourism. Trial-and-error with natural consequences can be effective but it is limited in its application to lots of problems and in our settings may be downright dangerous. It is also a strategy that is more often associated with novices rather than expert performers.

Information processing

The information processing approach suggests that all decision-making is reliant on our memory systems. Previous experiences, our reactions and the outcomes are stored in long-term memory and these are compared with the present situation in short-term memory (or working memory) in order to understand what is going on and decide on a course of action. An appropriate response is then retrieved from the long-term memory and applied to the present situation. Information processing puts a much greater emphasis on solving a new problem through the application of existing information and this approach may include some trial-and-error but it allows for a more forward-thinking problem-solving approach than pure behaviourism. In fact, it allows us to learn general approaches to decision-making as well as particular approaches to solving specific problems.

An algorithmic approach involves learning a solution that always works and always carrying out the action that way. This can work even when the learner does not understand why the approach is effective. I remember as a young trainee being taught to 'teach' skiing and being given a set of exercises to learn for each class. My job was very simple: have learners complete the exercises in the prescribed manner so they are ready for the next set. If they took longer to complete them or need correction that was fine as long as I got the point where they could do them all. I now realize many of the exercises were to trick the skier into learning on their own. Following the rules meant I did not have any more decisions to make. Unfortunately once we get past snowplough turns life becomes more complicated and it just is not possible to have rules for everything. Or, alternatively, the set of rules would take so long to work through that we would get very old before coming to a conclusion.

Psychologists such as McMorris and MacGillivary (1988) have approached the problem of decision-making by constructing a list of questions that a performer will answer in order to arrive at a decision. This approach is referred to as a hierarchical framework in that the more direct solutions are explored first. A mountaineer may ask: can we walk un-roped here? If the answer is no, the next question might be can we move together if we were roped up? The next solution may involve moving together with intermediate runners and so on and so on... An argument against this approach is that it can take a long time to reach the right answer. McMorris suggests it is possible that we actually start further down the hierarchy when a solution is obviously impossible. For instance, if we are already roped up and using intermediate runners then the next secure option is likely to involve fixed belays so when things get more difficult we start with that option.

A heuristics approach to decision-making sounds very sophisticated but really it boils down to using 'rules of thumb' to select an appropriate strategy. This approach is not about optimizing the outcome but it is about selecting a strong strategy with a better than average chance of success. For example, a hillwalker may be taught 'never walk more than 1,000 metres without some kind of check-off point'. This strategy is not so much about getting a great outcome but it minimizes lots of consequences of getting it wrong and the walker does not need to think about the appropriateness of not breaking the rule very often. It also does not rely on learning a set of steps to reach a solution. Lots of group management decisions that people are taught on instructor training programmes will come into this category – simple messages that avoid lots of problems most of the time like keeping a less competent person closer to the coach.

Another popular approach to strategic planning is means–end analysis. It is also one that lots of coaches in adventure sports will be familiar with. Means–end analysis really just means starting at the goal and working backwards. It is a good approach for activities that have a clear destination. It is often the approach that we would use when planning a route on a mountain or down a river such as in Figure 9.4. It is a good way of coming up with a plan that does not leave us stranded but perhaps it is not so good in terms of choosing between alternative strategies.

Compensatory and non-compensatory decision-making

Logically we should evaluate all the potential benefits and disadvantages of each choice we have when we make a decision between alternatives. This would be called a compensatory decision-making strategy because every factor is taken into account. It sounds great in theory but in fact there can easily be an overwhelming number of factors to consider for anything but a simple choice. The evidence is that we often revert to non-compensatory decision-making where effectively some factors are completely ignored when we make our decision. There are number of main ways that we can reduce the factors we consider.

A conjunctive strategy means setting minimum standards for each factor. We then do not ask how beneficial a factor is: we just ask is it at the required standard

FIGURE 9.4 Sometimes it is all about ending up in the right place and everything else is secondary

or not. This approach simplifies the judgements we are making and gives a framework for acceptance or rejection. In a sense this is the sort of decision we tend to make when we evaluate coaches for an assessment or looking at competence within a role. It works when not achieving one aspect of our goal undermines the whole approach no matter how good the other parts are.

Elimination by aspects is a strategy for reducing the options. We might use this approach when there is lots of choice and a particular characteristic of a solution may be unsafe or just unpalatable. For example, if we have a group planning a mountain walk when heavy rain is expected we may eliminate all routes that would involve stream crossings. On our off-piste run we may eliminate all options that include walking out. Again this is one of the strategies that experienced adventure sports coaches will be familiar with even if they do not recognize it as a specific strategy that aids decision-making. This is one of the crucial things that we need to think about if we are coaching tactics – how do we actually make those choices ourselves and are we making those strategies for decision-making explicit to our learners and explaining why we think that approach to decision-making is appropriate?

A maxi-max strategy means we make our choice by picking the option with the strongest positive feature. With this strategy we ignore the weakness of each solution in an attempt to maximize the potential benefit. This approach can work if the weak aspects of the solution are not going to cause us real problems. This approach tends to be high risk–high gain. Its application for adventure sport is probably limited because often the consequences may be too dire. However, it may be appropriate for controlled situations, such as a competition day plan, where we think the increased risks may be worth the potential reward and the safe strategy will create a good change of the outcome we would like.

During a recent European White Water Rafting Championship, the GB Masters Raft Team was confronted with such a situation within the slalom discipline of the event. The sequence of moves between gates 2 and 3 could be accomplished through a technical and powerfully demanding sequence or one of relative ease, which was achievable but time costly. The faster but more technically demanding sequence had the potential of receiving a 50 second penalty, due to the increased risk of a missed gate. This higher risk but higher gain strategy came with the consequence of being placed lower in the rankings and potentially losing a podium position. As two runs were allowed the team decided on a 'one of each' approach but this still did not result in a medal. Oh well, back to the training!

A mini-max strategy means that we consider the weaknesses of each approach and pick the solution with the strongest weak feature. This strategy means we may well not get the solution with the most gains but we avoid the consequences of the worst aspects of the solutions on offer. It is the sort of solution that we would go for when we cannot afford for things to go wrong and this is more important than big gains. This way of thinking is well suited to emergency planning and therefore particularly useful to adventure sports coaches and performers. Maxi-max strategies tend to prioritize maximum gain – accepting higher risk for greater potential reward. Mini-Max strategies are conservative and are about minimizing risk – maximizing the chance of getting an acceptable result.

Intuitive decision-making in experts

The naturalistic decision-making approach championed by psychologists like Kahneman and Klein (2009) suggest that often experts in time-pressed situations do not actually consciously process alternative strategies and in fact they arrive at a single strategy and then evaluate it on its own merits. They will then adjust this strategy based on the evaluative process and only if it appears that it will not provide an acceptable solution do they go back to the starting blocks and formulate a new plan. The problem with this approach is that you already need to be an expert with many hours of experience for this level of intuitive decision-making. This approach to understanding good decision-making has been effective when experts seem to be able to consistently make decisions that are shown to be more effective than we initially expect. The main appeal of this approach is that discovering the cues that these experts attend to can be helpful in informing training and education programmes for others.

One attempt to examine tactical decision-making in sailing was by Araujo *et al.* (2005). They had sailors of different abilities complete races on a computer simulation. A major finding was that the inexperienced sailors appeared to make more exploratory behaviours where they adjusted their craft to see what would happen. The study also highlighted that expert sailors were more able to prioritize the most important information and that they seemed to do this quite automatically. Araujo *et al.* criticized the assumption that expert decision-making is always a rational process based on recall of a 'best' solution and that in a dynamic environment tactical decision-making is actually a continuous process of responding to relevant cues in the environment. James Jerome Gibson used the term 'attunement to affordances' to explain how with experience we become better able to automatically process the opportunities in our environment. As pathways to a goal are often neither completely right or completely wrong we need to be aware of this when we evaluate tactical decision-making. Expert performers will stay flexible in the way they tune their overall strategy to solving the problem responding to changes in the situation as they occur.

Psychologists who focus on failures in expert decision-making have called the infallibility of intuitive expert decision-making into question. The heuristics and biases approach to expert decision-making, supported by Daniel Kahneman, looks at situations where expert decisions have been shown to be wrong sometimes with disastrous results. An area in adventure sport where the heuristic and biases approach has been applied is in decisions that backcountry skiers make about snow stability and avalanche risk. McCammon (2004) identified six kinds of heuristic traps that can occur in decision-making when adventure sports participants make decisions during recreational activities: familiarity, consistency, acceptance, the expert halo, social facilitation and scarcity (these are explored more in Chapter 12).

Common problems in decision-making include:

- Hypothesis locking when we hold onto a view regardless of incoming information.
- Entrapment where we have already invested in a solution so we continue to pursue it.
- Expectation bias when we only attend to information that confirms our earlier appraisal.
- Hindsight effects where we interpret past events as more likely than they were.
- Framing where presenting a problem different way would result in a different solution.

How are training tactics different?

As tactics are about selecting an approach to a problem rather than technical accuracy it is very hard to teach tactical decision-making through a traditional demonstration and replication model. This is particularly true in situations where the effectiveness of a decision will not be known until we see future events unfold for instance where an opponent's behaviour or unpredictable changes in conditions come into play. It is also often impossible to be sure how an alternative strategy would have worked out because the outcome is a product of an interaction between the environment and the performer's behaviours rather than a simple cause and effect relationship. For this reason, part practice and simplification practice strategies can lead to flawed learning where a technically accurate response can provide positive reinforcement of an untested or even questionable tactical approach. This is a major reason why we need to be very cautious of overemphasis on skills, drills and part practice. As a trainee ski instructor, Chris Hodgson was taught a plethora of stepping and pressure control exercises. I did learn to execute a wide range of motor patterns but the reality was that these did little for my skiing performance or my understanding of ski teaching because ultimately I did not understand what I was being asked to develop or how and when it would fit into my skiing. I now look at that time as a lost opportunity because the lesson was never embedded into a skiing context.

In traditional sports, Bunker and Thorpe (1982) proposed a model known as 'teaching games for understanding' as a response to a perceived over-emphasis on decontextualized skills and drills practice. Since then the Bunker-Thorpe model has been both highly influential and widely debated. A key criticism is that it can become a 'cognitive-first' approach, which runs counter to much of the more current motor skill acquisition theory. On the other hand, it emphasizes practice that includes genuine opportunities for decision-making as the cornerstone of sporting development. The teaching games for understanding approach suggests that coaches should set up interactive and naturalistic practice that includes key constraints that encourage learners to adopt beneficial approaches to problem solving and also that the decision-making aspect of sports performance is deliberately empathized and unpicked by the coach. An adventure sport coach using this approach might employ a climbing route with steep sections but good resting positions to encourage their learner to adopt a 'climb quickly between rests' approach.

Tactical decision-making needs to be practiced in context. Learners need lots of interaction with opportunities to make decisions and experience the consequences of these decisions. Grehaigne and Godbout describe this as a constructivist approach (see more in Chapter 2) because the learning situation must be learner- rather than content-based. We can approach strategic decision-making from a theoretical perspective but the tuning and testing of tactical decisions ultimately can only occur in an experientially based context. However, there may well be a need for a cognitive process when learners will need to analyse the activity and explore the reasons for success or failure. Grehaigne and Godbout refer to 'repeated hypothesis-verification cycles' where learners will link experiential and cognitive activities in order to improve their own understanding of the rules they apply to solving tactical problems. The goal is to develop what Bunker and Thorpe described as 'game sense' that will result in positive behavioural changes and choices.

How will we know that a learner has game sense?

We will see it in the choices they make on how to apply their skill set. A skier will travel an intelligent route down the mountainside. They will accelerate to an appropriate speed before making any turns than drop into an appropriate rhythm. They will stretch the turns on one side and move laterally to position themselves so that they can proceed more directly down the fall line on the crucial section and as the slope flattens they will lengthen the turns to maintain speed. Each of these decisions on their own could be accidental but in combination they paint a picture of a skier who knows exactly how to approach each section of the slope and responding to angle, snow quality and future terrain.

Coaching decision-making

Tactical understanding is complex and is central to the success of coaching this aspect of performance. The learner needs to be provided with an environment where tactical implications become increasingly progressive rather than overwhelming. As soon as the coach needs to intervene and tell the learner how to solve the tactical problem the opportunity for development in the tactical decision-making realm is lost. Coaches might see a coaching session in which they explain choices to learners as a lesson with a tactical focus however the lessons here are unlikely to proceed past the knowledge phase.

A useful model for coaches interested in providing situations with a tactical choice is Newell's constraint-led practice model (1986) shown in Figure 9.5. Newell viewed behaviour as an emergent response from the interaction of the individual's attributes, the task the wish to achieve and the environment in which the task takes place. When any one of these elements is changed the interaction changes and the emergent response is different. As coaches, if we want performers to develop alternative behaviours then we can achieve this by managing any or all of the three elements; in other words, constraining them. For example, if we want our mountain biker to develop a more aerodynamic position on the bike then a ride against a severe headwind (environmental constraint) will mean that the rider is forced to adjust to the practice situation. There will be a direct feedback system in place as the rider responds to the situation and tries to find an optimal position for them. The beauty of the approach is that they are likely to achieve an outcome that is to some extent unique and includes their own limitations and strengths. A less flexible rider will find a different compromise than a more flexible one. They might also find other tactical solutions like riding in a wind shadow.

The coach's role within this model is normally to set up quality practice/learning situations by setting an environment and task and behaviours will emerge in an effort to solve the problem (individual constraints can also be used,

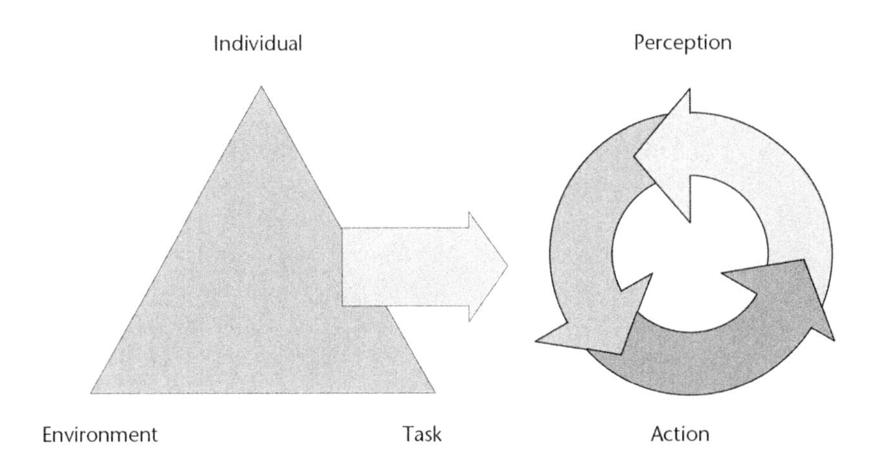

FIGURE 9.5 A constraints-led perspective on learning emphasising the interaction of performer, task and environmental constraints

for instance, forward paddling blindfolded). The learner will become immersed in a cycle of action and perception where they evaluate what is happening and the opportunities as they act and react within, and on, this dynamic environment, which may well be changing because of their actions. Perception and action are by necessity tied together as we act the situation changes and as the situation changes we continue to react. For example, when sailing a boat into an area of clean wind that we have spotted the vessel reacts to the changes and we act on the boat accordingly. The boat then reacts to that adjustment picking up speed and we need to adjust to that by sheeting in as the apparent wind moves, and so on.

There is a genuine tension between stability of solutions and adaptability. On one hand, we want to be sure that performers will respond in an appropriate way each time they are in a similar situation and that success is not down to random chance. On the other hand, we want the learner to be able to adapt to the subtle differences in their environment, their own physical condition and the specific task demands. Remember that earlier we said that we wanted our learners to become adaptive experts. If we want to develop tactical awareness and decision-making we need to control the variability in the practice situation so that the variance is not so great we get random solutions – this will improve consistency and stability. However, we need to ensure there is always a degree of variability in the practice conditions we set so that we avoid a deterministic and predictable system where the response needs no adjustment or tuning and become stereotyped because our environment is seldom stable or predicable. The coach's role is to play on the boundary between a system that is too difficult to predict and one that is too easy. As the learner improves they will naturally need a more dynamic situation in order to be challenged but we still do not want them to be overwhelmed.

A novice skier needs a uniform slope with little in the way of aspect or gradient shifts and consistent snow. As they improve we can slowly increase the complexity of the terrain. There is an important distinction here between difficult ground that is a technical challenge and complex ground that is a tactical challenge. More complex ground is likely to include some higher technical challenges as well but we need to ensure that we do not increase technical difficulty too much so that it overshadows the tactical aspect. Our expert skier should be comfortable moving through transitions of slope and snow and moving between groomed terrain and moguls, making necessary adjustments without having to come to a stop each time something changes. The temptation will be to stop and 'prime' our learner every time there is a change but what we actually need to do is accurately set up the task and select the environment that allows the learner to explore without the need for our continuous instructions. If the lesson is not quite working then we adjust the task instructions or the environment until it does – we do not solve the problem for the learner ourselves.

The use of video analysis has become quite common in motor skill development but it also offers a vehicle for tactical exploration outside of 'real time' activities. Video analysis can be used in a reviewing format where the learner's actual performance and situation is unpicked retrospectively and various solutions to a problem are explored along with the outcomes of the choice made at the time. Modern activity style cameras like the ubiquitous Go Pro provide a good opportunity to gather video footage of a performer in a natural setting. A coach on a mountain bike, skis or powerboat can follow their learner without intervening capturing a record of line speed and technical choices the rider, skier or sailor makes. Another way to use video is to provide the learner with video clips of novel situation that they have not been in by looking at other performers. The live action can be frozen providing an opportunity to discuss 'what happens next'. In the analysis it is essential that the main discussion is on the tactical decisions rather than technical execution. The coach and learner should examine the actual decisions made as well as alternative course of action. The appropriateness of choice may well be a little fuzzy and this is something to accept rather than shy away from. Sometimes even a 'bad' choice can work. One thing that has to be remembered is that the performer needs to have the ability to execute the plan, so discussing something beyond their ability (physically, technically or psychologically) can occasionally be useful but often is not.

Conclusion

Coaching tactics can be difficult and frustrating. The gains our learners make are often nowhere near as obvious in the short term as technical gains can be. However, if we neglect this aspect of performance we are doing our learners a disservice by limiting their potential. We are also likely to be guilty of keeping them dependent on us to make decisions on their behalf, unable to recognize the conditions for themselves to use what they have learned.

Key messages are that we need to help learners develop strategies in lots of sporting situations. It is vital that they learn to recognize all sources of likely information for themselves and perhaps develop deliberate 'scanning techniques' for common situations. Weighing up evidence carefully and knowing what they want to achieve and the kind of approach they want to adopt is vital. They need to know are they working to minimize risk, economize on effort or maximize their enjoyment because the strategy they formulate is likely to be different for each of these outcomes.

We need to coach leaners to continue to check the evidence that their decisions were based on. And also that it is okay to change strategy if the environment throws up an unexpected challenge, things are not going to plan or their capabilities change as they become fatigued or they get in to a position to be more successful than they had thought. It is a natural human condition to want to stick to the plan and feel consistent but it can be the wrong choice and can limit our outcomes or even become dangerous. Because we had to change the plan does not mean out initial assessment was wrong.

Performers at all levels need to practice in representative situations frequently where they can experiment with strategy and reactive choices. This can take some management to ensure it happens in an environment with enough leeway or backup systems in place but we do have to avoid the easy option of presenting 'the solution' and then getting learners to action it. Scenario-based learning and the use of constraints can help us provide learners with opportunities to gain real feedback about their choices. Reviewing these in regard to tactical choices and reflecting on decisions made during actual pressured performance can also provide learners with more of an insight into strategy and tactics. Ultimately tactics is one quarter of the PPTT model and we should ensure that at every level of learning we offer participants the opportunity to develop this aspect. The alternative is that perhaps we are really more of a 'technical consultant' than a rounded adventure sports coach. Tactics are a crucial aspect of performance in all adventure sports and there is still a lot of potential from a practical perspective to incorporate tactical aspects into coaching, but also to recognize tactics more formally within coach education for the adventure sector.

References

Araujo, D., Davids, K. and Serpa, S. (2005). An ecological approach to expertise effects in decision-making in a simulated sailing regatta. *Psychology of Sport and Exercise*, 6, 671–692.

Bunker, D. and Thorpe, R. (1982). A model for the teaching of games in the secondary school. *Bulletin of Physical Education*, 10, 9–16.

BASI Alpine Manual. Available at: www.basi.org.uk/shopitem/the-new-basi-alpine-combination-manual.aspx retrieved 2 December 2014.

Collins, L. and Collins, D. (2012). Conceptualizing the adventure-sports coach. *Journal of Adventure Education and Outdoor Learning*, 12, 81–93.

Cooper, D. (2012). *Rough Water Handling: A Practical Manual, Essential Knowledge for Intermediate and Advanced Paddlers*. Bangor, Wales: Pesda Press.

Ferrero, F. (ed.) (2006). *British Canoe Union Coaching Handbook*. Bangor, Wales: Pesda Press.
Goddard D. and Neumann, U. (1993). *Performance Rockclimbing*. Mechanicsburg, PA: Stackpole Books.
Grehaigne, J-F. and Godbout, P. (1995). Tactical Knowledge in Team Sports From a Constructivist and Cognitivist Perspective. *Quest*, 47, 490–505.
Kahneman, D. and Klein, G. (2009). Conditions for intuitive expertise: A failure to disagree. *American Psychologist*, 64, 515–526.
McCammon, I. (2004). Heuristic traps in recreational avalanche accidents: Evidence and implications. *Avalanche News*, 68, 1–10.
Nash, C. and Collins, D. (2006). Tacit Knowledge in Expert Coaching: Science or Art? *Quest*, 58, 465–477.
McMorris, T. and MacGillivary, W. W. (1988). An investigation into the relationship between field independence and decision making in soccer. In: *Science and Football*, T. Reilly, A. Lees, K. Davids and W. J. Murphy (eds), London: E. & F.N. Spon, 552–557.
Newell, K. M. (1986). Constraints on the Development of Coordination. In: M. Wade and H. T. A. Whiting (eds), *Motor Development in Children: Aspects of Coordination and Control*. Dordrecht, The Netherlands: Martinus Nijhoff, 341–360.
Twight, M. and Martin, J. (1999). *Extreme Alpinism: Climbing Light, Fast and High*. Seattle, WA: Mountaineers Books.

10

TRAINING PRINCIPLES FOR ADVENTURE SPORTS

John Kelly and John Metcalfe

Introduction

The principles of training and nutrition as they relate to specific adventure sports is beyond the scope of a single chapter and the umbrella 'adventure sports' contains a myriad different activities (and sub-activities) with each having their own physiological demands and training requirements. However, despite these numerous permutations there are training themes and processes common to all adventurous sports. It is not the purpose of this chapter to address the specific training principles in great detail. Our philosophy is to discuss these principles in the general context of contemporary adventurous sports with an emphasis on an applied approach. For a deeper scientific understanding of the training and bioenergetic principles you may wish to refer to more specific texts (Beachle and Earle, 2008; Foran, 2000; Cissik, 2012; McArdle *et al.*, 2014).

Training for adventurous sports

The first step in the training process is to ascertain exactly what it is you are training for. This may sound obvious, but the adage 'think before you sweat' is never more apt than here. An error at this stage may lead at best to inefficient training, or worse detrimental training. The more detailed you are at this stage the more efficient your training will be. Initially you need to perform a bioenergetic analysis of your sport, the simplest way to do this is to define the activity. Let us use surfing as an example. Surfing can be described as a sport comprising high-intensity bouts of exercise punctuated with medium-intensity activity (see Table 10.1). This basic framework can be determined through simple observation. It is important to note that this information will be anecdotal and subjective so it is vital that you gather it from well-informed athletes and coaches, and where possible triangulate

TABLE 10.1 Sub-activities of surfing

Activity	*Description*
1. The paddle-out	The surfer is in a prone position and paddles out to the line-up using the arms. This activity may require duck-dives that require the surfer to push the surfboard powerfully under approaching waves before resurfacing and continuing paddling. These activities may be required several times before arriving at the line-up
2. Sitting and maintaining position	Once at the line-up, the surfer sits balanced on the board and waits for approaching waves, or paddles against opposing rip currents to maintain position
3. Powerful paddle strokes	In order to get on to an approaching wave the surfer assumes a prone position and quickly accelerates the board by employing several powerful paddle strokes
4. The 'pop-up'	Once the wave has successfully been caught, the surfer must drive explosively from the prone position to the upright position
5. Riding the wave	Once in the upright position the surfer must powerfully manoeuvre the board along the face of the wave.

Source: Metcalfe and Kelly, 2012

this information with other reliable sources. Although the data are not empirical, the richness of this information will enable you to contextualize and understand the demands of the sport in an applied setting. This now allows you to further characterize the sub-activities and identify major demands and movement patterns.

The next step is to perform a temporal analysis to determine the time spent in each of the sub-activities. Meir and co-workers reported that 44 per cent of the time surfing was spent paddling (Figure 10.1), 35 per cent was spent sitting waiting for waves, 5 per cent was spent actually riding waves with the remaining time comprising other activities such as duck-diving, retrieving the board and wading (Meir *et al.*, 1991). This exercise can be a simple pen and paper observation using a tally chart, or via video footage and specific analysis software. Most importantly, you should have clearly defined parameters beforehand for each sub-activity.

Next, support these observations with more-detailed information regarding the physiological demands of the sport. Unfortunately, scientific data that describe the physiological responses to, and factors that contribute to success in, adventure sports are rare compared with those from mainstream sports. However, in recent years, investigations have slowly begun to gather momentum and a small but growing number of physiological studies have been published. Several adventure sports are now Olympic sports and have begun to attract scientific research.

FIGURE 10.1 In a temporal analysis the coach will determine the amount of time spent in each sub-activity, such as paddling, sitting or riding

Caution is advised when interpreting these studies as scientific enquiry typically demands controlled data collection in specifiable and repeatable conditions. While this gives insight into the relationships of physiological variables under laboratory conditions, such data often lacks authenticity, and does not provide an understanding of what happens under the variable conditions inherent in adventure sports. It is therefore ideal to look at applied research that seeks to describe the anatomical and physiological requirements of high-performing practitioners in the field. If we return to surfing as our example, Mendez-Villanueva and Bishop (2005) reported that during a simulated competition heat the mean heart rate of surfers was 84 per cent of their laboratory-measured peak heart rate and that they spent over a quarter of the time in excess of 90 per cent heart rate peak. This now gives an insight into the intensity of the activity. In addition to academic journals, such data are often available online, in sport-specific texts and from the sport's governing body.

Exercise intensity

One purpose of your analysis is to ascertain the intensity of work required for the sport. From this you can then determine: the training intensity, the work:rest ratio and the nutritional requirements of your adventure sport.

The term intensity is part of the daily parlance of coaches, athletes and sports scientists; however, it is often vague and ill defined. A major aspect of preparation is knowing how hard you will need to work in the sport and also to be able to monitor how hard you are working during training. This is extremely important as it enables you to train specific metabolic pathways that you will be using in the activity.

The two main metabolic pathways are characterized as anaerobic and aerobic. The anaerobic energy systems do not require oxygen in order to resynthesize high-energy compounds and as such can liberate large amounts of energy quickly. There are two anaerobic energy systems: the phosphogen system and the anaerobic glycolysis system. The former relies on stored high-energy compounds and has a duration of approximately 6–12 seconds when working maximally. The latter requires glucose or glycogen (see nutrition section) as a substrate and has a duration of approximately 60–180 seconds. These energy systems burn bright but not for very long. The aerobic energy system requires the presence of oxygen and is therefore dependent on the 'fitness' of the cardiovascular system. A benefit of this system is that it can use carbohydrate and fat as substrates. It is the most efficient of the energy systems but resynthesizes the high-energy compounds at a much slower rate. It is beyond the scope of this chapter to detail these pathways any further.

High-intensity work requires a predominant energy contribution from the anaerobic energy systems and lower-intensity work from the aerobic energy system. There are several ways of quantifying the exercise intensity (and thus metabolic demand) of adventurous sports, these include: exercise heart rate as a percentage of maximum; volume of oxygen consumed as a percentage of aerobic capacity; the volume of exercise at or above predetermined thresholds; and power output to name a few. Each method has merits and drawbacks but heart rate monitoring is the most practicable method and is applicable to a wide range of adventurous activities.

Heart rate monitoring

Heart rate monitoring is a method of observing how hard the heart is working, which in turn gives us an indication of the metabolic demands of the activity. Heart rate monitors are relatively inexpensive and, in addition to real-time information, they can record the data, which can be downloaded and analyzed at a later time. At its simplest the real-time data can inform you how hard you are working while undertaking the activity and in the subsequent analysis you can ascertain work to rest ratios, which can then be used to inform training and nutritional strategies.

Determining maximum heart rate and training zones

A relatively accurate and cheap method is to run up a hill (between 5–10 per cent gradient) for two minutes. You should be exercising maximally at the end of the run. Your heart rate at the end of this test will be within a few beats of your maximum. This is physically demanding so it is recommended that a GP's approval is given beforehand. A slightly less accurate method is to predict your maximum heart rate using the Tanaka equation:

$$\text{Maximum heart rate} = 208 - (0.7 \times \text{age})$$

(Tanaka et al., *2001)*

Once you have determined your maximum heart rate, you can use a heart rate monitor to determine how intense (as a percentage of maximum) you have been working during the activity (Table 10.2). You can also use this information to construct and monitor your anaerobic and aerobic conditioning workouts.

Conditioning exercises for adventure sports

The majority of adventure sports are dependent on the weather, which means that ideal conditions are sporadic at best. This often means that it is difficult to use an adventure sport as a training tool in itself. Furthermore, in order to capitalize on ideal weather conditions when they do occur you need to be in great shape. The cornerstones of any fitness training plan are: duration, intensity and frequency. With regard to adventure sports, these parameters are often dictated by the environmental conditions thus making it problematic for adventure sport practitioners in general to plan specific sport-based training workouts. It is clear that in order to capitalize on ideal conditions and improve it is important to be physically conditioned beforehand.

General conditioning

Functional strength

Most adventure sports require flexion and extension movement patterns at the hip, knee and ankle (referred to as 'triple extension' in conditioning parlance). In addition, adventure sports require the body to be orchestrated in a coordinated and sometimes powerful manner. As such, Olympic lifts and ballistic exercises (such as: squats, power cleans, power snatches, split jerks, presses, rows and pulls) that develop functional strength should form the basis of an adventure athlete's training plan. In addition to working the muscles over the full range of motion and helping minimize injury, these exercises also enable you to maximize your return on your efforts because they work major muscle groups simultaneously, thus freeing up time and energy to devote to other aspects of your technical training specific to your activity. This is an important aspect to note as the technical mastery of skills is often the most important contributor to performance and competitive success.

TABLE 10.2 Suggested heart rate training zones

Training	*Energy system*	*Intensity*	*Perception*
Recovery	Aerobic	<55% maximum heart rate	Very light
Zone 1	Aerobic	55–75% maximum heart rate	Easy
Zone 2	Aerobic	75–80% maximum heart rate	Medium
Zone 3	Aerobic/anaerobic	80–90% maximum heart rate	Medium hard
Zone 4	Anaerobic	90–95% maximum heart rate	Hard
Zone 5	Anaerobic	95% + maximum heart rate	Maximum effort

Adventure activity-specific exercises

Specificity is a major training principle. In short, the body adapts specifically to the stressor (in this case training) that is applied. It follows that if the training is not correct then the subsequent adaptation will not achieve the desired outcome. For this reason it is important that your initial appraisal of the activity is correct. Adventurous activities occur in some of the most unstable and changing sporting environments – especially water sports – and logically they require core stability and balance. As such, functional exercises that enhance neuromuscular responses to an unstable environment, such as those performed on balance boards and stability balls, are routinely purported to be key aspects of adventure training. Such exercises feature heavily in anecdotal training advice; however, they may not be the most appropriate training methods. Again, let us use surfing as an example: a surfboard is relatively unstable only when it is stationary or slow moving; it becomes increasingly stable with increasing velocity. As such the board is at its most unstable during the initial power strokes, pop-up and dropping down the wave, but once moving along the wave face it becomes increasingly stable. This stable platform at speed provides a further rationale for the inclusion of the Olympic and ballistic exercises highlighted earlier – wobble board and fit ball training will not help here and may even be detrimental.

In the absence of being able to use the sport itself as training, it follows that movement-specific exercises should be included in the gym-based sessions for adventure sport athletes. You should spend time identifying movement patterns and pay particular attention to the length, speed and direction the force is applied and mimic these in the conditioning exercises you choose. In addition to sport-specific exercises you should also include exercises that develop the other musculature in order to avoid imbalances (Table 10.3). The inclusion of yoga-based exercises is an excellent and efficient way to address this matter.

Modulation of training

Once the requirements of your adventure sport have been determined, your next step is to structure your training. Periodization is the term given to the planning of the training period. This is typically over a year and is referred to as a macrocycle (Bompa, 1999). The macrocycle is then subdivided into mesocycles each of which focuses on predominant sequential aspects of training in order to arrive at peak

Table 10.3 Suggested repetitions and sets for resistance training outcomes

	Repetitions	*Sets*	*Rest (minutes)*
Muscular endurance	15+	3	1
Strength and power	10–15	3–5	3–5
Strength	<6	3–5	3–5

fitness for a competition or an event. Figure 10.2 details a hypothetical simplified plan for an adventure sport athlete aiming to reach peak condition during autumn/early winter.

Month	Jan	Feb	March	April	May	June	July	Aug	Sept	Oct	Nov	Dec
Mesocycle	AR	Base fitness		Strength	Power		TC	Specific	Peak fitness			AR

FIGURE 10.2 Simplified example of a periodized plan

Note: AR = active rest; TC = training camp.

Source: Adapted from Metcalfe and Kelly, 2012.

The proposed merits of periodization are described extensively (Bompa, 1999) and employed almost ubiquitously by coaches and athletes. Detractors note that predicting one's training over a year is akin to trying to predict the UK weather on a specific date several months from now: you might have a rough idea based on the season, but that is about all. In short there are too many variables to make accurate predictions on which to base periodization, these variables include: training adaptation, mood, lifestyle, commitments, illness, sleep patterns and chronobiology to name a few.

Periodization and adventure sports

Although it is fickle at the micro level, the weather follows seasonal variations with an increased probability of favourable conditions for different adventurous sports at different times of the year (snowboarding, winter mountaineering, surfing, etc.) This coupled with scheduled competitions and events means periodization may be of some benefit.

Figure 10.2 is a traditional example of a periodized plan. During the Base Fitness mesocycle you should aim to develop your aerobic power and muscular endurance, ideally through aerobic exercise and participating in the sport when conditions allow. High repetitions (15+) of squats, presses, rows, pulls and sport-specific exercises should also be included. In the strength mesocycle your goal is to maintain your aerobic power while developing your strength. The resistance exercises can be similar to the subsequent cycle, but repetition maximum range should be 10–15.

A typical power phase should also include power cleans, power snatches, split jerks, squat thrusts and plyometric exercises. The goal of this mesocycle is to develop your power production in order to execute explosive movements that are crucial to your performance in your chosen sport. The purpose of the training camp is to allow a period of consolidation of the physical and technical aspects of the training plan. The goal of the specific cycle is to further hone the fitness you developed during the previous stages in preparation for your main event where peak fitness is desired.

Periodization and adventure sports concerns

The widely used periodized model has been questioned recently mainly because, despite its popularity, there is little empirical evidence to support it. Furthermore, periodization is a mechanistic model applied to a complex adaptive organism – a human being – and it is highly unlikely that there is a one-size-fits-all plan for any given objectives (Kiely, 2011). While a periodized plan makes sense on paper, it is difficult to accurately predict an athlete's response to training and therefore it is erroneous to advance-plan preparation programmes. Possible reasons for the lack of predictive power are that an athlete's adaptation to any training session is the interaction of several responses including: the training load, genetics, training history and transient states (biological functioning, psychological frame of mind and social factors). In a similar vein, meteorologists find it difficult to predict long-term weather conditions due to transient influential factors. It is therefore a difficult task for an adventurous sport practitioner to predict both biological adaptations and weather conditions in order to accurately design a detailed training plan.

The solution probably lies somewhere between the two schools of thought. With regard to your training plan, you should manipulate the mesocycles to address your specific goals and be flexible enough to react to the transient biological, meteorological and everyday conditions. This will require you to dynamically adapt the exercise intensity and volume of your training in order to maintain your desired training load.

Body composition

Different adventurous sports require different anatomical and physiological characteristics. A simplistic example would be a fell runner who requires highly developed lower body musculature whereas a kayaker requires upper body muscular development. However, body mass is generally considered an influencing factor in any sport where there is movement against gravity or where acceleration, deceleration and agility are important. An obvious example is rock climbing during which the body is lifted vertically against gravity. As most adventure sports require the body to be moved in some form or other, body mass may be an influencing factor. If we use mountain biking as an example, some researchers have reported stronger correlations when secondary predictors of performance such as peak power output and aerobic capacity are normalized to body mass compared to the absolute values (Baron, 2001; Gregory *et al.*, 2007) whereas others have not (Laursen *et al.*, 2003).

In a broad sense, body composition refers to the relationship between fat mass and fat-free mass. Body fat is inert mass and in most cases contributes little to performance (Martin *et al.*, 1998) with perhaps the exception of open water swimming, were it provides buoyancy and insulation. When concerned with bodyweight management, monitoring body mass alone is often misleading as it also includes muscle mass. A better method would be to monitor body fat percentage. This can be achieved using skinfold callipers or bioelectrical impedance. Typically the lower the fat mass the greater the strength/power to weight ratio, which translates to better performance, or a lower energy cost of the activity. Body fat percentages for elite athletes in adventurous sports range from 5–10 per cent for males and 10–20 per cent for females. Body fat loss may be achieved by either eating less, expending more or usually a combination of the two. The following section will aim to address some of the topics surrounding this matter.

Nutrition for adventure sports

This section will outline the importance of an appropriate diet to allow optimal performance in adventure activities. Human performance can benefit from dietary manipulation. As with training, your nutritional plan should start with a needs analysis of the event in which you are competing. You will need to understand the physiological and also the nutritional requirements of the sport. For example, the Yukon 1000 is a self-supported canoe or kayak event along a 1,000 km stretch of the Yukon River. There is limited information on the physiological demands or nutritional demands of this event. On a smaller scale, the Devizes to Westminster International canoe race is competed for over a 24-hour period. Again, sound nutritional strategies are called for not only to optimize performance, but also to make the event more enjoyable. Changing the form of transportation, there is the Tour Divide, a 2,700 mile self-supported mountain bike race from the Canadian to the Mexican border. How do you 'fuel' such an event? Where will the food come from? How much should you eat? When should you eat it? Of course in an ideal world these questions could be answered, but out there on the trail, it may be that you can only eat what you have, or can find, and you can only eat when the opportunity presents itself. How do you carry sufficient fluid to maintain adequate hydration? The Tour Divide demands that you are cycling for between 14 to 21 hours per day, that is a lot of fluid and calories. Other events that are non-competitive still require the same assessment and planning. Big wall climbing, alpinism and sea kayak expeditions all require considerable thought and planning given over to providing an adequate nutrition. Twight (1999) provides an overview of nutrition to support alpine assaults; Hörst (2003) includes a chapter on diet in his work *Training for Climbing*; and a section on nutritional value may be found in Doug Cooper's *Rough Water Handling* (2012). These central figures acknowledge that a sound diet will not make you a more skilful mountain biker or sea paddler, but there is no doubt that it will allow you to train well and train hard to acquire those skills and perform during the activity.

Events that are generally short, but very intense, might not require any nutrition during the event. For example, a short fell race of six miles (Parbold Hill Race) would not require any additional calories while racing. This duration of event can be completed successfully with on-board stores of energy. Extending the event duration naturally increases the need for feeding strategies to be put in place.

Metcalfe *et al.*, (2011) investigated the intensity and energy cost of marathon mountain bike racing. Marathon mountain biking was defined as distances from 90 km through 24-hour races and into multi-day stage races. Ten well-trained athletes completed a single 95 km race through North Wales where the intensity of the race was estimated by heart rate recording, giving an average heart rate of 150 beats per minute for the duration of the event. This equated to 80 per cent of their maximum heart rate, intensity zone 3 (hard exercise). Correspondingly the average energy expenditure over the five hours and 47 minutes of the race was 5,039 kcal; or 14.3 kcal per minute. In order to maintain this level of exercise intensity, and to maintain pace, fuel has to be taken on board or the exercise will stop.

You will also need to consider your own needs. How much energy do you require just to tick over? This is known as basal metabolic rate, or resting metabolic rate, given in kilocalories (REE). It may be measured or predicted in a number of ways. The most accurate method requires expensive equipment, a laboratory, a trained technician and a professional capable of interpreting the results. While most universities in the UK offer this service, that level of accuracy is only needed in research studies. A cheap and usable alternative is to estimate your resting energy expenditure using an equation. There are several available. A popular equation developed by Mifflin *et al.*, (1990) predicts REE from body mass (kg), height (centimetres), age (years) and gender. Below is the equation, with a worked example for a 48-year-old male, 175 cm tall and weighing 75 kg.

$$\text{Male REE} = (\text{mass} \times 10)+(\text{height} \times 6.25)-(\text{age} \times 5)+5$$
$$\text{REE} = (75 \times 10)+(175 \times 6.25)-(48 \times 5)+5$$
$$\text{REE} = 750+1094-240+5$$
$$\text{REE} = 1{,}609 \text{ kcal}$$

The equation is slightly different for women: REE $= (\text{mass} \times 10)+(\text{height} \times 6.25)-(\text{age} \times 5)-161$.

For our hypothetical athlete, his resting energy expenditure is approximately 1,610 kcal. Although metabolism is a complicated topic, we can say that if he eats less than this value, he would lose weight; if he eats more he would gain weight. The REE is only a 'resting' value and we can add on any activity completed during the day. For example, he might have a job as a mechanic, which does involve some physical activity. REE may be increased by a factor of 1.15 for this particular job role, equalling 1,851 kcal. Further to this he is training to complete a mountain bike marathon. He trains an hour per day, except a two-hour ride on Saturday and three on Sunday. Giving him a total of 10 hours training per week. Energy expenditures for many different activities have been calculated previously, and the information is widely available, McArdle *et al.*, (2014) being a good source. There are also plenty of online websites and apps that do a similar job. It would be worth having a look at MyFitnessPal. This app estimates your resting energy expenditure, and gives a good estimation of various activities, and foodstuffs.

Back to our athlete, the intensity of an activity does have an effect on energy expended, but for argument's sake, let us say that all training this week is completed at a moderate intensity. This would equate to an energy expenditure for cycling of about 10 kcal per minute or 600 per hour (for someone of this mass). Therefore, Monday's energy expenditure would be approximately 1851+600 = 2,451 kcal; Sunday's would be 3,651 kcal. This has to be replaced. It is also very useful to track energy in alongside energy out on a daily basis. It is common for people to eat the same energy volume of food daily. This is problematic for a couple for reasons. First, you tend to overeat on days where activity is low; this leads to an excess of calories that ultimately are converted to fat and stored. Second, you under eat on days were activity is high. This depletes energy stores, especially carbohydrate, and is detrimental to training on subsequent days. Again, the use of an online tracker helps with this process.

It is critical to replace energy lost during the day and during training, but equally important is gauging the composition of food as well, the percentages of energy derived from carbohydrate, protein and fat. Most guidelines suggest about 55 per cent carbohydrate, 30 per cent fat and 15 per cent protein. For people engaged in sport and physical activity, it is probably prudent to increase the amount of carbohydrate in the diet to around 65 per cent, with 20 per cent fat and 15 per cent protein. Other researchers such as Cordain and Friel (2012) recommend a much higher percentage of protein and lower carbohydrate intake. If we apply this to our athlete, his total energy expenditure for the day was 3,651 kcal, giving him a breakdown of 2,373 kcal from carbohydrate, 730 kcal from fat and 547 kcal from protein. However, 2,373 kcal is an enormous amount of carbohydrate: it would require 600 g of carbohydrate to be consumed. There is about 4 kcal of carbohydrate per gram. Table 10.4 gives the breakdown of food to support that day's training, along with the gram weight in carbohydrate. Note that somewhere he has to fit in three hours of riding too: If he is not riding, he is eating! Also note

TABLE 10.4 Dietary breakdown over 24 hours

Breakfast	*Snack*	*Lunch*	*Snack*	*Dinner*	*On bike*
Muesli 100g 80 g	3 pancakes 23 g	Packet pasta 78 g	Alpen bar ×2 50 g	Large baked potato 56 g	Gel ×3 66 g
Skimmed milk 13 g	2 tbsp maple syrup 24 g	Half melon 24 g		Tin of beans 58 g	Energy drink 75 g
Large banana 30 g	Large banana 30 g				
Total 123 g	77 g	102 g	50 g	114 g	141 g
Grand total					607g

that this is only carbohydrate, he still has to consume about 1,000 kcal of fat and protein. So, what makes a good diet for an athlete and why?

We have evolved to use many different food sources for the everyday cellular processes of life. Frank Booth and Manu Chakravarthy (2004), have suggested that early humans existing as hunter gatherers acquired food almost exclusively by engaging in physical activity. The consequence of this lifestyle was the evolution of physically robust and aerobically conditioned humans. This evolutionary landscape promoted genes, which enhanced physical performance, and genes, which allowed for efficient energy storage and thrifty use of fuel sources (Neel, 1962).

The acquisition of food is no longer coupled directly with physical activity – they are now often seen as separate behaviours. Recently, the last hundred years or so, western humans have become concerned with weight management, primarily for health reasons, but aesthetics too. This has led to a quest for the one diet that will nourish health while maintaining an appropriate weight. A cursory web search would reveal close to 100 different 'diets'. While some were prescribed to aid a particular medical condition, the majority were aimed at weight loss. Questions that stem from this are: is there a diet that is aligned with health? Is there a diet that improves performance? And, is there a specific diet that is both healthy and performance enhancing? The answer to these questions is, probably. But, each individual will have differing dietary needs, and different responses to any particular diet.

The biochemistry of metabolism and nutrition can be an extremely complicated topic so the following section will try to decant and draw off the important useable points. A brief overview of the macronutrients (carbohydrates, proteins and fats) is presented to help you through this topic. It is beyond the scope of a single chapter to cover all aspects of dietary needs. Suffice to say that an athletic diet is a healthy diet. Food choices should include as much fresh produce as possible with the emphasis on a lot of fruit and vegetables. The vitamin and mineral content of food is not covered in this chapter, but the consumption of a varied diet that is high in fruit and vegetables will ensure sufficient quantities of these micronutrients. Athletes, as much as everyone else, should move to a diet that avoids simple sugars, trans fats and highly processed foods.

Carbohydrates

Carbohydrates are a class of organic molecules. In their simplest form they are arranged as simple sugars or monosaccharides. They are abundant in nature, but as nutrients they enter the human body as glucose, fructose and galactose. Glucose has a particularly important position as it is the carbohydrate that we use for energy. When 1 g of carbohydrate is used fully, it provides 4 kcal of energy. Monosaccharides may also pair up to form disaccharides such as lactose, a combination of glucose and galactose found in milk, or sucrose, a combination of glucose and fructose commonly known as table sugar.

Complex carbohydrates are found as starches and fibre. The exact structure of the complex carbohydrate will determine its properties, such as how easily digestible it is, or what happens to it when it is cooked. Polysaccharides have many linked sugars arranged in straight chains or organized in highly branched arrangements. These tend to be the more starchy foods such as potatoes, bread and pasta. Another interesting polysaccharide is glycogen. This is how humans store glucose in the muscle, and also in the liver. Glycogen may be rapidly broken down and the glucose used for energy. It is a very good source of stored energy, but its storage capacity is limited to provide about 60–90 minutes worth of exercise. More trained individuals and people with a higher muscle mass are able to store more glycogen, but otherwise the limit is genetically determined. What this means, is that carbohydrate does need to be replenished often to maintain an adequate supply.

Carbohydrates during exercise

A diet high in carbohydrate prior to endurance exercise has a role: carbo-loading as it is now known is a well-recognized strategy for enhancing performance. Another useful benefit of carbohydrate is in extending exercise performance (or delaying fatigue) by ingesting carbohydrate during exercise. This is again, another area of research that has a large volume of support in the literature. To cherrypick some important experiments to highlight the point, Yaspelkis *et al.* (1993) found that time to exhaustion was significantly greater for carbohydrate conditions compared with a placebo. They concluded that ingesting carbohydrate during exercise is beneficial in staving off fatigue, by utilizing the available carbohydrate in the blood, thus sparing glycogen in the muscle.

One matter of importance is whether there is a limit on how much carbohydrate you can consume during exercise. This is of importance for several reasons. First, one would hope to maximize the amount of fuel taken on board. Second, too much carbohydrate, or taken too quickly, has been shown to increase the incidence and severity of gastrointestinal distress. In 2000, Jeukendrup and Jentjens demonstrated that there is a physiological maximum for how much exogenous carbohydrate may be transported and used during exercise. Athletes should endeavour to consume 1.0–1.1 g/minute of carbohydrate, approximately 60–70 g per hour (240–280 kcal/hour). This limit seems not to be affected by body size; the limit is similar in both trained and untrained individuals.

More recently Jentjens *et al.*, (2004) demonstrated that this limit may be exceeded if multiple carbohydrates are ingested. In their study, a combination of glucose and fructose elicited a higher rate of 1.3 g/minute (78 g/hour, or 312 kcal/hour) during two hours of cycling at 50 per cent of maximal aerobic capacity (VO_2 max). Of course, carbohydrate ingestion is only required for activities of an extended duration, perhaps those that last over 90 minutes. Shorter events can be completed on stored muscle glycogen. In addition, events up to 4 hours are probably well served with single carbohydrate solutions (glucose) rather a combination. This probably reflects the exercise intensity at which events are completed. As exercise intensity increases, so does the rate at which carbohydrate is used. As an example, hill walking is often completed over an extended period of time, but the intensity is moderate, and therefore carbohydrate will contribute less to the overall energy supply, and fat will contribute to a greater extent.

One final point on carbohydrate ingestion during exercise: feeding during a race is a skill and therefore has to be practiced. Although the scientific literature is thin in this area, there is much anecdotal evidence that supports the idea of practicing this aspect of racing. From a logistical point of view, it is worth experimenting with the various products available, bars, gels, powders, etc. to find a product that is palatable and easily consumed. In higher-intensity events, let us say short-course mountain bike racing, the intensity is so high that it precludes eating, partly because unwrapping food and the act of eating is difficult from a moving bike, and fluids seem to be tolerated better in these situations.

Carbohydrates in recovery

Recovery from a training session or big event is extremely important, as it will provide the basis for adaptation to occur, and provide a solid base for the next session. Repeated days of hard or long training or activity have been shown to reduce glycogen stores in the muscle to levels, which impair performance. This state is known as glycogen depletion. When it occurs during exercise it has been described by runners as hitting the wall, and cyclists as knocking or bonking. Whatever the term used to describe the glycogen-depleted state, performance suffers. This is usually characterized by a reduction in pace; in ultra-distance events hitting the wall results in walking rather than running. During training, chronic glycogen depletion is associated with an inability to complete hard sets, staleness, poor sleep and possibly injury. In order to recover fully, three things are required. 1. Rest, which includes adequate and quality sleep. There is an old adage among endurance athletes that says, "why stand when you can sit, why sit when you can lie down". You could probably add to this, "why lay down when you can sleep". Sleep is crucial for repair and adaptation. 2. Fluids should be consumed in response to thirst and not as a drinking regime, but rehydrating following exercise will improve subsequent performance and is particularly useful when maintaining a high carbohydrate diet. 3. Refuelling. The restoration of muscle glycogen stores ensures the performance in subsequent training sessions and competition is optimized.

Generally speaking, the rate at which glycogen stores are synthesized following exercise is quite slow, but can be adequately completed in 24 hours by following a high-carbohydrate diet. Costill *et al.*, (1981) reported that a diet consisting of 150–600 g of carbohydrate per day was sufficient to return muscle glycogen stores to normal following a glycogen-depleting exercise. It did not matter whether simple or complex carbohydrates were used. However, in some circumstances you might wish to increase the rate of glycogen synthesis; for example, if you are completing multiple training sessions in a day, or you have other commitments that do not allow a leisurely approach to feeding. In this case the time at which you ingest the carbohydrate is important. Ivy *et al.* (1988) investigated the effect of time of carbohydrate ingestion on muscle glycogen stores. Results showed that delaying carbohydrate feeding by two hours did slow the rate of glycogen storage, concluding that there is a 'window' of opportunity. More recently, Zawadzki *et al.* (1992) demonstrated that combining carbohydrate with protein increases the rate of glycogen synthesis beyond that of carbohydrate alone.

Investigators have now shown that speedy recovery from exercise using a carbohydrate protein mix, not only improves muscle glycogen synthesis, but does have an impact on subsequent performance. Thomas *et al.* (2009) compared the effect of chocolate milk, which is a combination of carbohydrate and protein, to that of carbohydrate drinks. The drinks were 'matched' for their energy content. Nine cyclists completed glycogen-depleting protocols, after which and within two hours of recovery they consumed either the chocolate milk, or the carbohydrate drinks. At the end of the recovery period, they then completed a cycle at 70 per cent of their maximum until volitional exhaustion. The chocolate milk improved performance in these trials by 51 per cent! Thirty-two minutes for the chocolate milk versus 21 minutes for the carbohydrate drink.

To summarize, carbohydrate is a critical fuel source for physical activity. Unless an individual is engaged in very intense or very prolonged exercise, carbohydrate intake can be achieved through eating a nutritious and varied diet containing complex carbohydrates. During exercise, it is often easier to consume carbohydrates in a liquid form, and although they are simple carbohydrates they are used almost immediately for energy. In recovery, carbohydrate with protein does increase the rate at which carbohydrate stores are replenished. This may be accomplished by carbohydrate protein drinks, or by following a diet rich in complex carbohydrates and quality protein sources.

Protein

Proteins are a macronutrient that is of paramount importance to the athlete. Proteins form structures within the body and are the primary molecules that form the architecture of muscle. In addition, they play a crucial role in muscle repair and maintenance of immune function. The essential amino acids must be consumed within the diet. If you follow a balanced and varied diet, then this generally does not present a problem. However there are some groups who need to give greater consideration to their protein source. As the essential amino acids are found in abundance in meat products (termed high-quality protein), vegetarians may struggle to ensure that the essential amino acids are eaten. Vegetable sources of protein never contain all of the essential amino acids and are therefore known as incomplete proteins. Vegetarians must ensure a mix of protein sources, which complement each other, and together provide the complete protein package.

Historically, eating large quantities of protein has been associated with weight lifters and bodybuilders. Anecdotally their argument is to provide the body with sufficient building blocks to build muscle following training. Current recommendations suggest that the daily intake required for protein is 0.8 g per kg of body mass, which, for our 75 kg athlete would give 60 g per day, which is about 200 g of chicken breast or 250 g of tuna. However these recommendations were developed from, and used for, a sedentary population, those individuals who engage in less than 30 minutes per day of physical activity. There still exists a disparity between current recommendations and the actual intake of protein by athletes.

One of the difficulties for researchers has been how to quantify protein needs. Protein requirements almost certainly will differ depending on factors such as your baseline training status, and whether you are embarking on a new form of training. Think back to the periodized plan earlier in the chapter – April, see the start of the strength training phase. In a clever study, Lemon *et al.*, (1992) investigated the protein requirements of novice weightlifters during initial intensive strength training. The data showed that a much higher protein intake was required to maintain nitrogen balance, 1.6–1.7 g per kg per day: 100 per cent more than the current recommended daily allowance. Interestingly they concluded that there was an upper limit. Increasing the protein intake up to 2.62 g per kg per day, did not improve nitrogen balance, muscle mass or strength gains. This study (and others) suggests that diet may be periodized to track with your training programme. In a similar way to track daily calorie intake and expenditure, diet may be manipulated to enhance particular training adaptations, although we are still a long way off giving individualized advice on this aspect.

In summary, protein intake should come from a wide variety of sources, generally without the need for additional supplementation. There are some exceptions to this, for example, vegetarians need to ensure a wide a varied mix of proteins to provide all of the essential amino acids. The exact amount of protein required is as yet unknown and will be influenced by many factors such as training status and activity type. A sound recommendation is to provide 20 per cent of the daily calorific requirement from protein, increasing this at times when protein needs are higher, for example during strength training periods.

Fats

Fats are a group of compounds also known as lipids. Characteristically they are greasy to the touch. Gram for gram, fats are the most energetic food source; with 1 g of fat yielding 9 kcal of energy. This is as opposed to 4 kcal from a gram of carbohydrate or protein. Over the last four decades or so, fats have not done well in the public psyche. As with all food research, this is not without some justification as a high-fat diet has been associated with chronic diseases such as obesity, coronary heart disease and some cancers. However the picture is more complicated than that. Some fats are highly destructive and should be avoided at all costs. Saturated fats, found in some products should only be consumed in small amounts. Trans fats, fats that have been manufactured by humans and found in abundance in highly processed foods, should definitely be avoided. However, many other sources of fat, mono-unsaturated, poly-unsaturated and omega 3 must be eaten regularly. These may be found in cold water fish, such as tuna, or avocados, and nuts. Fats are crucial for long-term health, immune function and in the manufacture of hormones; they are also an important source of energy for the exercising human.

Fat is the most energetic food source, and even the leanest athlete still has sufficient fat stores to fuel several marathons back to back. However, liberating the energy from fat requires a greater volume of oxygen than does carbohydrate. At low exercise intensities, fat is used preferentially, but as exercise intensity climbs fat contribution is lower as carbohydrate contribution increases. One of the key adaptations to training for endurance sports is a shift in the contribution from fat at any given exercise intensity. If the body can use more of its fat store, then muscle glycogen will be spared for use later in the event. It is possible to train the body to use more fat and less carbohydrate; for example, long training sessions at a low intensity with no extra carbohydrate. Interestingly, it may also be possible to improve performance by manipulating the diet. Lambert *et al.*, (1994), showed an enhanced endurance performance following two weeks of a high-fat diet, compared with a diet that was higher in carbohydrate. It should be noted that the intensity of exercise in this study was only moderate, generally lower than that involved in competitive sports, nonetheless for some activities, expeditions for example, this would be very useful.

In summary, fats should contribute somewhere between 20–30 per cent of your diet. Choose fats that have a better composition, mono and poly-unsaturated fats from lean meats. Include a varied selection of food sources such as seafood, poultry and nuts, and avoid highly processed foods.

Putting it all together

To summarize this chapter; people wishing to engage in adventure sports or activities can improve their performance by following a period of training and following a healthy diet. Initially a bioenergetic analysis of the activity should be undertaken, which would highlight the duration and the intensity of the activity. Further a dietary plan should be put in place to support the training load and improve the performance during the event. The diet should reflect the demands of the training and track energy expenditure on a daily basis. Begin by determining overall calorie expenditure and then determine protein requirement, remembering that this might change dependent on the training demand. After this, 20–30 per cent of the overall requirement should come from suitable fat sources. The remainder should be composed of carbohydrate, preferably complex carbohydrates from fruit, and vegetable sources.

References

Beachle, T. R. and Earle, R. W. (2008). *Essentials of Strength Training and Conditioning.* Champaign, IL: Human Kinetics.

Baron, R. (2001). Aerobic and anaerobic power characteristics of off road cyclists. *Medicine and Science in Sports and Exercise* 33, 1387–1393.

Bompa, T. (1999). *Periodization: Theory and Methodology*. Human Kinetics.

Chakravarthy, M.V. and Booth, F.W. (2004). Eating, exercise, and "thrifty" genotypes: connecting the dots toward an evolutionary understanding of modern chronic diseases. *Journal of Applied Physiology*, 96(1), 3–10.

Cissik, J. (2012). *Strength and Conditioning: A concise introduction*. London: Routledge.

Cooper, D. (2012). *Rough Water Handling*. Bangor, Wales: Pesda Press.

Cordain, L. and Friel J. (2012). *The Paleo Diet for Athletes: The Ancient Nutritional Formula for Peak Athletic Performance*, NY, NY: Rodale.

Costill, D.L., Sherman, W.M., Fink, W.J., Maresh, C., Witten, M. and Miller, J.M. (1981). The role of dietary carbohydrates in muscle glycogen resynthesis after strenuous running. *The American Journal of Clinical Nutrition*, 34(9), 1831–1836.

Foran, B. (2000). *High Performance Sports Conditioning*. Human Kinetics.

Gregory, J., Johns, D. and Walls, J. (2007). Relative vs absolute physiological measures as predictors of mountain bike cross-country race performance. *Journal of Strength and Conditioning Research*, 21(1), 17–22.

Hörst, E. J. (2003). *Training for Climbing*. Falcon. USA.

Ivy, J. L., Katz, A. L., Cutler, C. L., Sherman, W. M. and Coyle, E. F. (1988). Muscle glycogen synthesis after exercise: effect of time of carbohydrate ingestion. *Journal of Applied Physiology*, 64(4), 1480–1485.

Jentjens, R. L. P. G., Moseley, L., Waring, R.H., Harding, L.K. and Jeukendrup, A.E. (2004). Oxidation of combined ingestion of glucose and fructose during exercise. *Journal of Applied Physiology*, 96, 1277–1284.

Jeukendrup, A.E. and Jentjens, R. (2000). Oxidation of carbohydrate feedings during prolonged exercise. *Sports Medicine*, 29(6), 407–424.

Kiely, J. (2011). Planning for physical performance: the individual perspective. In: D. Collins, A. Button, and H. Richards (eds),*Performance psychology: a practitioner's guide*. London: Churchill Livingstone Elsevier.

Lambert, E.V., Speechly, D.P., Dennis, S.C. and Noakes, T.D. (1994). Enhanced endurance in trained cyclists during moderate intensity exercise following 2 weeks adaptation to a high fat diet. *European Journal of Applied Physiology*. 69, 287–293.

Laursen, P., Ahern, S., Herzig, P., Shing, C. and Jenkins, D. (2003). Physiological responses to repeated bouts of high intensity ultra-endurance cycling – a field study case report. *Journal of Science and Medicine in Sport*, 6(2), 176–186.

Lemon, P.W.R., Tarnopolsky, M.A., MacDougall, J.D. and Atkinos, S.A. (1992). Protein requirements and muscle mass/strength changes during intensive training in novice bodybuilders. *Journal of Applied Physiology*, 73(2), 767–775.

McArdle, W., Katch, F. and Katch, V. (2014). *Exercise Physiology: Nutrition, Energy, and Human Performance*. Lippincott Williams and Wilkins.

Martin, J. C., Milliken, D. L., Cobb, J. E., McFadden, K. L. and Coggan, A. R. (1998). Validation of a mathematical model for road cycling power. *Journal of Applied Biomechanics*, 14, 276–291.

Meir, R. A., Lowdon, B. J. and Davie, A. J. (1991). Heart rates and estimated energy expenditure during recreational surfing. *Australian Journal of Science and Medicine in Sport* 23, 70–74.

Mendez-Villanueva, A. and Bishop, D. (2005). *Physiological Aspects of Surfboard Riding Performance. Sports Med* 35(1), 55–70.

Metcalfe, J. and Kelly, J. (2012). Land-based conditioning for UK-based surfers. *Professional Strength and Conditioning* 25, 23–28.

Metcalfe, J., Aitkins, S.J. and Kelly, J. (2011). Heart rate responses and energy cost of mountain bike marathon racing. *Journal of Cycle Coaching*. 3, 11–17.

Mifflin, M.D., St Jeor, S.T., Hill, L.A., Scott, B.J., Daugherty, S.A. and Koh, Y.O. (1990). A new predictive equation for resting energy expenditure in healthy individuals. *American Journal of Clinical Nutrition*, 51, 241–247.

Neel, J.V. (1962). Diabetes Mellitus: A "thrifty" genotype rendered detrimental by "progress"? *American Journal of Human Genetics*, 14, 353–362.

Tanaka, H., Monahan, K. G. and Seals, D. S. (2001). Age-predicted maximal heart rate revisited. *Journal of the American College of Cardiology*, 37, 153–156.

Thomas, K., Morris, P. and Stevenson, E. (2009). Improved endurance capacity following chocolate milk consumption compared with 2 commercially available sport drinks. *Applied Physiology, Nutrition and Metabolism,* 34, 78–82.

Twight, M.F. (1999). *Extreme Alpinism. Climbing Light, Fast and High*. Seattle, US: Mountaineers Books.

Yaspelkis, B.B., Patterson, J.G., Anderla, P.A., Ding, Z. and Ivy, J.L. (1993). Carbohydrate supplementation spares muscle glycogen during variable-intensity exercise. *Journal of Applied Physiology*, 75(4), 1477–1485.

Zawadzki, K.M., Yaspelkis, B.B. and Ivy, J.L. (1992). Carbohydrate-protein complex increases the rate of muscle glycogen storage after exercise. *Journal of Applied Physiology*, 75(5), 1854–1859.

11
USING MENTAL SKILLS IN YOUR ADVENTURE SPORTS COACHING

Jane Lomax and Paul Gray

Introduction

Over recent years coaches have increasingly recognized the need to include a focus on mental aspects of performance within training sessions. In the past, coaches were generally comfortable with coaching the technical, and perhaps physical and nutritional, aspects of performance but tended to leave the mental aspects to develop as a natural consequence of the practice environment. To some extent this did indeed happen but nowadays there is a recognition that coaches can do much to contribute to the training of mental skills with a more overt approach within the practice and competition environment.

This chapter aims to support coach's awareness of the psychological components of performance and help them consider how they can encourage the development of good habits within participants from an early stage. Starting the process early is important as mental skills training is not only for the elite but also for all levels of performance. Mental skills training normally includes goal setting, confidence building, concentration, imagery and arousal or anxiety management (Burton and Raedeke, 2008; Navin, 2011; Pyke, 2013). Coaches can contribute positively to the development of all of these skills and indeed could extend the range to include attribution training and motivational aspects. Choices of practice structure and communication skills particularly can support this and the benefits will be seen in increased and prolonged enjoyment of activities together with improved coping skills under pressure. These are both particularly important given the lifestyle choices made by those who train hard to improve performance and the dynamic nature of the environment adventure sports coaches generally work in.

This chapter will focus on ideas that integrate mental skills within the coaching sessions. Although many of these ideas can be utilized generically it is important to note that the use of mental skills often needs to be individualized and situationally specific. It is like picking a chocolate from a box of Quality Street, they are all chocolates but all have different flavours, shapes and tastes. What you, as coach, or your performer chooses one day may not be the same the following day!

Goal setting within coaching

Goal setting is probably the most commonly cited mental skill because of its versatility, so provides a logical start point. A simple tool on the face of it but often underestimated. When used effectively goal setting can underpin and facilitate the development of many mental aspects of performance. Effective goal setting can build a positive coach–participant relationship to support long-term involvement and sustained success over time. The nature of goals set will vary depending on the coaching context and the timescales available. Goal-setting literature advocates a range of acronyms to support effective goal setting some with different descriptors attached to the initials. All are aiming at a similar approach but for this chapter we will use SMARTERP, as outlined below.

To support the delivery of a specific coaching session, ask yourself the following questions as you set out to plan your outcomes and task progressions:

S **SPECIFIC** What is the purpose of this session? Of each task?
Specific goals are more effective than 'do your best' ones, but being specific is often easier to say than do. A specific focus to each task will help choices of practice structure, mode of communication, level of feedback and extent of participant involvement, as well as encouraging concentration skills. If the goals are appropriate to the needs and current abilities of the individuals the tasks will be motivational too.

M **MEASURABLE** How will you know your participants have improved? Will they be able to see or feel a difference from the start of the session?
Performance may take longer than one session to master but understanding what you are trying to do can come first and you need to know what is changing.

A **AGREED** Have you decided all the session goals or are you able to involve the participants in any way?
Participant involvement in the direction their training is taking helps satisfy our innate need to be self-determining and the sense of empowerment gained from agreeing goals can have a powerful motivational and confidence building impact. This will depend, though, on the experience level of the performers you are working with.

R **REALISTIC** What can your performers already do? What capabilities do they have to extend that performance? How will you ensure all participants experience success?
The goals used need to challenge performers and normally need to be differentiated between individuals within a group, but they also need to be realistic within the time frame available.

T **TIME-PHASED** How many tasks have you got planned within the time available? How much time will each performer get to practice each task? How will these goals develop from one session to the next?
Participants need an idea of the mid- and long-term picture.

E **EVALUATED** What can participants do at the end of the session better than at the start? What went well? What needs more practice? What help is needed now?
Reflections are an important part of the learning process but are much easier if the goals are clearly defined at the start. How we attribute our successes and failures affects our confidence and desire to come back, so careful thought is needed to ensure participants have a positive experience.

R **RECORDED** How will you record goals set?
Difficult, while working in the outdoors, but helpful to do if possible as a good reminder of where participants have come from when there is a lull in progress and confidence or motivation.

P **POSITIVE** How have you phrased your goals?
Whatever you are concentrating on you are most likely to do, so a positively phrased goal helps encourage a focus on the actions necessary to complete the task at hand rather than asking participants to 'avoid doing X'.

Encouraging performers to explore goal setting

Adventure sports environments present many challenges that performers can pitch themselves against to progress, this makes the use of goal setting all the more interesting. Competitive sports are driven by outcomes – who is best, first, fastest or most aesthetic? Successful completion of these events can bring both extrinsic rewards through medals, fame, sponsorship deals and intrinsic rewards through a sense of achievement and pride. For example, after his gold medal-winning performance in the C2 Slalom event London 2012 Etienne Stott reported that: "It's weird. It could have been a disaster and now it's a dream … getting to the final was amazing" (BBC website). Outside of formal competition, an outcome goal can include climbing a specific peak such as Mont Blanc. Outcomes here may not be rewarded with fame or financial gain but will bring the individual a great sense of pride and achievement.

Encouraging participants to aspire to achieve outcome goals gives structure, direction and purpose to training and practice. However, whether we are first, or better than others at climbing a specific route, is only partially under our control. We can train to be as good as possible but if someone else is that little bit better on the day, or the environmental conditions change and prevent a trip proceeding, we will not achieve that accolade. Some coaches focus much energy into outcome goals, pitching performers against each other, tapping into the natural competitive tendencies of individuals as an ego-orientated climate is developed, even punishing mistakes. Indeed, hiring and firing of coaches and funding decisions are often based on just this premise. However, an overemphasis on outcome goals can lead to a roller coaster of emotions for the participants – anxiety and confidence levels are up and down as there can only be one 'winner' on each occasion. To achieve desired outcomes and maintain performers in a more stable mental state over time coaches need to consider their definition of 'success'. To help outcome goals can be underpinned by both performance and process goals that are more under the performer's control as indicated in Figure 11.1.

OUTCOME GOAL

Win a medal, gain a top 20 placement

Climb a specific grade,

Paddle a specific stretch of white water

Achieve the next level of instructor qualification

PERFORMANCE GOALS

These are normally measurable stepping stones on the way towards achieving an outcome

Achieving a specific level on a fitness test as a marker within a training programme

Split times

Achieve a specific hip angulation within skiing (performance analysis software will help here)

Frequency of executing a specific move within a practice run

PROCESS GOALS

These are the everyday focus of practice sessions – the smaller stepping stones that permit the achievement of both other goal types. These are often the coaching points used by coaches within session tasks

Drive skis through the turn; drop hips into the middle of the turn

Look for the eddies as an opportunity to break out and take a rest

Reach forwards to make sure the paddle is vertical on entry to the water

FIGURE 11.1 A layered approach to goal setting

A layered approach to goal setting like this gives coaches a number of 'success' measures so even if the overall outcome is not achieved there may be a number of other goals that have been met. This helps the debrief process and recovery towards the next effort and reduces frustration and disappointment where the outcome goal was not achieved. A healthy balance of emphasis between each goal type will help coaches provide a motivational climate to the session according to the needs of the individuals involved.

Within the planning of a specific session the outcome goal relates to what coaches would like the participants to be able to do at the end of the session that they could not do at the start. The process goals provide the focus for performance development in each task and are often identified in demonstrations and instructions. Coaches can encourage participant involvement in the use of these goals through use of questioning to identify which element of performance they would welcome practice on. This helps individualize goals, differentiate tasks and impacts directly on the next mental skill we focus on: confidence. Longer-term use of goal setting is covered in the planning chapter (see Chapter 8).

Building confidence

Confidence is about having the belief that we can achieve success. Some of us are generally more confident across a range of life activities whereas others are not, but whatever our start point our confidence can be improved. A word of warning, though, there is a point beyond which we could be guilty of generating 'false confidence' or 'overconfidence' where performers might think they are better than they actually are, which can lead to problems.

Adventure sports coaches have the added difficulty of working within dynamic environments where rapidly changing conditions can cause confidence to desert an individual at any moment. A healthy self-confidence is a real buffer to coping with adverse conditions and the pressure that challenging and dynamic activities bring. Coaches can borrow ideas for confidence development from Bandura's work on self-efficacy, or situationally specific self-confidence, which is depicted in a number of texts (Horn , 2002; Weinberg and Gould, 2011) and suggests that our behaviour and thought patterns are directly influenced by our expectations of success. These expectations are influenced by:

Performance accomplishments – previous successes. This is the most powerful determinant of self-efficacy. Coaches need to choose their goals and task progressions carefully to ensure participants have the opportunity to experience success often enough to develop the robust self-belief required to cope with pressure of performing in a dynamic environment. Goals set and practice structure are important tools to help coaches achieve this.

Vicarious experiences – In addition to building up a bank of performance accomplishments, coaches can use the opportunity for participants to see others succeed (vicarious experiences) to good effect by careful selection of models within their use of demonstrations to encourage a mind set of "If they can do it, so can I". Coaches should consider carefully the order participants attempt a climbing task for example and spend time talking with and observing participants while walking to the crag to work out who is the most confident and nervous before even arriving so that a rough order is already sorted before starting.

Many practice environments also provide the opportunity to observe others performing, so coaches can direct attention to other climbers working on the crag or skiers on the slopes where a ride on a chair lift can provide excellent vantage points. Both of these are particularly powerful confidence builders if the person demonstrating or being watched is as similar to the participant as possible. Needless to say, using such vicarious experiences is more likely to be successful in developing self-confidence if the model being shown is a positive and successful one!

Verbal persuasion – There will be many examples of coaches in adventure activities talking performers through difficult moments – whether it be a first-time abseiler nervous of heights or an intermediate snowboarder working their way down their first black run. The adventure sports coach is a great external source of verbal persuasion for the participant, though there could be a credibility issue if the coach tries to persuade a performer they can do something and then they fail!

Verbal persuasion comes from other performers and spectators too and the 'art' of coaching is to decide whom is the prime source at what time. The impact on performance varies depending on what it is others are persuading the participant to do! Some performers are good at verbally persuading themselves already and will happily talk to themselves, some internally and some out loud. However, most self-talk is negative and full of frustrations so taking control of self-talk is an increasingly popular approach to mental skills training and the role of the coach here is outlined in more detail below.

Physiological and emotional arousal – It is not the level of physiological and emotional arousal *per se* that will have an impact on self-confidence but rather the performer's perceptions of these. Where a climber is experiencing butterflies, sweaty palms and racing heartbeat as you might expect before embarking on a climb, if that climber perceives this heightened physiological arousal positively that they are 'up for it' then confidence is likely to be increased; where these symptoms cause worry and doubt the confidence will rapidly disappear. Helping participants interpret arousal symptoms in a more positive light will enhance confidence.

Imaginal experiences – These are a powerful tool too and will be explored later in this chapter but encouraging performers to relive good performances is always helpful, as is mentally rehearsing successful outcomes of the task at hand.

Positive thinking – getting the right mind set: Self-talk

Many of us talk to ourselves while we are performing. Galwey and Krieger suggested that our mind is split into two – Self 1 being the 'chattering mind'; Self 2 is our natural mode of performance. The Inner Game approach was all about keeping Self 1 quiet or at least positively occupied so that Self 2 could get on with performing uninhibited by Self 1. This is a challenge to many of us as when Self 1 is 'chattering' and we are talking to ourselves, sadly we are often telling ourselves off, expressing frustration, reminding ourselves of what we are trying to avoid doing and sometimes overanalysing the movement components. None of these thoughts are likely to help us perform well so coaches can put energy into helping participants use positive self-talk to keep Self 1 productively engaged or aim to quieten it to allow Self 2 to run off uninterrupted.

Whatever we are thinking we are most likely to do next, so maintaining a positive mind set is crucial to maintain confidence and the ability to make important decisions. Coaches can help performers take control of that mind set through the use of the following strategies.

Strategies to help positive thinking and self-talk

1. Use positively phrased key words or short statements that relate to good performance and are easily repeated in our heads for example 'smooth' when trying to carve C-shaped turns on skis.
2. Neutralize negative thoughts or turn them into more positive ones. Easier said than done! To stop negative thoughts in their tracks some find it helpful to actually say 'stop' to themselves or consider a red light switching on or just raise their hand in a stop motion. Then it may be possible to neutralize those thoughts with a cue word such as 'calm' or preferably replace them with a more positive alternative. This takes practice!
3. Remind yourself of previous good performances – through imagery or talking through the event. Very helpful prior to your next turn!
4. Mentally rehearsing the movement or route choice you are about to complete. Some can do this in images others prefer to feel the movements they will make.
5. Learn to use a pre-performance routine for security and comfort.
6. Stay in the 'here and now', sometimes referred to as 'mindfulness' (Williams, 2008). Encourage performers to put aside their feelings about previous performances and the implications of what is to come and focus on the task at hand.

> I wanted to focus on the first three strokes. I wanted to nail them and hopefully the rest would sort itself out, which it did.
>
> *(quote reported from Ed McKeever after his Olympic Gold Kayak performance, London 2012)*

7. 'Bin Your Baggage' – The analogy of a 'bin' helps 'park' your life concerns at the side of the training environment. Participants can use this bin to place all their worrying thoughts, to free their mind to focus on the training session at hand. This works best if at the end of the session participants revisit the 'bin' and decide which worrying thoughts they can leave in the bin and which need to be recovered and then dealt with. This revisiting and dealing with the

concerns is central to this strategy working. 'Binning your baggage' helps participants focus on their training more clearly, then prioritize and manage the things that are bothering them.

8 Rationalize your fears. Galwey suggests we have Fear 1 and Fear 2 akin to the Self 1 and 2 reported earlier. Fear 1, like Self 1, is harmful and is based on illusion so the size of the moguls, waves or rocks suddenly take on enormous proportions and we convince ourselves that we will fall and hurt ourselves. Fear 2, though, enables us to see danger with a heightened sense of detail and the adrenalin rush we get from this can help us achieve feats of performance we could not normally imagine. Galwey suggests we use our sense of reality to help change the shape of our illusions and tame Fear 1.

Develop imagery skills

Imagery is another powerful and versatile mental skill that can contribute to all mental aspects of performance. Hale (2004) advocates imagery's contribution to four major mental aspects of performance: commitment, confidence, control and concentration. Imagery has value for both motivational and cognitive processes.

'Imagery' is about using all the senses to recreate the execution of a performance in our minds and the more vivid and 'real' the image the more helpful it is likely to be. Imagery can support learning of new skills, emotional control, readiness to perform as well as mentally practicing the skills and decisions we are likely to be faced with. Some participants may find using all senses too challenging when visualizing, i.e. using visual elements of performance only, can be sufficient. Others may find it easier to feel the movements as seeing images alludes them, so the use of imagery is very individual. Higher levels of performers generally aim to develop the ability to use all senses in a very precise manner to help with performance preparation, reviewing, confidence pick-ups and error detection and correction.

Coaches can encourage participants to use imagery to:

- Mentally practice specific skills while waiting for a practice turn – for example, run through paddling movements on the bank before entering the water, to encourage participants to maximize the benefits of physical practice.
- Observe, analyse and plan their route then practice performing the route in their head before setting off (see Figure 11.2). This can be built up in smaller sections and gradually worked towards longer ones.
- Mentally practice away from the session to speed up skill development.
- Reinforce learning movements that are closer to a target movement.
- When a mistake has been made, recognize that and then practice replacing the negative image with an image of the desired movement to improve the speed of recovery.
- After a good attempt, relive that and develop a repertoire of 'best performance images'. Reliving these moments helps confidence and mood and participants who are in a good mood are more likely to do well and train harder.

FIGURE 11.2 A skier takes time at the top of the slopes to image the line he will take down the mountain before setting off

Source: Photoshoot Whistler 1415 © Blake Jorgenson

Some participants may find it easier to do this by envisaging themselves running the route as if they are watching themselves on the TV (known as external imagery) whereas others may be able to feel as though they are doing the movement themselves (internal imagery). Both forms of imagery are useful in different situations so it is a good idea to encourage practicing both. More recent use of video and performance analysis within coaching can be helpful in developing the external imagery, though the internal approach helps participants replicate feelings associated with the movements. However, coaches do need to take care with the use of imagery. It is a powerful tool so coaches need to be secure that performers are imaging successful performances.

Example: An elite water skier once shared with me that she was having problems landing her jumps. When asked whether she used imagery it turned out she did, but imaged herself falling on landing. Our job then was to put her imaging skills into 'rewind' mode to determine where in the image performance was array and then replace this section with a more appropriate response, and continue to work that through to get to a successful landing on a consistent basis. Then the jump had a chance of holding the landing in reality.

To develop this level of sophistication within the use of imagery takes time, but is achievable. It may take practice outside of the training environment, or extra time while within training, but it is an investment worth making. When looking to improve performers' ability to image the PETTLEP guidelines (Wakefield and Smith, 2012), introduced earlier in the book (see Chapter 8), are a helpful start point and we revisit them here:

P **PHYSICAL** Use items of equipment, e.g. paddle, when trying to image.

E **ENVIRONMENT** Concentrate on a realistic/similar environment as possible to that in which you aim to perform.

T **TASK** The image should be identical to the desired performance.

T **TIMING** Collins and Collins suggest participants should use 'real time' and the imaged performance should take the same time as the real performance. Electrocardiogram trace evidence from neural activity in the thigh muscles of slalom ski racers when imaging their route through the poles prior to starting a race would certainly support this. However, there may be some occasions or individual participants who find imaging in slow motion helpful, for example, some elite level water skiers have reported finding imaging their trick routines on the bank to be more helpful in slow motion. So consider individual needs here.

L **LEARNING** Update your images as you gain more competence.

E **EMOTION** Include the emotional component within the image if possible to help develop control and coping skills as well as confidence.

P **PERSPECTIVE** Normally participants should be encouraged to use an internal perspective so they can get in tune with the feelings of the movements, though there may be times when an external perspective could also be helpful.

Imagery practice should be short and last for a few minutes at a time. Some performers find it helps to be relaxed before they start practicing imagery, whereas others prefer to be up and simulating performance so there is a need to go with what works for the individual. Some individuals are naturally able to visualize a range of imagery situations, but others find it difficult from one perspective or to even visualize. Consider the following:

> Interestingly I find this very difficult to do. I struggle at the bottom of a climbing route to visualize the way. I am more reactive to how my body feels while climbing. Guess it's like the box of chocolates analogy, I would never pick the blue wrapper (imagery) but choosing the purple wrapper (self-talk) gives me great pleasure (boosts my confidence). And yet I climb with someone who visualizes every single time he approaches the wall.
>
> *(Paul Gray)*

Work with what your participant can do, and do well, then if the situation presents itself you could look to develop a wider range of imagery skills. Writing scripts that involve the different stages of performance and developing more in-depth images for specific elements of performance can be helpful (Hale, 2004). However, it is quite time consuming so coaches would need to have enough one-to-one time to achieve this or could bring in a sport psychologist to help.

Learn to concentrate

You have already heard that concentration can often be lost when performing under pressure and individuals can be easily distracted, so it is helpful to train different elements of concentration subtly throughout the coaching process. Many of us will have been told at some stage in our lives to 'concentrate' and this is often delivered with a frustrated tone of voice. The question is though 'concentrate'? ... on what? Concentration is the ability to be focused on the right thing at the right moment in time. For example, a ski slalom racer would normally find it helpful to be focused two to three gates ahead and if that focus shifts closer they will be too late to make the turn through the gate. This focus of attention must be robust enough to resist distractions as there is precious little time to refocus between gates and athletes who tend to lose focus are seen skiing out of the course or missing a gate. However, we also need to be able to appropriately switch our focus of attention from one element of the display to another to read the dynamic nature of the environment.

Coaches therefore need to provide activities that encourage participants to focus in different ways, learn to switch from one type of attentional focus to another appropriately, resist distractions and recover from a loss of focus. Nideffer's (1976) model still provides a useful structure for the coaching of concentration skills and provides us with two dimensions to work with (Figure 11.3).

The first dimension shows that concentration varies from a broad focus, where we try and take in as much of the information available in the environment as possible, to a narrow focus, where we are focusing on something specific. Our gaze can be thought of as a camera lens that zooms in and out to focus on different

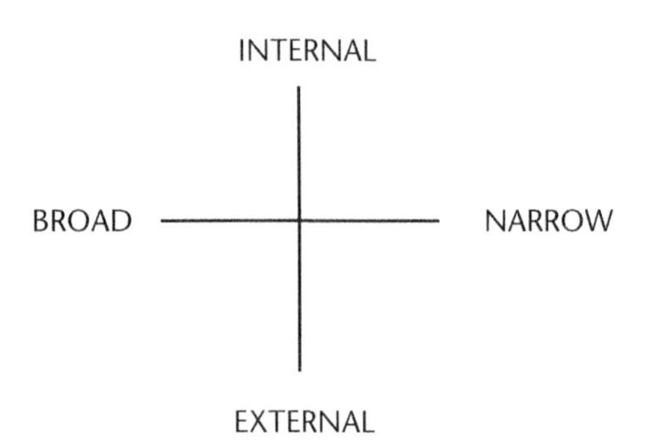

FIGURE 11.3 Nideffer's (1976) model of attentional styles

points and practice can be encouraged by deliberately focusing on different elements of the environment. The skier or snowboarder standing at the top of a run, for example, might be encouraged to take in as much information from the slope terrain – steepness, snow conditions (a broad focus), then practice focusing on specific elements of that display – an individual turn or specific mogul (a narrow focus) and vary points of focus between the two.

Participants need help to know the parts of the environment are relevant to help decision-making. For example, an inexperienced individual will naturally hone in on the hazards the environment presents e.g. rocks in white water and danger areas, whereas a more experienced performer will look for the opportunities that the environment presents e.g. eddies and opportunities for rest.

Training conscious control of focus raises awareness to where you are focused compared with where you should be. A good match here is helpful. However, under stress or heightened emotions, our control of focus can be lost and we can find ourselves in 'tunnel vision' and focusing on something far too specific or 'hyper-distractible' as our focus becomes too broad and we are easily distracted. Both of these have a negative effect on performance and mistakes are made. Coaches can help participants recover more quickly from these mistakes if they understand and have practiced focus shifts.

The second dimension of Nideffer's model suggests we can also be focused on something 'internal', i.e. what we want part of our body to do during a movement or something that is 'external' to us – a point ahead, a specific hold or object we are aiming for. Coaches can help practicing each of these focal points with their use of instructions. Coaches can monitor the focal points they encourage during a session to ensure they practice with internal, external, narrow and broad foci and any combination of these. Coaching manuals often include examples of coaching points that will help practice internal, narrow focus but it is often more of a challenge to get help with an external focus so it is important coaches look to balance the use of each element.

Our skiers could be encouraged to take in as much information as possible noticing the undulations of the slope to practice broad, external focus. When they start to plan the route to take down the slope this uses a broad, internal concentration. Then before setting off, the first few turns could be rehearsed and a focal point two to three turns ahead used to help navigate down the slope. Switching between different focal points can be helpful practice, particularly when trying to problem solve or help performers prepare to perform and recover from mistakes.

These experienced rafters (Figure 11.4) demonstrate appropriate use of an external, broad focus of attention permitting them to gather information about the environment they are about to paddle through so they can choose the line they wish to take the raft through the rapid (internal, broad focus). They may well also use some cue words to keep the power in their strokes (narrow, internal focus) and at times switch to a narrow external focus when picking out a specific slalom gate. The art of good concentration is to use each of these foci at the right moment and switch between them appropriately.

FIGURE 11.4 External/broad focus in action

Controlling emotions

Heightened emotions can negatively affect a number of performance aspects. Adventure sports, by the nature of the activities, can often take performers outside their comfort zone and there can be perceptions of potential physical, emotional and financial harm or injury. Heightened levels of arousal can be experienced at all levels of performance whether it be a first-time abseiler who is nervous of heights, a skier or boarder who finds a slope much steeper than anticipated or an experienced leader who finds a sudden change in environment presents an unexpected challenge.

Similar to confidence, some of us are just more anxious than others, but all of us can train to improve the control of emotions and anxiety. Most texts will distinguish between terminology – stress, arousal and anxiety – in an effort to understand the impact of emotions. Stress, which is often interpreted as negative within its colloquial use, is used by coaches in each challenge set to participants. Without it we would not get growth, but the art of coaching is to strike the right balance between challenge and growth (eustress) and over-reaching the participants' perceived capabilities (distress).

When faced with challenges, we experience heightened physical responses (arousal) with increased heart rate, sweating, for example. We need these to be ready to perform and coaches will normally ensure a warm-up activity to encourage this. Hopefully this also includes a cognitive component to engage mental aspects of performance too. Levels of arousal that help performance will vary depending on the individual, their perception of that arousal level and the activity itself. Archery for example would benefit from a low arousal level whereas a descent down strong white water would warrant a higher arousal level. Coaches can stimulate changes in arousal levels by the activities provided and their intensity, but once a participant starts to feel uncomfortable about their arousal levels they will experience anxiety or even panic.

There are many theories available to explain these relationships and their impact on performance, which can be read in more detail elsewhere (Weinberg and Gould, 2011; Horn, 2008). Here we are drawing from these theories to give practical ideas for the adventure sports coaches to use. Returning to the Quality Street analogy, different flavours in the box to be used when it suits the mood and the situation!

Performing 'in the zone'

A popular phrase these days, developed from the Hanin's (1980) Zone of Optimal Functioning Theory, which suggests that there is a range, or 'zone', of arousal levels that each participant can experience and perform well. Once arousal levels fall below this, coaches can help the participant to increase their arousal levels to somewhere more productive (psyche up) and where arousal levels start to become overly heightened coaches can help participants to reduce those levels to a point that is more helpful (psyche down).

The coaches' challenge is to know the performers well enough to work out how wide this zone is for each performer. Some participants will function well over a range of arousal levels; others may be much more particular. Getting the preparation right for each individual in a group is thus a challenge – group pep talks may only work for some, pushing others' arousal levels too high with potentially disastrous effects on performance! Using the notion of 'being in the zone' is appealing in its simplicity and coaches can encourage strategies as seen in Table 11.1 below,

Many strategies are similar, just the manner they are applied are different. Judging who needs which approach is a challenge for coaches as reading arousal levels is difficult to do accurately if working off body language alone. Gaining a more accurate impression may be helped by discussion of observable behaviours with participants, i.e. what I observe of the participant, as the coach, to indicate they are at a specific level of arousal – a change in body posture in a kayak, the amount of chatting they do, where they position themselves within a group at the top of a rapid. Coaches can then attempt to help them recognize behaviours and control them.

Understanding anxieties

Arousal levels *per se* are generally neutral, so physiological arousal can be increased to quite a high level without necessarily causing a problem. However, once a

TABLE 11.1 Strategies to assist coaches when wishing to psyche participants up or down

Strategies to psyche up participants	*Strategies to psyche down participants*
Physical workout to increase physical and mental alertness	Physical workout to run off excess emotions
Music – upbeat	Music – calming
Cue words and self-talk to stimulate effort – 'drive', 'go', 'push'	Cue words and self-talk to calm – 'smooth', 'steady'
'Here and now' – focus on next task	Positive self-talk
Image previous achievements	'Here and now' – focus on next task not outcome or past mistakes
Mentally rehearse yourself succeeding at the task you are about to perform	Image previous achievements
Interpret your arousal positively	Mentally rehearse task about to perform
	Relaxation/tension control, reduce anxiety
	Keep things in perspective

Source: Adapted from Butler, 1996

participant starts to interpret their arousal levels as unhelpful or start worrying about them this can lead to anxiety. Anxiety can present itself in different forms, normally categorized into either physical (somatic) or thinking (cognitive) symptoms. Somatic anxiety symptoms include increased heart rate, sweaty palms, butterflies, feelings of nausea and frequent toilet visits. Cognitive anxiety symptoms include worrying thoughts either relating to the tasks, the environment or consequences of actions.

Heightened anxiety levels have a negative impact on performance. Cognitive anxiety causes worry, over-analysis, missing of important cues and shifts of concentration from helpful cues to harmful ones. The information-processing capacity is thus less efficient and both the decisions made and the execution of the movements themselves can be less efficient. Somatic anxiety symptoms often dissipate once performance starts so a good warm-up can help. But where these symptoms persist or reappear during performance they are likely to cause increased muscle tension above the level that is useful for performance. Excess muscle tension reduces efficiency in movement skill execution, which can result in a loss of fluidity of movement or a snatched, jerky paddle stroke, for example.

Where this persists and is allowed to reach extreme levels participants can experience 'the yips' or 'choking'. Yips and choking are related to having a mind set that is not fit for purpose (Rotherham *et al.*, 2012). Yips can result in a sudden loss of form, overfocus on movement mechanics, shaking and an inability to execute a movement that participants are normally able to do. Choking results in a participant who is performing well 'throw it all away', concentration is shifted from the here and now to the end result so participants are distracted. For example, a climber could shift their focus at the top of a climb onto walking off the crag rather than focusing on the move itself and mistakes are easy to make as a result. Yips and choking can occur separately or at the same time, are often triggered by life events and the underlying emotional components need to be addressed if the performer is to be helped. If they are not dealt with, they can ruin performers' careers as they become so fixated on that one element of performance that it threatens to disrupt the rest of their participation in not only the event at the time but from then on. Not a pleasant experience!

Learning to manage heightened arousal levels and dealing with anxieties as they arise can be a more successful long-term strategy to support performers than unpicking the yips or choking once they have set in, which is difficult to do successfully and strategies of trying new equipment may only provide a short-lived solution.

Coping with anxieties

Given that involvement in adventure activities often takes participants outside of their comfort zone, an awareness of how to help manage arousal and anxiety levels is an essential part of the adventure sports coach's role. It is worth noting though that many individuals love that element of 'risk ' or perceived risk and thrive off the adrenalin buzz obtained from pushing their limits or trying a more-testing environment to pitch their skills against. At the top end this can take participants to extreme environments that others would never dream of tackling but on a daily basis means participants need to be challenged at whatever level they are working at. The sensation-seeking element of participation in adventure sport is an important motivator and, when managed well, can lead to participants achieving feats of performance they had no idea were possible. Managed badly risks driving the participant from the activity for good and can even put them in real danger.

A range of strategies are available to manage anxieties, some quick fire ones that can be used in a field setting and others that can be used at home or prior to an event to aid preparation. In the past, anxiety symptoms were matched with the intervention (Davidson and Schwartz, 1976), but recent thinking recognizes the interplay between cognitive and somatic components (Hardy and Fazey, 1987) and would utilize the Quality Street analogy more i.e. develop a range of strategies (flavours) and pick the one that suits the individual and the mood best. Coaches need to consider the strategies they are comfortable working with, as some may feel working with deep relaxation strategies is more the remit of a sports psychologist than a coach. Everyday strategies are discussed below.

Reducing somatic anxiety, or heightened physiological arousal

Breath control – taking deeper, slower breaths perhaps coupled with counting to three or five slowly to encourage deeper breaths to help calm the individual.
Tension control – tightness often first appears in the neck and shoulders, which will quickly affect performance.

If participants can be encouraged to step back from the activity and take control of rising tension then this can be checked at a manageable point. Training tension control in muscles can be helped with a simple exercise of lifting your shoulders up to your ears, tensing all the muscles as hard as you can, then releasing those muscles, letting the tension drain away from the muscles. Practice can reduce this to a small tension-relaxation exercise that can be done briefly during swift breaks in performance. When adapted to paddling, hold your paddle as normal and then try and pull the paddle apart (tension) then relax. Also try to 'shrink' the paddle. This can be done at the top of a rapid and helps reduce body tension. It takes two minutes to have an effect!

Those individuals who want to extend the practice of relaxation throughout the body could use a progressive muscular relaxation technique that adopts the same idea to relax different limbs of the body in turn to obtain deep relaxation. Use of 15–20 minute tapes can help the night before an event to gain a good night's sleep; off season is a good time of year to develop these deep relaxation skills.

Reducing cognitive anxiety

Cognitive symptoms can be experienced for some time before participating and are thus emotionally draining and confidence sapping. Strategies for keeping a positive mind set and maintain confidence are essentially the same as those that will help reduce cognitive anxiety so please revisit that section. There are also relaxation strategies with a more cognitive component including meditative approaches or music and images of peaceful places to calm the thought processes. Whether these are more or less helpful than the physical versions will be down to individual taste – which chocolate to choose!

Coping with sudden emotional switches

Excitement is part of the adventure experience (Apter, 1992). For the participant in a playful mood (Kerr, 1997), low levels of arousal may be boring to them and they will seek higher levels of arousal to excite themselves. Those of a more serious mind set may find lower levels of arousal relaxing and high levels of arousal anxiety inducing. So getting a feel for each participant's mood helps read the arousal level that will get the best from each individual. Be warned though: the excitement that seems so appealing one minute can instantly switch to anxiety and is a quick mood swing that can take both participant and coach by surprise. Coaches can take heart though – if the switch happened one way it should be possible to reverse that switch and help the participant re-focus on their initial sense of excitement using any one of the strategies above.

Putting it all together – performance routines

Participants generally like to feel as secure, confident and in control as possible before embarking on a new challenge, particularly one that extends them, involves pressure of competition, difficult conditions or has important consequences. The adventure sports coach can help performers bring their mental skills together in a manageable pre-performance routine to match the situation they are facing and take control of thoughts and feelings immediately before performing. Routines can be developed over time to prepare for the start of performance or utilized to recover from mistakes more quickly or help restart after breaks. Performance routines can also help cope with changes faced in the environment by bringing composure and clarity of focus. Left to develop on their own, performers may resort to a reliance on superstitions, such as a 'lucky sock syndrome', so some structure to a pre-performance routine with distinct stages can help give the performer control. Once practiced, performance routines can block out distractions, assist in the calming process and provide a consistent set of behaviours to encourage consistency in performance.

For example, after making a mistake:

- Remove the reaction — acknowledge the error and then remove it
- Recover — controlled breathing, relaxation
- Review — what to do next, review and adjust performance plan, decide action
- Visualize/image — next action
- Cue in to the event — use key words or statements as a 'trigger'
- Lock onto your trigger — hold your attention on the relevant cue
- Respond — trust your training has been geared to this moment and action

The earlier good habits are started the better, as once these routines are established they are difficult to change.

Post-performance reflections and review

This is an important area of performance development that, through logistical difficulties and lack of time, is often neglected. Adventure sports coaches may have more opportunity than other sports with down time in the evenings on multi-day trips, in transit to and from sites, when packing equipment or even in natural breaks during a day's activity. Post-performance time can encourage reflections on learning and recognition of achievements. Coaches can take the thinking full circle by reflecting back against the goals set and encourage dialogue rather than merely giving feedback, thus involving participants in their own development.

Timing is a factor as immediately after completion of a task may not be the best moment as emotions could be high. Here coaches could adopt a 'hot de-brief' approach with minimal input and then a more detailed reflection once emotions have calmed. Finding the right balance for each individual is a challenge particularly if the performer is competing away from the coach. A young ski racer once reported to me 'the worst bit was the silence in the car driving home' so coaches of youngsters may need to involve parents in the process too.

Listening to the reasons athletes give for their performances can be enlightening. What they attribute their levels of performance to can give coaches important indicators of confidence levels and ownership of performances. After a good performance encourage the attribution of success to something that is stable, internal and within the performer's control. For example, their own abilities, the work put into training and the process goals adopted that day. This keeps confidence more stable and encourages expectations of success more than the performer who attributes their success to others' misfortunes or 'being lucky'. Where a performer has a poorer performance, though, the attributions need to be considered to help them recover emotionally. 'There I told you I was no good' is not going to help, so focusing on something less stable, less in their control and external may be more helpful in the short term. However, coaches need to recognize when a crisis management strategy is turning into a performer making excuses and not taking responsibilities for performance. Here coaches need to encourage mind sets that will refocus on action planning for growth again as soon as possible.

The key to success – effective communication

We can talk about mental skills in coaching at length and read all the books and research we like, but at the end of the day whether it works or not will come down to the communication skills of the coach and the match of these to the performers. The coach–athlete relationship is the link between theory and practice. A comment here, a look there, is all it takes to change the atmosphere and messages sent by the coach and received by the performers in an instance. What we say is important, yes, but not as much as the way we say it or even the way we behave. We use video and performance analysis freely with our participants these days, so why not do so with our coaching? Checking the match between our behaviours and what we say and do can be quite illuminating and could explain why, sometimes, the reactions we get in performers are not what we expect!

Concluding comment

Hopefully this chapter has given you food for thought of some subtleties that can make a difference to the dynamics of that coach–performer interface and encourage you to explore the application of mental skills within your coaching. Where more in-depth work is required you may want to refer to a qualified sports science support worker or even a clinical psychologist, but the contents of this chapter are aimed at the application of mental skills to the coaching process rather than dealing with the more complex individual issues that those practicing in sport psychology might expect to work with.

References

Apter, M.A. (1992). *The Dangerous Edge: The Psychology of Excitement.* New York: The Free Press.

Butler, R (1996). *Sport Psychology in Action.* Butterworth Heinemann.

Burton, D. and Raedeke, T.D. (2008). *Sports Psychology for Coaches.* Champaign, IL: Human Kinetics.

Davidson, R.J. and Schwartz, R.E. (1976). The psychobiology of relaxation related states: A Multi-Process Theory. In: D.I. Mostofsky (ed.), *Behaviour Control and Modification of Physiological Activity.* Englewood Cliffs, NJ: Prentice-Hall, Inc.

Galwey, W.T. and Krieger, R. (1997). *Inner Skiing.* Revised edition. New York: Random House.

Hale, B. (2004). *Imagery Training.* Leeds: SportscoachUK Coachwise Solutions.

Hanin, Y. L. (1980). A study of anxiety in sports. In: W. F. Straub (ed.), *Sport Psychology: An Analysis of Athlete Behavior,* Ithaca, NY: Mouvement, 236–249.

Hardy, L., and Fazey, J.A. (1987). The inverted-U hypothesis: A catastrophe for sport psychology? Paper presented at the Annual Conference of the North American Society for the Psychology of Sport and Physical Activity, Vancouver, Canada.

Horn, T. (2008). *Advances in Sport Psychology* 2nd Edition. Champaign, IL: Human Kinetics.

Kerr, J. (1997). *Motivation and Emotion in Sport: Reversal Theory.* East Sussex: Psychology Press.

Navin, A. (ed.) (2011). *Sports Coaching: A Reference for Students, Coaches and Competitors.* Wiltshire: Crowood Press.

Nideffer, R. M. (1976). Test of attentional and interpersonal style. *Journal of Personality and Social Psychology,* 34(3), 394–404.

Pyke, F. (ed.) (2013). *Coaching Excellence.* Champaign, IL: Human Kinetics

Rotherham, M., Maynard, I., Owen, T., Bawden, M. and Francis, L. (2012). Preliminary Evidence for the Treatment of type I 'Yips': The Efficacy of the Emotional Freedom Techniques. *The Sport Psychologist,* 26, 551–570.

Wakefield, C. and Smith, D. (2012). Perfecting Practice: Applying the PETTLEP model of Motor Imagery. *Journal of Sport Psychology in Action,* 3, 1–11

Weinberg, R.S. and Gould, D. (2011). *Foundations of Sport and Exercise Psychology.* 5th Edition Champaign, IL: Human Kinetics.

Williams, R. (2008). *Mental Techniques for Climbing.* Retrieved from www.ukclimbing.com/articles/page.php?id=1126 (accessed 21 November 2014).

12

RISK MANAGEMENT

Chris Hodgson

Introduction

Risk management is one of the main competencies of the adventure sports coach and Collins and Collins (2012) identify this element of the role as 'welfare and safety' skills. It can easily be argued that any outdoor or adventure-based professional has to manage welfare and safety and this is true, but the nature of adventure sport performance and adventure sports participants means that the range of judgements may be greater for the coach than for a teacher or guide. During leadership and coaching qualification courses and assessments managing risk will play a large part in the outcome of a candidate, but the reality is that in most assessments the parameters for risk management judgements will actually be quite limited in comparison to the wide range of situations that an adventure sports coach will find themselves in. Particularly when learners reach higher levels of competence and autonomy, which will be much more common for the adventure sports coach than for most adventure educators.

This chapter will explore general principles behind risk management within the adventure sector but will pay particular attention to the subtle but significant differences that the adventure sports coach will need to consider. The concept of risk–benefit balance will be a strong theme as will how the coach manages the tension between retaining control of the situation and empowering adventure sports participants to make their own decisions. Risk management in adventure education has been explored in a number of texts and so this chapter will not provide a step-by-step process for risk management. Instead it will highlight where our focus might need to be different or adapted for the adventure sports coaching paradigm.

Risk by degree

All adventure sports carry a degree of inherent risk. At a beginner level the risk encountered by an adventure sports participant, in a professionally organized activity, should be similar to the level encountered in an education setting. As a beginner, that participant may have a desire to undertake difficult and demanding activities but they are unlikely to have either the technical skills to do so or a real understanding of the judgements necessary. The coach's responsibility for this learner will be to provide a well-controlled activity where risks are well understood by the novice and no higher than that encountered in other aspects of everyday life. In fact, the reality is that the acceptable level of risk is likely to be less than other aspects of the participants' life. Marcus Bailie (2007) explored this in his report 'by comparison'. Bailie compared causes of death statistics that included 22,000 alcohol-related deaths, 3,500 road traffic accidents and a figure of 150 adventure activity deaths (across all activities – most of these not part of organized coaching).

The issue for adventure sports coaches is that participants that they work with will often not fit the educational model. An adult sportsperson engaged in white water paddling may in fact be comfortable with a very different level of risk. In *White Water Safety and Rescue*, Franco Ferrero (1998) described how four hypothetical paddlers on a trip together would not only be exposed to different levels of danger because of their skill based and physical attributes, but also would be prepared to engage with activities with a different degree of personal risk. In the example, the least skilful paddler in the group chooses to run a rapid that more skilful paddlers portage. Ferrero makes the point that it would be foolish for a leader to allow a learner to undertake an activity that they were almost certain to fail on if the consequences are likely to be serious injury. However, the reality is that the adventure sports coach is much more likely to be making these kind of difficult decisions where a learner may be happy to take risks, which are on the edge of what we personally might see as acceptable.

An adventure sports coach does need to consider what they personally will deem to be acceptable risk for their clients. To an extent this is going to be different from coach to coach. It is possible to be involved in coaching activities where the risks are identical to those we would see in mainstream adventure education settings and if this is where the coach is comfortable then that is fine as long as they have recognized that in advance and they take on learners with appropriate aspirations. Other coaches will be prepared to allow capable students to take higher risks in pursuit of their sporting goals. For example, a climbing coach working with an expert climber may find himself or herself discussing plans that involve routes with extremely difficult moves and sketchy protection. The potential for a fall resulting in serious injury would be an inherent part of that activity and something a performer would have to accept. This coach needs to have a clear personal philosophy that is consistent with the potential outcomes of this scenario. Even if they are not going to be present during the climb in a supervisory or advisory capacity and feel legally distant from the activity, there is still an ethical and moral dilemma as they are helping a participant who is clear that they will be taking on this level of risk.

There is nothing wrong with a coach having a conservative personal philosophy on risk taking, but the performer and coach need to have compatible explanations. It may be that the time comes when a coach needs to consider stepping away from a learner themselves or might refer them to someone else because their expectations on risk become incompatible with those of the coach. It would be hard to see where this would be necessary in an education setting and could be a new experience for the coach.

Risk-benefit analysis

The classic risk management model for the UK is based on an industrial model that was designed primarily for factory and other 'workplace' settings. The Health and Safety at Work Act requires risks to be reduced 'as low as reasonably practicable'. Philosophically this approach to adventure sports participation or coaching leaves us in a pickle. Given that adventure sports participation by its nature is completely discretionary and involves engaging in activities that are fundamentally risky, any model that asks us to reduce risk to a minimum level at all times is unrealistic and would effectively eliminate many opportunities for participation that adventure sports enthusiasts enjoy. Fortunately even the government's own report on managing risk in the adventure setting recognizes the inherent problem with the 'as low as reasonably practicable' model and recommends a risk–benefit assessment as a starting point for activity decisions.

An important point made by Bailie is that ongoing involvement in adventure activities can actually extend lives by providing some protection against the five biggest killers: heart attacks, cancers, smoking, obesity-and-unfitness and alcohol. He also warns about the 'Hatfield effect' where deliberately avoiding an activity perceived as dangerous can actually lead to exposure to a statistically much more dangerous alternative.

If we are going to make good judgements about risk exposure then we need a realistic understanding of the likelihood and consequences of an incident in an activity and the effectiveness of controls. For example, what are the chances of a head injury during a skiing activity and how much protection does a helmet provide in that situation? Our appraisal of situations should be evidence based and we should be able to explain where that evidence comes from.

Legal liability and responsibility

Despite a significant focus on risk management and responsibility within the sector it is not uncommon for outdoor professionals to have a fairly thin knowledge of legal requirements and implications. Informal conversations and the way in which the media reports on issues tends to create a climate where legal systems and the courts are seen as irrational and part of a compensation culture. The reality is that the picture for adventure sports coaches running appropriate activities for capable and informed learners is nowhere near as pessimistic as some would have us believe. In fact, courts have often been quite clear in their support, or at least tolerance, of fully informed risk taking by adult adventurers.

A major question for a criminal or civil court case is: what would other experts do in the situation? Peer opinions are generally provided in the form of expert witness testimony. Legally if we adhere to the standard of behaviour that other professionals would expect to then we are unlikely to be found be negligent. However even if an activity is relatively safe if we do not taken common or easy risk-management steps then we could be found to be at fault (this is known as 'the Bolam test'). There is also an implication here that our practice will be up to date. Currently few professional ski teachers or guides would take clients on an off-piste tour without avalanche transceivers. Airbag rucksacks are becoming increasingly common and one day may be seen as standard practice for professionally lead off-piste activities.

Consent to take risks is a central legal principle that we need to consider and this is often referred to as a case of *volenti*. An adventure sports participant who willingly accepts a level of risk inherent in the activity has done so themselves and they are entitled to do that. The exact level of risk that they have consented to is variable and will depend on the circumstances and their knowledge base. Their age will also come into play for minors: there is not a hard line for consent to take risks but the courts will ask what is reasonable for the individual to be able to consent to. They do need to be considered capable of understanding the implications of the risk. This may need specialist knowledge in some cases or a situation may be 'self-evidently dangerous'. A non-obvious risk might need to be explained by the coach while an obvious one would not. However, a prudent coach may still provide a warning and instructions on appropriate behaviour. An important point is that the *volenti* defence does not mitigate for a lack of good practice by the coach; for example, a participant on a racing circuit can expect that crash barriers and gravel traps would be up to a reasonable standard for the activity (Fulbrook, 2005). An off-piste skier would expect avalanche transceivers to be in good working order and safe travel techniques to be employed where necessary.

Formal and written risk assessment

The industrial model of risk management has a strong emphasis on written risk assessments and formal risk management plans. In a fixed environment with predictable risk these can be effective in limiting exposure to unnecessary risk. They are particularly useful when decisions on safety can be made by an expert and then disseminated to other personnel in terms of guidance and instructions. Behaviours can be audited and reports about compliance can be kept to prove a culture of adhering to and checking safe working practice. In the world of adventure sports coaching written risk assessments are much less useful because the coded behaviours that work in a factory might be downright dangerous on a mountain or a river. An adventure sports coach needs to be able to manage risk in a dynamic manner making adjustments as they see fit in accordance with their own expert knowledge. Does this make written risk management procedures useless? No, because there still things that can be achieved through formal records and *a priori* planning.

Adventure facilitators and coaches often have justifiably negative views of health and safety paperwork. Perhaps we need a balanced view on this topic and we should consider what paperwork can do well and what it cannot do. A benefit of formal risk assessment procedures is that you can prove that you have considered what the activity involves and what steps might be necessary to manage that risk when the activity starts. Paperwork is good at showing that staff members are appropriately experienced and that equipment choices for an activity have been considered. It is also quite good at identifying any formal backup systems that are in place like a checking in procedure.

Paperwork cannot, and never should, take the place of sound judgement and effective decision-making. It would be foolhardy to deploy underqualified and under experienced coaches and rely on them following written operating procedures to the letter. The key to sensible paperwork is that you can show you have deployed the right person to the right place and activity with the right resources. You then rely on them (or you!) behaving in an intelligent, thoughtful and competent manner. A progressive approach to responsibility and updating through reading and scenario-based training is a good way to facilitate the human side of risk management and this can be recorded. One point made by Marcus Bailie of the Adventure Activities Licensing Service is that more accidents are due to overconfidence or inattention than actually technical incompetence. This is important because sometimes adventure sports coaches see having the right person in place as the only safety measure necessary and the evidence is that even the expert may need a review process to ensure accurate responses to environmental and situational demands.

Ultimately risk management is a process and not something that can be 'completed' and filed away. The more coaches and organizations accept the process approach and that paperwork reflects this, the better. The worst kind of paperwork is the comprehensive, exhaustive type that implies that the process has been completed and now it is just a case of following the operating procedures accurately.

Problems in expert decision-making

A major aspect of risk management in adventure sport coaching is the dynamic decision-making of the expert performer or adventure sports coach. In fact, the requirement of this kind of risk control is a strong feature of many commentators' views on adventure risk management. Having the right person in charge of the activity is intuitively an essential element of managing safety in an adventure setting and most of the time this single part of a complex picture will mean that an activity is well managed; in fact, there is probably no substitute for having the 'right' leader. Unfortunately there are times when having an experienced and knowledgeable leader can actually end in an unexpected elevation of risk levels. Ian McCammon (2004) examined this paradox in relation to avalanche accidents involving expert participants. What McCammon discovered was that there was evidence that intelligent, experienced people, often with formal avalanche training, were regularly involved in accidents where in hindsight the danger seemed obvious. The heuristics and biases approach to decision-making, championed by Daniel Kahneman (2009), pays particular attention to when experts make poor choices.

Heuristics are rules of thumb that guide us through situations that we encounter. Some are highly specific to the situation but those we apply across many situations can be more powerful because we are often not aware that we are using them in our decision-making at all. McCammon identified six heuristic traps that he felt explained why these decisions were made by leaders with sufficient knowledge and experience to identify the risks and plan an approach that would avoid the situation that lead to the accident: familiarity, consistency, acceptance, the expert halo, social facilitation and scarcity.

Decision-making is fatiguing so rather than evaluate the situation afresh we often simply behave the way we have before in a familiar situation. The higher the level of training, the greater the risk appears of ignoring a hazard in familiar terrain. The fact that you have been somewhere before and had a positive outcome becomes too strongly weighted and the evaluation of risk becomes blunted. McCammon found this effect could be so strong that parties with advanced training behaved exactly like those with none on familiar slopes.

There is a strong human drive to behave in a consistent manner. In fact we can become very unsure of ourselves if we are asked to behave in a way that seems inconsistent; it undermines our sense of self. This drive can be so strong that it overrules other decision-making processes and critical new information gets ignored. McCammon found that parties who felt committed to the plans actually gave lower hazard scores in the same situation to those who did not feel they had committed themselves. Mark Twight, the American alpinist, argues that climbers need to learn when to fail and retreat before losing control of a situation and that this is actually quite difficult to do.

Acceptance means that we are conditioned to behave in ways that we expect will gain the approval of others. In terms of risk-taking behaviours there does appear to be a gender difference here and males are more likely to take greater risks to seek approval than females. This has been seen in avalanche statistics where McCammon reports that although females have a lower chance of being an avalanche victim, males in mixed gender groups appear prone to taking more risks in order to fit with the gender role stereotype and behave more competitively. It does appear that this effect is reduced by formal training and is a risk that should be a target for 'awareness' training in adventure sports participants. It may therefore be more of a problem that we need to address in our coaching of others than in our personal leadership.

In any group there is likely to be a hierarchy of perceived competence and a problem associated with this is the expert halo effect. Sometimes the influence of the expert can be rational but often the expert halo is a result of another attribute like technical skiing ability, age or just the individual being more assertive. Parties with an identifiable leader appear to take more risks than those who genuinely make decisions based on a consensus and this effect seems independent of the actual competence of the group. People put much more faith in the decision-making of a 'trusted other' than they do themselves even when abilities are similar.

People tend to feel more confident in groups and this influences decision-making even when the group is of no practical benefit. Even trained leaders can make riskier decisions as group size increases. Having other groups in the vicinity also increases the likelihood of risk taking. It seems that other groups convey a 'stamp of approval' to the decision to be in a location even if there is objective evidence the situation is hazardous. Even more surprising is that this effect was greater for parties with more advanced training. Inexperienced groups were not emboldened by the presence of others but groups with basic or advanced training were.

The final heuristic trap explored by McCammon was scarcity. There is a tendency to value resources or conditions that are less common. People are likely to take disproportionate risks to be the first to ski untracked snow and this is probably true of other rare but seemingly favourable environmental conditions that

FIGURE 12.1 Fresh powder: The sense that a resource is scarce can lead to disproportionate risk taking

Source: Photoshoot Whistler 1415 © Blake Jorgenson

present both an opportunity and a hazard such as a rarely formed ice route being 'in' or fickle surf break going 'off'. The hazard aspect gets underplayed because a sense that the opportunity is hard to gain and easily lost takes over. Another common mistake is allowing a session to run on longer than planned because conditions are good even though participants are becoming fatigued – the 'one more run' scenario.

What does this mean for our practice as coaches? Well, first of all technical training and a strong knowledge base does not necessarily make us, or our more advanced learners, less likely to be involved in an avoidable incident. Even those of us with excellent activity-specific knowledge are still prone to being swayed by often unconscious decision-making influences. Providing knowledge or testing knowledge in our learners will not necessarily keep them safe either. Advanced decision-making skills are as important as an advanced knowledge base and yet this aspect is often underplayed in training.

Understanding our own human fallibility and the influences that can affect our judgement might help us to avoid falling into one or more heuristic traps where our hard-gained sport-specific knowledge is undermined by our automatic human risk-calculation system. We need to be wary of situations that might reinforce an overconfident attitude or undermine an appropriately cautious approach. We need to get into the habit of questioning ourselves, and our learners, whenever we are in a situation where we recognize that we may be influenced by any of the heuristic traps that McCammon identified. We should be careful of shortcutting the evidence-based decision-making systems that we have learned and going on 'gut feel'. If we are tempted to do that we should just stop and do an audit of the situation: might heuristic decision-making processes have overly influenced us?

Systematic risk assessment

The more systematic our approach to evaluating hazards the less likely we are to overlook a key issue or be overly influenced by inappropriate cues. The coach's gut feel is a useful warning sign and an experienced facilitator should never overlook it but neither should we rely on a completely reactive system.

The Health and Safety Executive (2006), the statutory organisation in Britain responsible for guidance on and enforcement of health and safety, suggests an approach called 'five steps to risk assessment':

- Step 1 – Identify the hazards.
- Step 2 – Decide who might be harmed and how.
- Step 3 – Evaluate the risks and decide on precautions.
- Step 4 – Record your findings and implement them.
- Step 5 – Review your assessment and update if necessary.

However, there is little mention of where you start when you identify hazards and this is often the source of problems. Marcus Bailie and I identified three approaches to systematic identification of hazards in *Adventure Education: An Introduction* (2011) and these were the priority approach, the chronological approach and the geographical approach. The most intuitive approach is the priority-based approach where the most significant hazard is identified and then we work down a hierarchy. The problem with this approach is that it relies on us spotting each hazard without any further cues. For this reason it is the method most likely to result in omissions. Now it may be a good way to present a completed set of risk management paperwork, but that does not always make it a good way to manage the process. The geographical and chronological approaches have more of a natural structure to them and the choice between them is generally down to the specific activity. Activities with a clear timeline often work best with the chronological approach. Things that happen in an area with boundaries, but less-predictable sequencing, can work better with the geographical approach.

A river trip or mountain bike route is a good example of where a chronological approach makes sense as hazards, and choices, are encountered in an organized way as we proceed through the activity. A surf beach or sailing lake might be better evaluated through a geographical 'sweep' approach because participants will move in a less predictable way and will encounter the same areas (and hazards) again and again.

An effective quality control process is to tackle hazard identification from more than one perspective and then compare results. Even better, we may be able to get a second observer to contribute. We call this approach triangulation and we can have triangulation by process, triangulation by observer, or both. Triangulation is one way to avoid simple oversights in our risk-management processes. However, it is not foolproof by any means because trained coaches will often view things in similar ways and therefore make the same mistake or omission. In fact, this is a common criticism of triangulation as a checking system and it is why a different framework or even framing of the problem can throw up different results.

Coaching risk management

It is quite common to involve learners in adventure education in the risk-management process as part of their learning. For adventure sports coaches this really is essential as we are ultimately interested in having clients become independent, which is potentially different from the aims of an adventure educator or sports coach where the activity may be a vehicle for other development.

A major element for coaching risk management is an open and inclusive environment where decisions and judgements can be evaluated. As Collins and Collins point out in Chapter 1, expecting judgement to develop purely through exposure to the activity is naïve and we should be actively working with learners to develop this aspect. A number of deliberate mechanisms can be employed to develop the judgement side of risk management. These include:

- Formal mentors – mentors like the coach themselves can provide robust models of process-based risk management and this can be explored as a discrete part of the activity.
- Critical friends – learners should be encouraged to talk through decisions with peers and compare their observations and evaluations.
- Active reflection – it can be tempting to dismiss an activity without incidents as one that has been well managed; however, this is not always the case and it is good practice to review successful days as well as days involving incidents.
- A recording and evaluation approach – recording observations and outcomes can provide a rich source of data for later reflection. It can also allow the learner to see patterns rather than view events in isolation.

On a bigger scale, we should encourage adventure sports participants (and coaches) to see themselves as part of a learning community where knowledge and lessons are shared. It can be embarrassing to make close calls public but the benefits of increased information should be worth the cost if it results in avoiding catastrophic results for our learners later on. The sector is getting much better in this regard but this approach needs to be championed for it to become embedded in our culture. Again, patterns can emerge that the individual would never see on their own. This was one of the main lessons of McCammon's work.

Conclusion

Ultimately, risk management is a skill set that the adventure sports coach will develop over a long period of time. An important question for the individual is what level of risk and outcome they are personally prepared to tolerate for their clients, as this will guide the scope of activities and learner that they may be happy working with. Expert knowledge is our main tool in managing risk but with the expert label also comes a level of certainty, or trust, which unchecked can lead to a new source of problems. We need to guard ourselves against that effect and from time to time go back to basics, re-examine the judgements we make and re-evaluate our behaviours.

Ongoing updating of risk management skills and practice is essential if we want to be considered current in terms of the professional model of adventure sports coaching. It is also a requirement in terms of how we would be seen by any legal processes where we would be expected to be working in line with the expectations of professional bodies and other experts in our fields.

The adventure sports coach will use exactly the same set of skills and make judgements in the same manner as other outdoor sector professionals. However, the context for judgements can be different and the expectations and experience base of client groups means that the adventure sports coach may find themselves making decisions that have a greater demand on the judgemental processes and may not be quite as clear cut. This means the adventure sports coach may need to engage in individual or mentored personal reflection regarding this aspect of their role.

References

Bailie, M. H. (2007). *And by comparison*. Cardiff: Adventure Activities Licensing Service.

Berry, M. and Hodgson, C. (2011). Risk management: philosophy and practice. In: C. Hodgson and M. Bailie, *Adventure Education: An Introduction*. London: Routledge, 46–62.

Collins, L. and Collins, D. (2012). Conceptualizing the adventure-sports coach. *Journal of Adventure Education & Outdoor Learning*, 12, 81–93.

Ferrero, F. (1998). *White Water Safety and Rescue*. Wales: Pesda Press.

Fulbrook, J. (2005). Outdoor Activities, negligence and the law. Hampshire: Ashgate.

Kahneman, D. and Klein, G. (2009). Conditions for intuitive expertise: A failure to disagree. *American Psychologist*, 64, 515–526.

McCammon, I. (2004). Heuristic traps in recreational avalanche accidents: Evidence and implications. *Avalanche News*, 68, 1–10.

13
PROFESSIONALISM AND THE ADVENTURE SPORTS COACH

Bill Taylor and Islay McEwan

Introduction

This chapter concerns itself with professionalism and its impact on the adventure sports coach in a leadership, guiding or coaching role. As discussed earlier in the book, the adventure sports coach may fulfil several roles within a given organization. Therefore, with specific reference to the concept of professionalism we use the terms guide, instruct, leadership and coaching as interchangeable and that, for simplicity, we refer to the outdoor sector to cover all contexts and activities related to the adventure sports coach. This chapter seeks, not so much to provide answers, as we would suggest that there are few definitive ones to give, but rather to raise important points and ask pertinent questions about what it means to be an outdoor professional. In doing so, we hope to offer a current assessment of where we are as a sector in terms of imbedding professional practice into our delivery and also to indicate the level of confidence we may have with regard to claims to be professional.

Questions surrounding 'What does it mean to be an outdoor professional?' have been with us for some time. Although we may not pay much attention to them on a daily basis, questions about our professional practice have been brought to bear in order to inform and crystallize our thoughts on particular matters and individual situations in which we might find ourselves. We would argue, however, that the questions asked of us, or that we ask ourselves, have had little internal logic and that the nature of the questions themselves has ebbed and flowed depending on the current atmosphere of the sector. When under pressure, individual elements within the wider outdoor adventure field have a tendency to retreat into their own notion of professionalism. Outdoor education has cited that its educational professional ideals are central to individual advancement and enhancement and those leading and coaching in adventurous activities have rallied around the principle of professionally informed safety judgements and risk management. As the outdoor sector is a conglomerate of different activities, ideals and interest groups, talk of professionalism will mean different things to different people.

The idea that those who feel under pressure to justify and establish themselves as legitimate distinct professionals are most vocal about their professionalism, we suggest, is particularly relevant when considering the outdoor sector (Stronach *et al.*, 2002). We would further argue that the need to ask ourselves questions about which professional identity will serve us best, will become increasingly important as we attempt to establish, or rather re-establish, what we do as being worthy, valuable and an important element in the nexus between adventure, health, education and recreation (McEwan and Taylor, 2010; Taylor and McEwan, 2012). There is a dearth of empirical evidence and published research in this area of professionalism in the outdoor sector. While the professionalization of sports coaching has had some attention (Taylor and Garratt, 2007; 2008; 2010a; 2010b; 2013), the outdoor sector generally has been left to internal conversations and emerging debates. As such, much of what we write here is tentative, based on first principles, informed by our outdoor histories and our research within the professional practices of allied occupations.

In the following chapter, we will consider a number of main components that historically have been regarded as underpinning an occupation's claim that their practice is professional and the wish to enhance the standing of those working within the particular sector. We must first, however, reflect on the defining features of professionalism, professional practice and the professionalization of an occupation. In doing so, we need to acknowledge the diversity within our sector – one which sees volunteers and those fully paid – deliver similar experiences in the same environmental domain. Within this section, we explore the nature of professional knowledge and argue that any leader, or coach, working within such environments should be able to think and act autonomously while working within a framework that upholds ethical decision-making, with and on behalf of those for whom they are responsible. Second, we look at the nature of training and education in the field and review the role of mentoring, reflective practice and continuous professional development (CPD) and their roles in maintaining currency and developing professionally informed practice. Here, we argue, we need to be mindful of the lessons learned in other occupations, such as those in teaching and health provision, where the research concerning ongoing professional development suggests that much of it fails to enhance practice (Gould *et al.*, 2007). Last, and drawing on lessons from other occupations that have undergone similar journeys, we will outline a number of ongoing questions that will emerge as the nature of what we do in leadership, guiding and coaching in the outdoor continues to alter to meet the demands of clients, governing bodies and others allied to the outdoor sector.

Defining professionalism

The terms professional, professionalism, professionalization and a profession seem to resist definition. Not only are the terms used interchangeably, but also, few authors writing on the subject agree a working starting point for their meaning. Generally, we can consider the term 'professional' as a set of beliefs, ideals and commitments that inform and underpin both individual and group practices, ethics of engagement and thoughts (Freidson, 1973; 2001; Taylor and Garratt, 2007; 2008). Furthermore, 'professionalism' is an embodiment of these traits in the actions of individuals and groups. So, while being professional is mainly a state of mind, professionalism is the manifestation of these beliefs, ideals and commitments being put into action; that is, one's professional practice. When we talk of ongoing 'professionalization', we refer to the processes by which groups and individuals undertake activities in order to position themselves as a profession. We may use the phrase 'undergoing professionalization' to describe those who wish to enhance their occupational standing, which also includes those who are continually re-educating themselves as the demands made on them become more complex and exacting. A 'profession' itself is an occupational group that holds identifiable traits, core beliefs, a set of ethics that guide practice, a distinct knowledge base and, to some degree, is recognized by others as belonging to a particular occupational domain or employment field. While early writers on the professions considered only those in full paid employment as being worthy of the name, more recent consideration suggests that many of the elements of being a profession have been observed in practice within the voluntary sector (Lawson, 2004).

Turning to the question 'Can we legitimately claim that coaching and leading in the outdoor adventure sector is professional?' – the answer is, 'probably; in some situations, maybe'. There is no doubt that many of those who are active as leaders, guides, instructors and coaches are committed to professional development and professional ideals. Some will earn their living from such activities, while others will engage only in these roles in their spare time, separate from their normal paid employment. We could argue that it is not the fact that some individuals earn money from the activity that counts as professionalism, but rather the way in which they approach their engagement and the values they hold while doing so.

Professions as an ideal type: Do we measure up?

In western society, we have elevated a number of occupations to a position where they are seen as the 'ideal professions'; medicine, law and the church are commonly cited as those occupations that are considered to be archetypal professions (Freidson, 2001; Lawson, 2004). In doing so, authors in the field have drawn out common traits that have been presented as evidence of this higher occupational position, and which, in turn, have become characteristics to which others may wish to aspire. A number of authors have suggested that for a claim for professional status to be upheld, certain qualities need to be in place. In the following section, we review these characteristics and chart where the outdoor sector measures up, making reference to those leading and teaching others.

Body of knowledge

Established professions possess a distinct body of knowledge that is particular to the profession in question. This knowledge is mainly generated from within the occupation itself, is individual to the professional setting, nuanced to the main activity, and is often accompanied by its own language and use of particular terminology (Beck and Young, 2005). The defining feature is that the knowledge itself is operationalized and demonstrative at a sophisticated level of practice application. It is not just the demonstration of a practice that is important, but also the accompanying cognitive processes used to justify the underlying decisions that are of central importance (Shulman, 2005). In addition to this, to act as a professional is to understand how to access and generate this rarefied knowledge, an understanding that is difficult for those outside the sector to achieve. In this area, it could be suggested that outdoor leadership and coaching has a strong claim.

Within outdoor activities, there has long been the generation of novel and bespoke methods of delivery, leadership and teaching. In addition, the knowledge base developed has been endorsed by outsider agencies as being valuable and, thus, held up as an indication of expertise. Those working at leading and guiding in a variety of outdoor settings have long dealt with environmentally led dynamic risk assessments. Making judgements on the balance between adventure, learning and acceptable risk, while considering those being led and the aim of the activities in the outdoors, requires complex and informed decision-making. In many situations, these judgements draw on a depth and breadth of experiences and skills that take time to acquire and refine. There is little doubt that the risk-management principles displayed by many in the outdoor sector are both sophisticated in conception and indications of 'best practice'.

One could argue that many of the situations that an outdoor leader and coach would find themselves in are distinct and, thus, require particular forms of knowledge. In the field of white water safety and rescue, the advances made in understanding and 'practical wisdom' (sometimes referred to as *phronesis* [Standal and Hemmested, 2011]) have been accompanied by the development of bespoke solutions, equipment and systems, which themselves have been exported into the mainstream rescue services. Not only has the white water paddling world generated new knowledge and practice, but in many situations practitioners are also seen as the 'field-based experts' delivering professional training and education programmes to a number of outside agencies.

These two examples go some way to illustrate the nature of rarefied knowledge and help to support, to a degree, the claim that in some situations, professional knowledge and the accompanying phronesis can be identified within the outdoor leadership and coaching fields (see Figure 13.1). Our diversity, however, is also our weakness and internal learning from within and across the sector is hampered by a lack of a strong organizational centre and limited opportunities to share our expertise via journals and generic publications.

FIGURE 13.1 The ability to make judgements requires complex and informed decision-making and are strong indicators of a 'professional'

Source: Photo by Dr Mark Tozer

Higher education

Engagement with higher education is something that the archetypal professions have long held as being central to their practice. The medical and legal professions' educational processes are based on a long-term commitment to university level education where they exert control over the nature of the learning and control access to courses. The outdoor sector has limited control over these elements. While the requirement for recognized qualifications within the outdoor arena is growing and the moral position surrounding leading and coaching in the outdoors without any qualifications is problematic, the situation within the UK remains that there is no legal requirement, in most cases, for individuals to hold any level of qualification. Indeed, the historical roots of much of Britain's outdoor sector bear witness to this: the Youth Hotel Association, the Scout movement, the Ramblers Association and many of the National Governing Bodies (NGBs) of outdoor and adventure activities have a long and proud record of providing opportunities in the outdoors by voluntary and *ad hoc* provision. Those with both the experience and commitment to provide voluntary leadership and instruction to the next generation of practitioners have played a crucial role in introducing others to the outdoors.

There are a number of external pressures on the activities and individuals involved in them to embrace a qualification culture. Insurance companies are increasingly asking for evidence of competence and training before issuing cover for those wishing to lead and coach others in the outdoors. The move towards a European-wide regulated workforce may see minimum standards being put in place and become a requirement for those wishing to take charge of learners in an outdoor setting. Some activities already have well-established qualification structures, for example, in diving and sub-aqua, it is, among others, the PADI system, and for the professional mountaineer, the International Guides certification holds considerable international kudos. There is a growth of certification schemes that acknowledge the international nature of some leading and coaching in the outdoors and which have been established to certificate those working both at home and abroad in a variety of environmental settings (British Association of International Mountain Leaders [BAIML], 2014). The development of the United Kingdom Coaching Certificate (UKCC) over the last eight years has formalized a cross-sport approach to coach education, training and assessment. Indeed, at the higher end (the scheme runs from level 1 to 4) the level 4 award is now benchmarked at post-graduate university level. Most of the high-level awards aforementioned require considerable time, financial and personal commitment in order to achieve, and, by the nature of the award, bestow elements that are associated with expertise and a degree of professionalism (Taylor and Garratt, 2013).

Aligned with the outdoor sector's partial engagement with higher levels of education, is the notion that there has been an intellectualization of the processes of leading and coaching within the field. As 'what we know about what we do' has increased, the depth and breadth of understanding demanded by clients, educators and the sector itself, has, in turn, grown. We are now expected to have a basic working knowledge of the psychology of risk management, and pedagogical and learning principles, as well as having an environmental ethos and commitment to minimize our impact. Increasingly, the outdoors is used as a therapeutic medium to help deal with the strains and stresses of modern life, and in these applications the development of an expertise in counselling maybe required. Expectations are changing and now people are being guided up Mount Everest, led down the Grand Canyon, dog sledged to the North Pole, taken to dive sites that 20 years ago were the sole preserve of the then expert and young people crew sailing boats across the Atlantic Ocean. All of these activities, when led by others, draw on greater degrees of expertise and understanding which, we would argue, are indicators of an engagement with higher levels of education and professional knowledge. This extension of the remits of our operational practice requires not only that we understand what to do, but also that we think deeply about how to do it.

Professional bodies

In addition to the elements already mentioned, traditional professions are supported by independent professional bodies, which carry out a number of duties.

As well as providing support for their membership via legal advice and insurance services, these professional bodies also have the ability to control and sanction members who practice outside agreed terms of reference. For example, organizations such as the General Medical Council can suspend doctors if they are found to be acting in an unprofessional manner. Other professional organizations have a degree of control over the initial education of their membership and will further endorse CPD opportunities and additional professional qualifications in order to retain control over their members' learning. Indeed, for some professions, membership of the controlling body is a prerequisite for the right to practice and, within this endorsement, they have the ability to regulate and control membership entry and professional standards.

The outdoor leadership and coaching practitioner faces a different situation. While membership of outdoor organizations may offer considerable benefits, no outdoor qualification has a protected title to it (anyone can call themselves a Mountain Guide if they avoid using the full title and do not claim membership of the international body) and, while it may be difficult to claim continued currency if you operate outside of the NGBs of sport, it is still possible to do so. This position is a one of weakness if the outdoor sector wishes to claim professional status.

Client-based practice

Another tenet that has been associated with the professions, is the commitment to place the needs of the client at the forefront of practice: doctors undertake the Hippocratic Oath, lawyers will advise their clients to the best of their ability, despite what may be best for them as individual professionals. Professionals profess to know better, to be the knowledgeable other, but also to act in a manner and disseminate their knowledge, guided by a 'sense of service' and an altruistic ethos. This service ideal may seem old fashioned, however, for many who view some professions as a vocation calling, this moral contract with society acts as a point of departure and base for professional relationships (Taylor and Garratt, 2010a; 2010b). So, this begs the question: do adventure sports coaches act in such a manner, and would they, if asked, indicate that their actions and behaviours are framed within an ethical commitment to place the needs of the learner at the heart of the process?

There is no doubt that much of the origin of outdoor provision can be traced back to the ideas inherent in muscular Christianity and the belief that the outdoor environment is a source of regeneration and recreation. As mentioned before, many of the bodies central to the birth of an outdoor education and adventure education movement were built on concepts of mutual aid and communityship. Is it possible for the outdoor leader and coach, however, to claim to work with these ideals in mind? Much of the intent of those working in the outdoors is to equip their charges with the skills and confidence to 'go it alone'; to prepare them for independence and to be confident in situations where they no longer require the safety net of having others take charge of the activity. In environmental settings where the management of both subjective and objective risk is paramount, the leader and coach will make judgements, individually and collectively, which allow learners to benefit from the opportunities inherent in risk-based activities without being subject to unjustifiable danger. Indeed, at times not only are we working in a risk-based environment managed by us for the benefit of the learner, but also, we make key decisions without the direct permission of the client in the belief that it allows them both learning and safe experiences. This fine balancing act, we would argue, is a professional act that requires, at its heart, knowledge of people and the domain in which adventure is undertaken. It can only be successfully managed if there is a degree of altruism and commitment to put the needs of the client first. Most of us involved in leading and coaching others in the outdoors, understand that much of our professional engagement is in a domain which is neither exacting for us, nor one which, if we were undertaking the activity for our own recreation, we would choose. These inherent commitments and sacrifices that we take on board as part of working with others, go some way to supporting the claim for a 'service ethos' and professional framework that will guide our working practices.

Autonomy

Linked to the notion of a 'service ethos' is the ability and implicit permission for professionals to act in an independent and autonomous manner. Of course, the traditional professional occupations work within the structures that are laid down by their professional bodies and operate inside the legal frameworks of society. They do hold close, however, in their claim for professionalism, the ability to make autonomous decisions, suggesting that because they deal with unique and contextually bound situations, it is difficult to be guided by previously prescribed solutions or one-size-fits-all answers. This ability to act independently, as well as to justify the actions undertaken, is a central tenet of exercising 'professional judgement' and this, in turn, is underpinned by engagement in higher levels of education and the possession of a deep and mature knowledge base.

Certainly, the adventure sports coach, when operating at the higher ends of the risk spectrum, is dealing with complex and unpredictable environmental conditions and leading and coaching in these domains requires the consideration of multiple and often complex options. It is in these circumstances, we would argue, that autonomous action is paramount to securing a safe and fruitful experience. Notwithstanding this, where the outdoor sector falls down is in the lack of explicit training targeted to support this form of professional judgement and practice. While many practitioners have the technical expertise to exercise the possible actions open to them, we would suggest that there is a lack of education relating to the ethical dimension of acting as an independent and autonomous leader or coach. Inherent within any decision-making at this level is a contextually based judgement whereby the consequences and ethical impact of the decisions made are fully understood and balanced against, and within, a cost–benefit analysis.

While we do not suggest that all outdoor leaders, guides, coaches or instructors operate in such a domain, we do support the idea that any claim to be professional at any level should acknowledge the right to make these independent decisions and that these should be informed by ethical and moral understandings.

Are we professional yet?

Using the criteria outlined above, and we accept that there are other ways of assessing professionalism, we could legitimately ask ourselves the question 'Are we, as a sector, professional?' Acknowledging that the sector is diverse, disparate and ill-defined, we wish to suggest that within the sector as a whole, there are elements of practice that exhibit many of the hallmarks of a professional occupation and professional practice. It is not uncommon to hear discussions around professional practice and its effect on delivery and behaviour. When asked a direct question about their professional status, few, if any coach or leader working within the sector would answer, 'no, I am not professional in what I do'.

What we may be able to say with some confidence is that some elements of our sector are being professionalized and that they are subject to both internal and external pressures to be more professional in nature. As we continue to claim a rightful place in the contemporary sporting and recreation landscape where occupation standing, access to funding and legal support for our outdoor activities continues to be important, moves towards understanding and embracing professionalism seem to be at the heart of all our futures.

The development of professional knowledge

If we accept that in exercising professional knowledge and judgement, we are often making unique decisions about distinctive situations, the potency of traditional forms of coaching and outdoor leadership education is called into question. Standard coach-education programmes have historically focused on the gaining of technical knowledge and, to a degree, pedagogical practices. As mentioned before, the attention devoted to the development of professional practical wisdom demonstrated by in-field decision-making has been somewhat lacking. Addressing this shortcoming, and at the same time acknowledging that the professional practitioner needs to display continued currency in their field, professional organizations and educational researchers have turned to mentoring, the use of reflective practice and CPD. It is to these three elements that aid the development of professional practice, which we now turn our attention.

Mentoring

Bloom (2013) suggests that the act of mentoring someone to help and guide an individual's development is often informal, *ad hoc* and unstructured. Most of us can remember particular individuals who played an important role in introducing us to the outdoors – they may have been a teacher, youth leader, friend of the family or significant other. They may not have called themselves a mentor, but nonetheless, we learned from them a great deal, often in a practical setting. In addition, many of us who have taken up coaching and leadership roles in the outdoors, have undertaken a form of observational apprenticeship (Borg, 2004; Shulman, 2005). That is, where the act of being in and around more experienced individuals and witnessing formative coaching leadership situations has allowed us to observe and internalize particular traits and behaviours. The old adage that 'we lead and coach in the manners in which we were led and coached' may hold true here.

This implicit and vicarious learning shapes many of the fundamental understandings that we base our professional practice on. The nature of the learning, however, in that it is unmediated, makes the quality of what we have picked up and embedded unclear. Furthermore, we may not even realize that some of these experiences are now replicating themselves in our own practice, even if they are undesirable.

Where the concept of mentoring seems to be most appropriate in terms of the education of adventure sports coaches and other outdoor practitioners is in development of phronesis or practical wisdom (Standal and Hemmested, 2011). Phronesis is an Aristotelian term meaning a form of practice expertise or wisdom that is demonstrative in nature. Its application lends itself to complex context-bound decision-making where there is no pre-existing solution or tried and tested answer. Such is the variety and nature of these situations, that to have someone else to refer to for help and advice can be invaluable. In these settings, experience can be of great benefit to learning, but only if the accompanying action is then considered and reflected upon. Having a mentoring relationship in which someone can act as sounding board and to help make sense of these novel contexts may help build deeper understanding and knowledge that can be newly articulated in future leadership and coaching roles.

Recent consideration of mentoring within the outdoor sector, as an aid to professional development, has attempted to formalize the process within coaching schemes without losing the strength of the *in situ* and bespoke nature of its applications. A number of NGBs of adventure sports have introduced mentoring as part of their education schemes with differing degrees of effectiveness. This has commonly seen situations in which more experienced, and higher qualified, coaches are mentoring less-experienced ones; the assumption being that learning with, and from, someone who has more experience will be of benefit. Research from within wider sport-coaching fields suggests that the process of mentoring others and the guiding of their development can be problematic on a number of fronts. Bloom (2013) among others (e.g. Cushion and Nelson, 2013), provides a note of caution when making assumptions regarding the benefit of mentoring. First, because of the one-to-one nature of many mentoring relationships, the educational process could result in a duplication of the mentor's particular working characteristics. This mirroring of values and traits may be avoided by the education of mentors to appreciate that their main role is to allow development of the mentee's own thought processes and behaviours. Additionally, there is some concern that, if mentoring is formalized within a coaching and leadership structure, then institutional agenda, hidden or otherwise, and the micro politics of different practices may have undue influences on the individual nature of the developmental experience. This has been recognized within the field of business and industrial leadership, where there has been a call for cross-domain and team mentorship relationships to be built (Ragin and Kram, 2007). The argument in this situation is that, because of the distinctive nature of professional judgements at high level, no one person could offer support and guidance across all areas of practice. It is not, we would suggest, difficult to see this concept being applied in the higher level of outdoor leadership and coaching. This is where practitioners are both multi-skilled in as much as they work across different domains, as well as multi-tasking because of the complexity of the nature of their practice. Here a team of influential others and mentors may be in a position to offer specialist guidance across a number of areas of expertise. There is, however, an inherent contradiction within mentoring in general: because of the bespoke and individual nature of the relationship, it is important that the guidance is not formulaic and, thus, limiting. Without significant training and resources, the quality of mentoring available may be variable, unknown and limited. In an effort to mediate the quality of this professional learning, we must place the needs of the individual at the heart of the relationship and be careful that, in our efforts to monitor quality, we do not impose those of the wider organizations inappropriately.

Reflective practice and professional learning

It would seem that these days everybody is a reflective practitioner. It is difficult to avoid the call to reflect and learn from our experience. There are numerous outdoor texts that espouse this, such as Kolb (1984) and Gibbs (1988), and, in doing so, suggest that reflection and learning have a simple relationship, i.e. that partaking in one naturally leads to the other. Accompanying the circular model representing the interaction between experience and reflection, these considerations often confuse reflection with remembering and place the focus on the individual nature of the action, reflection and possible learning nexus. In doing so, these pictorial representations are sometimes drawn as closed loops suggesting that the individual is both accountable and contained within his or her own learning. It is our understanding, however, that professional learning benefits from, and is accelerated by, social interaction and collective consideration. Furthermore, if experience in itself is such a productive teacher, then expertise would be the preserve of the elderly and we know that is not always the case. We suggest that reflective practice is more complex and, at times, difficult than is commonly suggested. In doing so, we support the views of Bradbury *et al.* (2010) and Frost (2010) in their call for reflective practice to be alert to the environmental constraints in which people professionally practice and also to be mindful of the structural, at times political, limits of our own reflections. In addition, for beginners new to the development of their own practice, it is difficult to reflect if one has limited experience and knowledge to draw upon. It is difficult to make sense of an experience, as a neophyte coach if it is your only experience and the novel nature of the practice renders it isolated and lacking other references. Like most forms of self-evaluation, reflective practice itself requires practice and commitment to devote time in which to undertake it, as well as the utilization of resources relating to the areas of development should they be required (Bold, 2011).

Turning to the work of Donald Schön (1983; 1987), we suggest that reflective practice does have a place within professional development in the outdoor sector mainly because of the nature of what we do. Schön's original concern was that such was the nature of professional practice in professions, such as architecture and medical surgery, whereby important decisions are made in moments of mass complexity that, without an approach to capture these learning experiences, experience itself may become impotent and fruitless. Referring to this complex world of multiple decision-making as the 'swampy lowlands of practice', he developed the notion of reflection on, reflection in and anticipatory reflection on practice. These states of reflection, when engaged with, ask the practitioner to make sense of contextually bound and the seemingly intuitive-based decision-making that characterize their practice. While not the intent of this chapter to review Schön's work, we draw the reader's attention to the potency of reflecting back on incidents and placing them in the wider context of environmental and institutional concerns. Schön suggested that critical reflection allows the cause, effect, strength and weakness of a situation to be identified and, thus, retained for future practice reference, or to allow identification of possible avenues for improvement.

A major tenet for professional advancement is to see our practice and our professional judgements as important opportunities for critical consideration. Situations that may seem unstructured and reactive in their management can be unpicked and reflected upon to reveal patterns, previously unseen, and these may help inform future behaviours. One area where reflective practice may be an aid to professional development is in reflecting upon critical incidents because of the interplay in many outdoor activities, between risk and learning, we as practitioners will sometimes find ourselves in potentially threatening situations. These threats may be to the physical, emotional or structural elements of delivery and a number of them may be ultimately managed to successful conclusion, at times without the learner involved even being aware of the context. These 'near misses' or 'close calls' are potent opportunities to revisit and revise practice. Those who professionally practice must continuously review this practice and acknowledge that 'what we do' is central to 'who we claim to be'.

Professional development and continuous professional development

A central characteristic in any professional group's claim for acknowledgment as the occupational lead in a particular field is that they, and their practice, are exemplars of best practice. In domains such as ours, where knowledge and innovations are driving coaching and leading delivery and personal performance to ever-higher levels, currency in our practice is central to our legitimacy. One method of attempting to maintain currency in the field is via engagement in CPD. Well established in other occupations such a health care and mainstream education, CPD has attempted to provide short course and/or intensive education in order to introduce innovations to practitioners or to up-skill their practice. Unfortunately, research has suggested that the effectiveness of traditional forms of CPD is somewhat doubtful. If the intent is to change and/or update practice, authors such as Cushion and Nelson (2013) suggest that slippage is evident between any CPD training event and importing new ideas back into the field. Reasons for this non-transferability are complex, but may be related to aspects of contextual relevance, the need for structural support and resistance to change from peers, managers or learners.

One of problems inherent in formalized systems of education for professional practice, such as CPD, is that it often takes place out of, and away from, the individual's learning practice environment. Because our expertise is contextually bound and our professional practice exhibits itself in what we do, the decontextualizing of education is, therefore, problematic. Without the presence of the enablers and constraints that help formulate our practice and that help to mould the appropriateness of our delivery, the importing of new material and thinking is intrinsically difficult. To be valued, any training needs to be applied, deemed to be effective and appreciated as an addition to our pedagogic practice. If earlier attempts to introduce new practices to our own delivery seem less than effective, practitioners will often reject the material and return to their original signature pedagogies (Shulman, 2005). Contextual relevance is critical and, thus, CPD that takes place in the environment of the practice seems to be more influential in shaping new practice and upskilling the practitioner.

While professionals working in coaching and leading in the outdoors may carry out day-to-day delivery in relative isolation, many of us work within establishments or institutions that may regulate our practice. Without the structural support in terms of resources or time in order to embed new practices, the introduction of novel ways of working maybe challenging. New ideas and ways of working need time and to be afforded patience before they are fashioned, interwoven and normalized into practice. Without the structural space and the appreciation that any new material may take time to import, pressures to return to old practices may be difficult to resist. Not only does this render the most recent CPD event impotent, but it can also encourage the professional (and potentially their employers if funding has been provided) to be conservative in their approach to future education or training possibilities.

In addition to requiring institutional support to embed new developments, professionals may seek tacit permission from within their peer network. Without implicit support from colleagues, peers and learners, novel approaches may be seen as untested, lacking a supportive history, or even be an act of heresy. To work within an autonomous framework often requires the agreement of others; colleagues may require practitioners to be 'on message' and could be in a position to curtail the development of new practice if not made aware of the potential benefits to both the individual and the collective. Others within the practice environment may feel threatened if new practices are deemed contradictory and intrinsically critical of past modes of practice that they still hold on to and practice. The pressure to conform and embody homogeneity should not be underestimated. The declaration of an evangelical convert returning from a training course with novel ways of working may not meet everybody's approval. In addition, those under our charge themselves may be resistant to new ways of working (Taylor and Garratt, 2013). When introducing new material and practice, we suggest the use of incremental change and alerting learners to the possibility of new and unfamiliar delivery. Learners can be conservative when engaged in learning in as much as they look for consistency in our practice in order to offset the uncertainty inherent in their own education.

The adventure sports coach and professional futures

Coaching, leading and guiding within the outdoor sector are going through an interesting time: not only are we dealing with a demanding and expectant client base, but there is also, we would argue, an ongoing professionalization of a number of elements within our practice. It is now possible to complete both undergraduate and postgraduate degrees in a number of outdoor sub-disciplines. Increasingly there are career pathways open to those wishing to make a legitimate living within the sector. The internationalization of adventure sports means that what we do have a currency beyond our home shores and the opportunities for cross-cultural learning and practice are ever developing (Duffy *et al.*, 2010). Advances in materials, belief in what we thought possible and our own knowledge are pushing the environment in which we practice to new heights and ever-demanding limits. At the same time, however, we continue to struggle within certain aspects of our sector to convince government, other related occupations, legislative bodies, legal systems and other stakeholders of the value and legitimacy of what we do. Furthermore, much of outdoor delivery still relies on considerable voluntary effort to make it happen and remains, in some quarters, the Cinderella of sport and recreation. Whether or not this reliance on the volunteer and mutual aid bodies will hinder professional growth remains to be seen. One thing that is certain is that when faced with potentially confusing and possibly contradictory futures, the questions surrounding what it means to be and to act as an outdoor professional will take centre stage in our development. In doing so, they will provide the momentum that may establish coaching and leading in the outdoors as activities of professional significance.

References

Beck, J. and Young, M. F. D. (2005). The assault on the professions and the restructuring of academic and professional identities: a Bernsteinian analysis. *British Journal of Sociology of Education*, 26(2), 183–197.

Bloom, G. (2013). Mentoring. In: P. Protac, W. Gilbert and J. Denison (eds), *Routledge Handbook of Sports Coaching*. London: Routledge, 476–485.
Bold, C. (2011). Transforming practice through critical reflection. In: C. Bold (ed.), *Supporting Learning and Teaching*. Abingdon, Oxon: Routledge, 189–202.
Borg, M. (2004). The apprenticeship of observation. *English Language Teaching (ELT) Journal*, 58(3), 274–276.
Bradbury, H., Frost, N., Kilminster, S. and Zukas, M. (eds) (2010). *Beyond Reflective Practice: New Approaches to Professional Lifelong Learning*. London: Routledge.
British Association of International Mountain Leaders (2014). Retrieved from http://baiml.org/index.asp (accessed on 1 August 2014).
Cushion, C. and Nelson, L. (2013). Coach education and learning: developing the field. In: P. Protac, W. Gilbert and J. Denison (eds), *Routledge Handbook of Sports Coaching*. London: Routledge, 359–374.
Duffy, P., Hartley, H., Bales, J. and Crespo, M. (2010). The development of sport coaching as a profession: challenges and future directions in a global context. Keynote lecture presented at the Canadian Sport Leadership conference, 18–21 November, Ottawa, Canada.
Freidson, E. (ed.) (1973). *The Professions and their Prospects*. Beverly Hills, CA: Sage.
Freidson, E. (2001). *Professionalism: The Third Logic*. Cambridge: Polity Press.
Frost, N. (2010). Professionalism and social change: the implications of social change for the 'reflective practitioner'. In: H. Bradury, N. Frost, S. Kilminster and M. Zukas (eds), *Beyond Reflective Practice: New Approaches to Professional Lifelong Learning*. London: Routledge, 15–24.
Gibbs, G. (1988). *Learning by Doing: A Guide to Teaching and Learning Method*. Oxford: Further Education Unit, Oxford Polytechnic.
Gould, D., Drey, N. and Berridge, E-J. (2007). Nurses' experience of continuing professional development. *Nurse Education Today*, 26(6), 602–609.
Kolb, D. A. (1984). *Experiential Learning*. Englewood Cliffs NJ: Prentice Hill.
Lawson, W. (2004). Professionalism: the golden years. *Journal of Professional Issues in Engineering Education and Practice*, 130(1), 26–36.
McEwan, I. M. and Taylor, W. G. (2010). When do I get to run on with the magic sponge? The twin illusions of meritocracy and democracy in the professions of sports medicine and physiotherapy. *Qualitative Research in Sport and Exercise*, 2(1), 77–91.
Ragin, R. B. and Kram, K. E. (2007). *The Handbook of Mentoring at Work: Theory, Research and Practice*. London: Sage.
Standal, O. S. and Hemmested, L. B. (2011). Becoming a good coach: coaching and phronesis. In: A. R. Hardman and C. Jones (eds), *The Ethics of Sports Coaching*. London: Routledge, 45–55.
Schön D. A. (1983). *The Reflective Practitioner*. New York: Basic Books.
Schön, D. A. (1987). *Educating the Reflective Practitioner*. San Francisco: Jossey-Bass.
Shulman, L. S. (2005). Signature pedagogies in the professions. *Daedalus*, 134(3), 52–59.
Stronach, I., Corbin, B., NcNamara, O., Stark, S. and Warne, T. (2002). Towards an uncertain politics of professionalism: teacher and nurse identities in flux. *Journal of Education Policy*, 17(1), 109–138.
Taylor, W. G. and Garratt, D. (2007). Notions of professionalism: conversations with coaches. *Leisure Studies Association Conference*, 3–4 July, University of Brighton, Eastbourne.
Taylor, W. G. and Garratt, D. (2008). *The Professionalisation of Sports Coaching in the UK: Issues and Conceptualisation*. Leeds: Sport Coach UK.
Taylor, W. G. and Garratt, D. (2010a). The professionalisation of sports coaching: relations of power, resistance and compliance. *Sport, Education and Society*, 15(1), 121–139.

Taylor, W. G. and Garratt, D. (2010b). The professionalisation of sports coaching: definitions, challenges and critique. In: J. Lyle and C. J. Cushion (eds) *Sports Coaching: Professionalism and Practice*. London: Elsevier, 99–118.

Taylor, W. G. and Garratt, D. (2013). Coaching and professionalisation. In: P. Protac, W. Gilbert and J. Denison (eds), *Routledge Handbook of Sports Coaching*. London: Routledge, 27–39.

Taylor, W. G. and McEwan, I. M. (2012). From interprofessional working to transprofessional possibilities: the new age of sports coaching in the UK. *Sport Coaching Review*, 1(1), 38–51.

INDEX

Printed in Great Britain
by Amazon